RACIS

C000053422

Racism

A Critical Analysis

Mike Cole

SWP
London July 2016.

PlutoPress
www.plutobooks.com

First published 2016 by Pluto Press
345 Archway Road, London N6 5AA

www.plutobooks.com

British Library Cataloguing in Publication Data
A catalogue record for this book is available from the British Library

ISBN 978 0 7453 3472 1 Hardback
ISBN 978 0 7453 3471 4 Paperback
ISBN 978 1 7837 1714 9 PDF eBook
ISBN 978 1 7837 1716 3 Kindle eBook
ISBN 978 1 7837 1715 6 EPUB eBook

This book is printed on paper suitable for recycling and made from fully managed and
sustained forest sources. Logging, pulping and manufacturing processes are expected to
conform to the environmental standards of the country of origin.

Typeset by Curran Publishing Services, Norwich
Text design by Melanie Patrick

Simultaneously printed in the European Union and United States of America

Contents

Acknowledgements

I would like to thank Silhouette Bushay, Gary Craig, Phil Griffiths, Sarah Lam, Tess Lee Ack, Alpesh Maisuria, Curry Malott, Karim Murji, Carl Parsons and Scott Poynting for their comments on and/or help with sections of this book. Special thanks to David Castle at Pluto Press. Any inadequacies, of course, remain mine.

Mike Cole

Introduction

'RACE': PAST ITS SELL-BY DATE

'Race' is a social construct. That this is the case is explained succinctly by neuroscientist Steven Rose and sociologist Hilary Rose.[1] As they note, in 1972 the evolutionary geneticist Richard Lewontin pointed out that 85 per cent of human genetic diversity occurred within rather than between populations, and only 6–10 per cent of diversity is associated with the broadly defined 'races'. Rose and Rose explain that most of this difference is accounted for by the readily visible genetic variation of skin colour, hair form and so on. The everyday business of seeing and acknowledging such difference is not the same as the project of genetics. For genetics, and more importantly, for the prospect of treating genetic diseases, the difference is important, since humans differ in their susceptibility to particular diseases, and genetics can have something to say about this. However, beyond medicine, the invocation of 'race' is increasingly suspect.

There has been a growing debate among geneticists about the utility of the term, and an entire issue of the influential journal *Nature Reviews Genetics* (Autumn 2004) was devoted to it. The geneticists agreed with most biological anthropologists that for human biology the term 'race' is an unhelpful leftover. Rose and Rose argue that '[w]hatever arbitrary boundaries one places on any population group for the purposes of genetic research, they do not match those of conventionally defined races'.[2] For example, the DNA of 'native' Britons contains traces of the multiple entries into the United Kingdom of occupiers and migrants. 'Race', as a scientific concept, Rose and Rose conclude, 'is well past its sell-by date'.[3] The popular political slogan 'one race, the human race' would appear to be accurate. 'Race' as a concept should be abandoned. For these reasons, following Robert Miles (referred to at length in this Introduction), if I need to use the term 'race' as an 'idea', as a social construct, I shall put it in inverted commas. As Miles explains:

> I am rigorous in believing that there is a very clear distinction between an idea and a concept … insofar as there is an idea of 'race' that is a historical reality … . [I] use the notion of racialization [the false categorisation of people into distinct 'races'] to then seek to explain the origin, development and use of that idea.[4]

Miss's use of the concept of racialization, a process that serves ruling-class interests by dividing the working class, promoting conflict among that class – the class with least access to power and wealth – and forcing down labour costs, is explored in this Introduction.

RACISM: A FRIGHTENINGLY REAL, BURNING AND OMNIPRESENT ISSUE

If 'race' is a social construct, racism, as I argue throughout this book, is a frighteningly real, burning and omnipresent issue. It is directed at people because of a number of perceived 'identities': 'race', ethnicity, nationality, religion or a combination of these. In addition, as I shall also demonstrate in this book, contemporary racism is multifaceted. For these reasons, it is important to adopt a broad concept of racism, rather than a narrow one, based on notions of overt biological inferiority as it was in the days of the British Empire in India, Africa and elsewhere; under slavery and its legacy in the United States; and as was the case with indigenous Americans and Australians dating back centuries. In these historical scenarios, notions of cultural inferiority coexisted with perceptions of biological inferiority. In the contemporary world, biological racism is less acceptable in the mainstream than is cultural racism.

Racism can also be unintentional as well as intentional (although the former can sometimes cause as much distress as the latter). The difference between these two forms of racism depends obviously on intention, and is summed up by the epithet – you do not have to be a racist (intentional) to be racist (which can be unintentional).[5] Racist pronouncements, intentional as well as unintentional, are often introduced with 'I'm not racist but ...'. Racism can be direct or indirect; it can be overt as well as covert. Moreover 'seemingly positive' attributes will probably ultimately have racist implications, as in 'they are good at sport', which may have the subtext that 'they' are not good at much else; or 'they have a strong culture', where 'they' are taking over might be a subtext. Racism can be dominative (direct and oppressive) as well as aversive (exclusion and cold-shouldering).[6] Finally, it should be stressed that racism can also become (more) apparent given certain stimuli.

CRITICAL RACE THEORY AND MARXISM

One of the challenges of writing a book about racism on three continents is to keep up with the frequency of its occurrence. I am not talking so much about overt intentional and psychologically or physically violent actions perpetrated by, and/or words expressed by, self-acknowledged or self-proclaimed racists, although there is plenty of that,[7] but more about racism's everyday mundane taken-for-granted acceptability. Although, as will soon be clear, my own theoretical orientation is neo-Marxist, which in terms of practice veers towards a socialism of the twenty-first century rather than the twentieth,[8] critical race theory (CRT), arguably the dominant radical paradigm with respect to the analysis of racism in the United States (and also a major presence in Australian academia, but less so in the United Kingdom) must be given credit for one of its central tenets, its insistence that racism is an unexceptional and constant occurrence for people of colour.[9] For many years when meeting a new acquaintance in the Anglophone world, I would try hard to take them at face value and not to make assumptions, whatever the visual or verbal clues, that they were racist. I do not do this any more, but assume intentional or unintentional racism, unless persuaded otherwise.

What is Critical Race Theory?

What then is CRT? Founding and leading UK-based CRT David Gillborn has defined it as consisting of a number of defining elements, and using several conceptual tools (see Figure 0.1).[10] Gillborn elaborates on each of the elements and each of the tools. Thus, racism as 'endemic' means that it goes far beyond 'crude, obvious acts of race hatred' to include 'the more subtle and hidden operations of power that have the effect of disadvantaging one or more minority ethnic groups'.[11] With respect to the crossing of epistemological boundaries, Gillborn argues that CRT's theoretical eclecticism allows it to bring various insights together in a new and challenging way that raise deeply troubling questions.[12]

As far as the limitations of civil rights laws are concerned, following William Tate, Gillborn argues that the laws to remedy racial inequality are often undermined before they can be fully implemented.[13] Moreover, 'CRT portrays dominant legal claims of neutrality, objectivity, color blindness, and meritocracy as camouflages for the self-interest of powerful entities of society'.[14] Critical race theorists not only criticize the inability of traditional legal discourse to deal with complex and comprehensive racism, they go further, by viewing legal discourse as 'one of the prime means by which such a critical perspective is denied legitimacy and the status quo is defended'.[15]

'Call to context' is a concept coined by leading US critical race theorist Richard Delgado, who insists on the importance of context and the detail

> **Defining elements**
>
> - racism as endemic... 'normal' not aberrant nor rare: deeply ingrained legally and culturally
> - crosses epistemological boundaries
> - critique of civil rights laws as fundamentally limited
> - critique of liberalism: claims of neutrality, objectivity, colour-blindness, and meritocracy as camouflages
> - call to context: challenges ahistoricism and recognizes experiential knowledge of people of colour.
>
> **Conceptual tools**
>
> - story-telling and counter-stories
> - interest convergence
> - critical white studies.

Figure 0.1 Critical race theory: a conceptual map
Source: D. Gillborn (2006) 'Critical race theory and education: racism and anti-racism in educational theory and praxis,' *Discourse*, 27(1), p. 20.

of the lived experience of minority peoples as 'a defence against the colour-blind and sanitized analyses generated via universalistic discourses'.[16] I fully agree with critical race theorists[17] that we should reject 'color blindness'. As Delgado and Stefancic explain:

> Critical race theorists . . . hold that color blindness will allow us to redress only extremely egregious racial harms, ones that everyone would notice and condemn. But if racism is embedded in our thought processes and social structures as deeply as many crits believe, then the 'ordinary business' of society – the routines, practices, and institutions that we rely on to effect the world's work – will keep minorities in subordinate positions. Only aggressive, color-conscious efforts to change the way things are will do much to ameliorate misery.[18]

Given CRT's roots in critical legal studies and the legal profession,[19] the call to context, according to Delgado and Stefancic,[20] is essential to understand the full background to any major dispute or issue.

A particularly striking aspect of CRT, Gillborn suggests, is the use of story-telling and counter-storytelling. Here, he explains, 'myths, assumptions, and received wisdoms can be questioned by shifting the grounds of debate or presenting analyses in ways that turn dominant assumptions on their head'.[21]

'Interest convergence' refers to the fact that 'white elites will tolerate or encourage racial advances for blacks only when such advances also promote white self-interest'.[22] Finally, 'critical white studies' is a wide-ranging field of study which focuses on white people and their sense of self, their interests and concerns. But Gillborn points out that since the mid-1980s there has been 'a significant increase in the amount of critical scholarship on the nature of "whiteness", work that is deconstructing the taken-for-granted myths and assumptions that circulate about what it means to be, and not be, a "white" person'.[23] Gillborn concludes that '[c]ritical scholarship on whiteness is not an assault on white people per se: it is an assault on the socially constructed and constantly reinforced power of white identifications and interests'.[24]

What is Marxism?

From a Marxist perspective,[25] social class is fundamental to capitalism, since capitalism relies for its very existence on the extraction of surplus value from workers: capitalists pay workers less than the value they produce, with the value added by workers' labour appropriated as profit by and for the capitalist when goods are sold (this is the labour theory of value, LTV).[26] This means that there is a permanent inherent conflict between the working class and the capitalist class. Class struggle is endemic to the capitalist system. It cannot be eradicated as long as capitalism exists. However it does not always, or even typically, take the form of open conflict or expressed hostility. It arises unavoidably from the tension generated by the zero-sum game (a benefit to one is at the cost of the other) between profits going to capitalists and wages or salaries given to workers. The objective interests of the capitalist and the worker are thus incompatible, and 'therefore generate not a tendency to permanent hostility and open warfare but a permanent tendency towards them'.[27]

Because of the cyclical instability of capitalism, periodic crises in capitalism mean that social revolution is always a possibility. However, as we shall see, the early socialists' prognosis that social revolution and socialism were inevitable and imminent has been undermined by subsequent historical developments, which are best explained by neo-Marxist theory.

If the LTV is one basis of Marxism, the other is the materialist conception of history. As Marx's co-writer Friedrich Engels explains, the materialist conception of history 'starts from the proposition that the production of the means to support human life and, next to production, the exchange of things produced, is the basis of all social structure'.[28] In capitalist societies, production is based on private ownership of the means of production, distribution and exchange, with workers forced to sell their labour power to capitalists in order to live. This combination of forces means that the way people relate to the physical world and the way people relate to each other are bound together in historically specific structural and necessary ways. As Marx put it, in the male-centred and sexist language[29] which was the norm in the nineteenth century:

> My inquiry led me to the conclusion that neither legal relations nor political forms could be comprehended whether by themselves or on the basis of a so-called general development of the human mind, but that on the contrary they originate in the material conditions of life .... In the social production of their existence, men inevitably enter into definite relations, which are independent of their will, namely relations of production appropriate to a given stage in the development of their material forces of production. The totality of these relations of production constitutes the economic structure of society, the real foundation, on which arises a legal and political superstructure and to which correspond definite forms of social consciousness. The mode of production of material life conditions the general process of social, political and intellectual life. It is not the consciousness of men that determines their existence, but their social existence that determines their consciousness.[30]

In other words it is the economic base, or the capitalist economy, that generates the legal and political levels of society. These are not neutral or objective but reflect the needs of the capitalist economy and capitalists. We tend to think the way we do because of the type of economic system in which we live. Marx also once noted that the:

> ideas of the ruling class are in every epoch the ruling ideas, i.e. the class which is the ruling material force of society, is at the same time its ruling intellectual force. The class which has the means of material production at its disposal, has control at the same time over the means of mental production, so that thereby, generally speaking, the ideas of those who lack the means of mental production are subject to it.[31]

Thus, in order to understand social, political, legal and intellectual life, which form the terrains of racism, and which have a massive effect on how we think and act, we need to make connections with the capitalist economy. Later in this Introduction, I try to explain how we come to think the way we do.

Engels referred to the combination of the LTV and the materialist conception of history as *scientific socialism*. In early scientific socialist writing, there is an undercurrent of the inevitability and imminence of socialism. This is particularly evident in the work of Engels and the Russian Bolshevik revolutionary, and leader of the Russian Revolution in 1917, Vladimir Ilyich Ulyanov, commonly known as Lenin.[32]

Although he did not write much about racism, Marx was well aware of its importance in the genesis of the industrial capitalist:

> The discovery of gold and silver in America, the extirpation, enslavement and entombment in mines of the aboriginal population, the beginning of the conquest and looting of the East Indies, the turning of Africa into a warren for the commercial hunting of black-skins, signalised the rosy dawn of the era of capitalist production.[33]

Taylor notes how Marx was also aware of three important features of capitalism, with respect to racialization.[34] First, capitalism promotes competition between workers for jobs, housing, education, health care and so on. Taylor calls these 'laws of false scarcity', whereby, as she notes, we are told there is not enough to go round:

> While the scarcity is false, the competition if real, and workers fighting over these items to better themselves or their families are often willing to believe the worst about other workers to justify why they should have something and others should not.[35]

The reality is that if wealth were to be distributed equally, and society run on socialist, rather than capitalist lines, there would be abundant jobs, housing, education, health care and so on for all.

The second feature of capitalism is that the ruling class uses racist ideology to divide workers against each other, and racialization is the perfect tool for this. As we shall see throughout the book, capitalism can thrive as long as workers blame other (racialized) workers rather than capitalists and capitalism for their structural location in societies.

Third, when one group of workers are super-exploited, it negatively impacts the working class as a whole. Thus, if capitalists can get away with paying very low wages to migrant workers (who often have migrated from capitalist economies with still lower wages, or no work at all), thereby generating greater surplus value and thereby profit, this lowers the wage level for all workers, racialized or not.

What is Neo-Marxism?

The development of neo-Marxism (the 'neo' – 'new' – in Neo-Marxism refers to theoretical developments in Marxism, post-Marx) needs to be seen in the light of the fact that inevitability and imminence of a general transition to socialism proved to be over-optimistic, and severely compromised. This fact meant that some aspects of Marxism had to be rethought. Specifically, what needed to be understood was the role of capitalist institutions in maintaining their power base.

As Leszek Kolakowski[36] has argued, the common element in theories designated as 'neo'-Marxist is a concern with the role of capitalist states' welfare institutions in retarding rather than advancing socialism. The defining features of neo-Marxism are a concern with culture (as in the notion of the forging of a hegemonic culture as elaborated by prominent Italian neo-Marxist Antonio Gramsci)[37] and with ideology (ideas that work in the interests of the ruling class, as in the concept of ideological state apparatuses outlined by French neo-Marxist Louis Althusser)[38] (both theorists are discussed in the next section). Neo-Marxist analysis should be seen as a supplement to rather than a replacement of Marxism.

Humanist Marxism and Structuralist Marxism

The neo-Marxism primarily employed in this book to understand racism can be divided into humanist Marxism and structuralist Marxism. The fundamental difference between the two is that the former emphasizes the power of the human will in breaking through the structures of capitalist society, while the latter reminds us of how powerful these constraining structures are. We should over-emphasize neither humanism (as this leads to idealism) nor structuralism (as this leads to determinism and defeatism).

Moreover, the humanist Gramsci and the structuralist Althusser should not necessarily be seen as polar opposites. While it is easy to see how the latter's writings have been used to stress domination by structures (such as interpellating subjects – see below) and the former's to stress struggle (as in hegemony and counter-hegemony – see below), there are passages in both writers' works that imply the opposite. Both forms of Marxism are in fact predated by Marx's famous dictum that stressed both the power of the structures of capitalist society and the power of workers to change history. I am referring to Marx's famous (1852) observation in the *Eighteenth Brumaire* that we make our own history (humanism), but not in circumstances of our own choosing (structuralism).[39] What is distinctive about my approach in this book is that rather than relying on Althusserian structuralist Marxism or Gramscian humanist Marxism, I argue that, in order to get a full understanding of the relationship between racism and schooling in the United Kingdom, the United States and Australia, it is informative to utilize some key concepts from both Gramsci and Althusser, as well as those of other (neo) Marxists, and of course those of Marx and Engels themselves.

One of Gramsci's key concepts is 'common sense'. Gramsci made a distinction between 'common sense' and good sense. 'Common sense' refers to thoughts and reflections that are felt to be the product of years of knowing what is right and necessary, but really mirror the interests of the ruling class. 'Common sense', then, is 'based on surface appearances and information, and does not reach deeper to give a systemic explanation for the disparities that exist in society'.[40] Engels described this is as 'false consciousness':

> Ideology is a process accomplished by the so-called thinker consciously, indeed, but with a false consciousness. The real motives impelling him remain unknown to him …. Hence he imagines false or apparent motives …. He works with mere thought material which he accepts without examination as the product of thought, he does not investigate further for a more remote process.[41]

'Common sense' connects racialization with popular consciousness. Thus, we might pick up in the street, read in a tabloid or hear from a politician, 'it's only common sense to restrict immigration to this small island', or 'become an official member of the Common Sense Campaign … [and] win back America',[42] or 'it's common sense that we should put jobs for Australian workers first and keep Asian workers out'.[43]

'Common sense' also works to reinforce racist stereotypes. Political activist and Marxist academic Keenga-Yamahtta Taylor gives the example of African Americans (although this can usually be applied to racialized groups in general) who, because of their worse housing, schooling, shorter life span and generally worse conditions are perceived to be inferior – 'they caused all this themselves' – which reinforces racism and racialization.[44]

Good sense, on the other hand, for Gramsci, is informed by a real political and economic awareness of capitalism, exemplified by Marxism and obtained by reading Marx. As educationalist Diana Coben has argued, good sense 'may be created out of common sense through an educative

Marxist politics'.[45] Good sense then would reveal that racialized groups are living in worse conditions because of racism, racialization and their structural location in capitalist society.

It is also useful to employ in our understanding of racism the concept of *interpellation*, as developed by Althusser. Interpellation is the process via which the politicians and the media, for example, claim to be speaking on behalf of the people: 'what the British have had enough of', 'what the American people want' or 'what Australians are sick and tired of'. Althusser stressed that it is individuals rather than classes or groups that are interpellated or hailed. For Althusser, the interpellation of subjects – the hailing of concrete individuals as concrete subjects, as in 'Hey, you there!'[46] – provides the absolute guarantee that everything really is so, and that on condition that the subjects recognize what they are and behave accordingly, everything will be all right: Amen – 'So be it'.[47] Althusser notes that it is a peculiarity of ideology that it imposes, without appearing to do so, 'obviousnesses as obviousnesses'.[48] Interpellation is the process by which ideologies function through concrete social institutions. This means that individuals as bearers of structures are transformed ideologically into subjects; that is, they live the relation of their real conditions of existence as if they autonomously determined that relation.[49] In other words, echoing Engels's notion of 'false consciousness', we tend to think and act in the interests of the ruling class, as if it was solely our choice to do so, and it is fully in our interests to do so. To give an example pertaining to racism, in the 2015 UK general election there was universal agreement about immigration among all establishment political parties, whose spokespersons could say with confidence that of course the British people want to restrict it.

More generally, this leads to the claim that there is no point in workers questioning their social class position under capitalism, let alone considering alternative ways of running the world, such as democratic socialism, or even social democracy:[50] 'socialism's been tried and it doesn't work. Anyway, people are basically selfish, and we need businesses and free enterprise to create wealth'.[51]

Interpellation is thus a fundamental process inserted within the ideological apparatus of the state, Althusser having made a distinction between the ideological apparatuses of the state (ISAs) (religion, education, family, law, politics, trade unions, communication, culture) and repressive state apparatuses (RSAs) (government, administration, army, police, courts, prisons).[52] Within the ISAs, subjects 'recognize' the existing state of affairs: 'it really is true that it is so and not otherwise'.[53]

Leading cultural theorist the late Stuart Hall has described how the interpellation process passes into common sense:

It is when it becomes 'just how things are' that it wins consent and enters common sense. And at that point the political regime or philosophy has achieved a more settled, long-term, deeper form of control.[54]

To reiterate, what is critical and crucial to the capitalist class and its supporters is that, in their stark determination to maintain hegemony, they make every effort to ensure that workers retain a belief that (racialized) capitalism is the best thing on offer, and do not look to antiracist or socialist alternatives.

The Gramscian concepts of hegemony and counter-hegemony are important complements to interpellation. Hegemony (from the Greek *hegemonía*, 'leadership') was used by Lenin to refer to the political leadership of the working class. Hegemony, as theorized by Gramsci, is the fusion of economic, political, intellectual and moral leadership that is brought about by one fundamental group, and groups allied to it through ideology. Thus a 'consensus' culture develops in which the working class identifies its own good with the good of the bourgeoisie, and helps to maintain the status quo rather than opposing it. However, crucially for Gramsci, hegemony is a process of contestation, and counter-hegemonic struggle is always possible. Hegemony has to be constantly worked for by both the bourgeoisie and the workers. As Eric Hobsbawm has argued, what is new in Gramsci is his observation that even bourgeois hegemony 'is not automatic but achieved through conscious political action and organisation'.[55]

However, hegemony fails to explain precisely how ideologies work, why they work with certain people and not with others, and crucially why certain ideologies work and others do not. For this we need interpellation. For example, the ruling class's success at keeping the racialization of others at the forefront of people's (false) consciousness is not logical (indeed, given that antiracism is in the interests of the solidarity of the working class as a whole, it is in fact illogical). But, as Stuart Hall once remarked, ideologies don't work by logic – they have logics of their own.[56] Because the successfully interpellated are largely trapped within one view of the world, it all makes 'common' sense – 'Yes, this is us.'

For Marxists, then, CRT's defining elements, as outlined for example by Gillborn earlier in this Introduction, need to be reconsidered in the light of what Marxism and neo-Marxism have to offer. Specifically, they need to be grounded in the economic and political realities of racialized capitalist societies, and with respect to this book, those of the United Kingdom, the United States and Australia. Thus, in order to *understand* racism in these capitalist societies and decipher Gillborn's insistence that endemic racism entails a consideration of subtle and hidden operations of power that disadvantage 'minority ethnic groups', we must focus on the ISAs and RSAs and the way in which they racialize and exploit different groups of people in different historical periods, and in different geographical locations, though often for the same reasons – the appropriation of more surplus value from racialized groups, and thereby more surplus from all workers, and/or to divide the working class and maintain hegemony.

With respect to the fact that CRT portrays legal claims of neutrality as camouflages for the self-interest of powerful elites, this needs to be supplemented by the identification of these elites as the *capitalist* class and its political agents. Allied to this, the status quo is indeed defended, but we need to know that it is preserved for that capitalist class and those political allies.

It is, of course, important for 'calling to context', as Gillborn notes, following Delgado, to listen to the lived experience of minoritized (for Marxists, read 'racialized') peoples, so that we can all better understand how and why they are racialized and for what reasons. This is not to patronize or belittle experiential knowledge as not valid in itself, but to facilitate moving forward in our mutual understanding of racism, in order to devise strategies to combat it. Story-telling is related to 'call to context', and I would argue that the same provisos apply.

I would agree that we should reject 'colour-blindness' (I prefer 'colour-discounting' – see note 14 to this Introduction) because racialization under capitalism can only be understood and addressed if we are aware of which particular groups of people are, via interpellation, being racialized – where and when and why, and how this is exploiting, oppressing and disadvantaging them.

With respect to 'interest convergence', the idea that 'white elites' encourage 'racial advances' only when such advances promote 'white self-interest' (Gillborn following Delgado and Stefancic), Marxists would argue that the self-interests being maintained are those of the (mainly) white ruling class (in the countries under consideration in this book) in its attempt to maintain ongoing hegemonic control.

Finally, while Gillborn may be right that critical scholarship on whiteness is not an assault on white people as such, I would take issue with him that the 'assault' should be on 'the socially constructed and consistently reinforced power of white identities and interests'. Rather, the 'assault' should be on the power of racialized capitalism. For Marxists, this rather than 'white supremacy' as defined by critical race theorists is the real hegemonic bloc.

CRITICAL RACE THEORY AND 'WHITE SUPREMACY': A MARXIST CRITIQUE

Rather than its limited usage to describe only extremist groups today, such as the Ku Klux Klan or hate groups, or actions in the past by the British Empire, or the colonizers in America and Australia, or practices in the pre-civil rights United States (see Chapters 1, 2 and 3 of this book), CRT employs the concept of 'white supremacy' as a descriptor of reality for everyday experiences of racism now. 'White supremacy' is seen as a more useful term than racism alone in certain contexts, for example in the United States, and in other specified countries, including the United Kingdom and Australia.[57] I have argued[58] that this is problematic, both through history and in the present. There are at least seven reasons for this. 'White supremacy':

- directs attention away from capitalist economics and politics
- homogenizes all white people
- inadequately explains non-colour-coded racism
- does not explain newer hybridist racism
- does not explain racism that is 'not white' against 'not white'
- is historically and contemporaneously associated with beliefs and values which are not necessarily associated with 'everyday racism', and historically and contemporaneously connects to fascism, whereas racism and fascism need to be differentiated
- is counter-productive in rallying against racism.

I shall deal briefly with each of these points in turn.

Directing Attention Away from Capitalist Economics and Politics

While, for Marxists, it is certainly the case that there has been a continuity of racism for hundreds of years, the concept of 'white supremacy' does not in itself explain this continuity, since it does not need to connect to modes of production and developments in capitalism. It is true that critical race theorist Charles Mills, for example,[59] provides a wide-ranging discussion of the history of economic exploitation, and that John Preston,[60] writing from within a CRT framework, argues that CRT needs to be considered alongside Marxism. However, unlike Marxism, there is no inherent need to connect with capitalist modes of production, or to make links to patterns of migration that are themselves strongly influenced by economic and political dynamics. Thus Gillborn[61] is able to make the case for CRT and 'white supremacy' without providing a discussion of the relationship of racism to capitalism. Throughout this book, I argue that for a full understanding of racism at any given geographical location and/or historical conjuncture it is necessary to employ the neo-Marxist concept of racialization.

The Neo-Marxist Concept of Racialization and Institutional Racism

Racialization refers to the categorization of people (falsely) into distinct 'races'. The neo-Marxist concept of racialization is distinct from other interpretations of racialization in that it purports that, in order to understand and combat racism, we must relate racism and racialization to historical, economic and political factors.

Specifically, the neo-Marxist concept of racialization makes the connection between racism and capitalist modes of production, as well as making links to patterns of migration that are in themselves determined by economic and political dynamics. Thus the concept is able to relate to these factors, which are the real material contexts of struggle (see Chapters 1, 2 and 3 of this book for a discussion of racialization in the United Kingdom, the United States and Australia respectively).

Robert Miles, a leading theorist of the Marxist concept of racialization, has defined it as an ideological process, where people are categorized falsely into the scientifically defunct notion of distinct 'races'.[62] Racialization, like 'race', is socially constructed. In Miles's words racialization refers to 'those instances where social relations between people have been structured by the signification of human biological characteristics [elsewhere in the same book, Miles[63] added cultural characteristics] in such a way as to define and *construct* [my emphasis] differentiated social collectivities'.[64] '[T]he process of racialization', Miles states, 'cannot be adequately understood without a conception of, and explanation for the complex interplay of different modes of production and, in particular, of the social relations necessarily established in the course of material production'.[65] It is this articulation with modes of production and with the ideological and the cultural that makes Miles's concept of racialization inherently (neo-) Marxist.[66] Miles insists that we employ the concept of 'racialization' rather than 'race' to analyse and understand why different groups are racialized in different locations in different historical and contemporary periods, and how this all relates to capitalist economic and political processes.[67]

The United Kingdom, the United States and Australia, as demonstrated in this book, are institutionally racist societies. This was recognized officially in the United Kingdom as long ago as 1999 by the Stephen Lawrence Inquiry Report,[68] which followed a lengthy public campaign initiated by the parents of black teenager Stephen Lawrence, after his racist murder in 1993. It needs to be stressed, however, that the resonances in institutional practices of this recognition have now in the United Kingdom virtually disappeared. Institutional racism is defined in the report as:

> The collective failure of an organisation to provide an appropriate and professional service to people because of their colour, culture, or ethnic origin. It can be seen or detected in processes, attitudes and behaviour which amount to discrimination through unwitting prejudice, ignorance, thoughtlessness and racist stereotyping which disadvantage minority ethnic people.[69]

From a Marxist viewpoint, the nebulous and ahistorical definition of institutional racism provided by Macpherson needs to have historical, economic and political foci. The definition also requires enhancement by the neo-Marxist concept of racialization. Last but not least, in line with the discussion of racism formulated at the beginning of this Introduction, I would also want to add intentional as well as unintentional or unwitting racism. I thus reformulate institutional racism as follows:

> Collective acts and/or procedures in an institution or institutions (locally, nationwide, continent-wide or globally) that intentionally or unintentionally have the effect of racializing, via 'common sense', certain populations or groups of people, through a process of inter-pellation. This racialization process cannot be understood without reference to economic and political factors related to developments and changes, historically and contemporaneously, in national, conti-nent-wide and global capitalism. Hegemony describes the ongoing attempts by the ruling class to consolidate a racist consensus. Counter-hegemony refers to continuing resistance to these endeavours.

It should be stressed that the interests of pro-capitalist politicians and capitalists do not always correspond, or coalesce around racialization. For example, it is often in the interests of establishment politicians to racialize certain groups of workers, for electoral gain, for example, while capitalists may prefer not to, in their pursuit of cheap labour power and great surplus value and hence profits. Marxist political economist Gareth Dale maintains that migrant workers are a perfect solution in times of intensified labour market flexibility, but also stresses the contradiction between capital's need for (cheap) flexible labour and the need for hegemonic control of the workforce by racializing potential foreign workers:

On the one hand, intensified competition spurs employers' requirements for enhanced labour market flexibility – for which immigrant
labour is ideal. On the other, in such periods questions of social
control tend to become more pressing. Governments strive to uphold
the ideology of 'social contract' even as its content is eroded through
unemployment and austerity. The logic, commonly, is for less political
capital to be derived from the [social contract's] content, while greater
emphasis is placed upon its exclusivity, on demarcation from those
who enter from or lie outside – immigrants and foreigners.[70]

The Homogenisation of All White People

Mills acknowledges that not 'all whites are better off than all nonwhites,
but ... as a statistical generalization, the objective life chances of whites
are significantly better'.[71] To take poverty as one example, in Chapters 1, 2
and 3 of this book, we see that poverty for white people is consistently less
than that of racialized peoples. Nevertheless, we should not lose sight of
the life chances of millions of working-class white people, who along with
racialized groups, are part of the 99 per cent, not the 1 per cent.[72]

Moreover, the term 'white supremacy' at least *implicates* all white people
as part of some hegemonic bloc of 'whiteness'. For Mills 'white supremacy'
is 'the basic political system that has shaped the world for the past several
hundred years' and 'the most important political system of recent global
history',[73] while the 'racial contract'[74] 'designates Europeans as the privileged race'.[75] To underline the point that he sees 'white supremacy' as a
political system in its own right, and that the racial contract is both 'real'
and 'global',[76] Mills asserts:

> Global white supremacy ... is *itself* a political system, a particular
> power structure of formal or informal rule, socioeconomic privilege,
> and norms for the differential distribution of material wealth and
> opportunities, benefits and burdens, rights and duties.[77]

Some critical race theorists argue that 'white supremacy' does not necessarily refer to skin colour, 'rather to structures of subordination and
domination'.[78] Charlotte Chadderton singles out my own work[79] as not
understanding this. My response would be that 'white supremacy' *is*
generally perceived as referring to skin colour. I also want to stress and
reiterate my view that Chadderton's 'structures of subordination and domination' are the very structures of racialized capitalism itself rather than
some white power bloc.

Inadequate Explanation of Non-Colour-Coded Racism

Mills acknowledges that there were/are what he refers to as '"borderline" Europeans' – 'the Irish, Slavs, Mediterraneans, and above all, of course, Jews', and that there also existed 'intra-European varieties of "racism"'. [80] However he argues that, while there remain 'some recognition of such distinctions in popular culture' – he gives examples of an 'Italian' waitress in the television series *Cheers* calling a WASP character 'Whitey' and a discussion in a 1992 movie about whether Italians are really white[81] – he relegates such distinctions primarily to history. While Mills is prepared to 'fuzzify' racial categories[82] with respect to 'shifting criteria prescribed by the evolving Racial Contract,'[83] and to acknowledge the existence of 'off-White' people at certain historical periods,[84] he maintains that his categorization – 'white/nonwhite, person/subperson' 'seems to me to map the essential features of the racial polity accurately, to carve the social reality at its ontological joints.'[85]

Mills is, of course, writing about the United States, and his analysis does not provide an explanation for non-colour-coded racism in the United Kingdom, where, as is shown in Chapter 1 of this book, there are well-documented analyses of such racism both historically and contemporaneously.

Robert Miles is aware of what I refer to as non-colour-coded racism. He stresses that racialization is a process and recognition that 'opens the door to history' which subsequently 'opens the door to understanding the complexities of who gets racialized when and for what purpose, and how that changes through time'.[86] Miles warns against avoiding the 'fundamental mistake' of drawing clear lines between what happens to white immigrants and black immigrants, adding that the 'black–white' dichotomy leads you into a 'huge cul-de-sac'.[87] 'White supremacy' provides no basis for an understanding racism directed at the Irish, at Jewish people, at Gypsy, Roma and Traveller communities, or of the widespread xeno-racism directed at Eastern European migrant workers since Poland joined the European Union (see Chapter 1). This racism has all the hallmarks of traditional racism, such as that directed at Asian, Black and other minority ethnic workers following mass immigration after the Second World War, but impacts on recently arrived groups of people.

No Explanation of Newer Hybridist Racism

Under this heading I include anti-asylum-seeker racism and Islamophobia. My reason for using the term 'newer hybridist racism' is because, unlike the forms of racism that are either essentially colour-coded or essentially non-colour-coded, anti-asylum-seeker racism and Islamophobia can be either colour-coded or non-colour-coded. These forms of racism can also encompass a combination of colour-coded and non-colour-coded racism. For example, racism directed at asylum seekers from 'sub-Saharan Africa' (itself a term with colour-coded racist implications), will be colour-coded, but may also be Islamophobic, which is not necessarily colour-coded, or it may be a combination of colour-coded (anti-Black) racism and non-color-coded racism (Islamophobia). That form of racism, experienced by Afghan and Iraqi asylum seekers, for example, is also ambiguous, and may or may not be more Islamophobic than colour-coded (see Chapter 1 for a discussion of newer hybridist racism, and Chapters 1, 2 and 3 for discussions of Islamophobia).

Lack of Explanation of Racism that is 'Not White' Against 'Non-White'

Charles Mills acknowledges that 'white supremacy' does not explain 'varieties of racial domination ... that are not white-over-non-white', and 'that is a weakness of the term that should be conceded'.[88] He gives the example of 'certain Asian nations'. In late 2015, Islamophobia in Myanmar (Burma) is an obvious example, and from my own personal experience, anti-Vietnamese racism is rife in Cambodia. Not-white over non-white racism is also a reality in South Africa. However, it has to be said that inter-ethnic racism is also a reality in the 'developed world'. For example, in the overtly xeno-racism UK Independence Party (UKIP) (see Chapter 1), there are black and Asian members and supporters.

Historical Context; Historical and Contemporary Association with Other Beliefs and Values; and Connections with Fascism

First of all, it needs to be pointed out that in certain periods of history, 'white supremacy' was the norm (see Chapters 1, 2 and 3). Second, white supremacist groups, conventionally defined, have tended to embrace a number of other beliefs and values which are not necessarily associated with everyday racism. These can include homophobia, Holocaust denial or claims that the Holocaust was exaggerated, antisemitic conspiracy theories (that Jewish people conspire to control the world), and engagement in military-type activity.

Some of these associated beliefs and values were epitomized by the now almost defunct white supremacist and fascist British National Party (BNP). When its then leader Nick Griffin appeared on the popular BBC discussion programme, *Question Time* in October 2009, he stated that Islam was incompatible with life in Britain, admitted sharing a platform with the Ku Klux Klan, and described gay men kissing in public as 'really creepy'. He said that 'legal reasons' prevented him from explaining why he had previously sought to play down the Holocaust, and that he had now changed his mind. He was challenged by fellow panellist Jack Straw, the then Justice Secretary, who said there was no law preventing him from giving an explanation.

It is important to distinguish between racism, and 'white supremacy' and fascism on the other. Aninda Bhattacharyya succinctly explains the relationship between capitalism and fascism. As he puts it, 'fascist organisations offer themselves to the ruling class as a deadly weapon to use against the left. But the use of this weapon comes at a price – stripping away any pretence that capitalism is a fair or progressive system'.[89] This is because fascism means that the ruling class has to use the full force of the RSAs rather than just rely on the ISAs.[90] Thus fascism is 'a weapon of last resort for our rulers, one that they turn to in periods of acute crisis but keep their distance from at other times'.[91] In other words, while the ruling class is quite happy to up the barometer of racism, it tries hard not to admit to doing that:

> The contradictory political relationship between the ruling class and fascism manifests itself as a contradictory ideological attitude and contradictory action. So the *Daily Mail* [a right-wing tabloid, aimed at the UK middle class] attacks Muslims, but also attacks the BNP for attacking Muslims. The mainstream parties denounce the BNP, but play to its agenda on issues like immigration.[92]

Fascism tends to have both a parliamentary and a street presence. This is typical of fascist complementarity, and dates back to Benito Mussolini, fascist dictator in Italy in the 1920s, 1930s and 1940s (he had the *squadre d'azione*), and Adolf Hitler, who had the 'Brownshirts' who played a major role in his rise to power in the 1920s and 1930s.[93] Antiracists, including Marxists, need of course to 'oppose both fascism and the racism that feeds it, both politically and on the streets, while understanding the distinctions and relationships between them'.[94] Bhattacharyya concludes:

> That means understanding that the 'right wing anti-fascism' of [sections of the media] isn't simply a matter of hypocrisy. There are material political motives for why the ruling class is ordinarily opposed to fascism … [but we] cannot ever rely on this right wing anti-fascism that can rapidly reverse into support for the Nazis.[95]

CRT obfuscation of 'white supremacy' and its collapse into the realm of 'everyday racism' critically undermines a serious analysis of 'white supremacy' in the conventional use of the term, and its connections to other obnoxious beliefs, values and actions, and to fascism.

'White Supremacy' as Counterproductive in Rallying Against Racism

As the crisis in capitalism deepens, it is absolutely essential for unity among the working class as a whole. Advocating 'white supremacy' as a descriptor of 'everyday racism' is useless as a unifier and counterproductive as a political rallying point. While the prospect of social revolution and socialism in the three main countries under discussion in this book (the United Kingdom, the United States and Australia) is off the agenda for the foreseeable future, it is inconceivable, in my view, that workers, racialized or not, could productively unite around anti-'white supremacy'. More constructive, from a Marxist perspective, is to demand an end to racialized capitalism.

CRITICAL RACE THEORY AND THE PRIMACY OF 'RACE' OVER CLASS: A MARXIST CRITIQUE[96]

Mills rejects both what he refers to as the 'original white radical orthodoxy (Marxist)' for arguing that social class is the primary contradiction in capitalist society, and the 'present white radical orthodoxy (post-Marxist/postmodernist)' for its rejection of any primary contradiction. Instead, for Mills, 'there is a primary contradiction, and ... it's race'.[97] For Kimberlé Crenshaw and colleagues, 'subsuming race under class' is 'the typical Marxist error'.[98]

Mills states that '[r]ace [is] the central identity around which people close ranks' and that there is 'no transracial class bloc'.[99] Given the way in which neoliberal global capitalism unites capitalists throughout the world on lines that are not necessarily colour-coded, this statement seems quite extraordinary.

'Race', Mills goes on, is 'the stable reference point for identifying the "them" and "us" which override all other "thems' and "us's" (identities are multiple, but some are more central than others)',[100] while for Crenshaw and colleagues, although they acknowledge that 'race' is socially constructed (an issue addressed at the beginning of this Introduction), with which Marxists would fully concur, 'race' is 'real' since 'there is a material dimension and weight to being "raced" in American society'.[101] I would agree, of course, that racism has real material effects on racialized peoples, and this is reflected throughout the book. 'Race', Mills concludes, is 'what ties the system together, and blocks progressive change.'[102] For Marxists, it is capitalism that does this.

Mills invites readers to:

> Imagine you're a white male Marxist in the happy prefeminist, pre-postmodernist world of a quarter-century ago. You read Marcuse, Miliband, Poulantzas, Althusser. You believe in a theory of group domination involving something like the following: The United States is a *class* society in which class, defined by *relationship to the means of production*, is the *fundamental* division, the bourgeoisie being the *ruling* class, the workers being *exploited* and *alienated*, with the state and the juridicial system *not* being neutral but part of a superstructure to maintain the existing order, while the *dominant ideology* naturalizes, and renders invisible and unobjectionable, class domination.[103]

This all seems a pretty accurate description of the United States in the twenty-first century, but for Mills it is 'a set of highly controversial propositions'.[104] He justifies this assertion by stating that all of the above 'would be disputed by mainstream political philosophy (liberalism), political science (pluralism), economics (neoclassical marginal utility theory), and sociology (Parsonian structural-functionalism and its heirs)'.[105] While this is true, my response to this would be, well, of course it would be disputed by mainstream philosophers, pluralist political scientists, neoclassical economists and functionalist sociologists, all of whom are, unlike Marxists, at one level or another apologists for capitalism.

Social class, I would argue, albeit massively racialized,[106] is the system upon which the maintenance of capitalism depends. It is possible, though extremely difficult, because of the multiple benefits accruing to capital of racializing workers (not least forcing down labour costs), and the unpaid and underpaid labour of women as a whole, to imagine a capitalist world of 'racial' (and gender) equality. It is not logically possible for capitalism to exhibit social class equality. Without the extraction of surplus value from the labor of workers, capitalism cannot exist.

Capitalism is dependent on racism both as a source of profiteering (in general appropriating more surplus value from racialized workers) and as a means of 'divide and rule', driving a wedge between non-racialized and racialized workers. These processes of 'divide and rule' were recognized by Marx, some 145 years ago:

> In all the big industrial centres in England there is profound antagonism between the Irish proletariat and the English proletariat. The

average English worker hates the Irish worker as a competitor who lowers wages and the standard of life. He feels national and religious antipathies for him. He regards him somewhat like the poor whites of the Southern states regard their black slaves. *This antagonism among the proletarians of England is artificially nourished and supported by the bourgeoisie. It knows that this scission is the true secret of maintaining its power* (my emphasis).[107]

That is one of the reasons why combating racism is so crucial for Marxists. As Keenga-Yamahtta Taylor puts it, without 'a commitment by revolutionary organizations in the here and now to the fight against racism, working-class unity will never be achieved and the revolutionary potential of the working class will never be realized'.[108]

INTERSECTIONALITY AND MARXISM

If CRT is a major Left paradigm for understanding racism in the United States and Australia, one of the foremost manifestations of contemporary feminism is intersectionality. As Marxist feminist Eve Mitchell puts it, '[t]oday, you could go into any university, on any number of liberal-to-left blogs or news websites, and the words "identity" and "intersectionality" will jump out [at] you as the hegemonic theory'.[109] What then is 'intersectionality'? Gillborn explains its connection to CRT. As he points out, critical race theorists 'often focus on how racism works with, against and through additional axes of differentiation including class, gender, sexuality and disability'.[110] Hence, there are a number of identity-specific varieties such as 'LatCrit', 'Asian-American jurisprudence', 'Native jurisprudence', and 'queer-crit',[111] as well as critical race theorists concerned with 'disability'. As Gillborn argues, this concern with intersectionality is especially strong in critical race feminism,[112] itself a variety of CRT. Indeed, the very concept of intersectionality is generally attributed to the aforementioned feminist critical race theorist Kimberlé Crenshaw in an article in 1989, in which she sought to challenge both feminist and antiracist theory and practice that neglected to 'accurately reflect the interaction of race and gender'.[113] As she reasoned, 'because the intersectional experience is greater than the sum of racism and sexism, any analysis that does not take intersectionality into account cannot sufficiently address the particular manner in which Black women are subordinated'.[114] A key aspect of intersectionality is its premise that multiple oppressions are not each suffered separately, but as a single, synthesized experience.[115]

Leading UK-based intersectionality theorist Nira Yuval-Davis states that unlike 'many feminists, especially black feminists, who focus on intersectional analysis as specific to black and ethnic minorities women or, at least, to marginalized people', she sees 'intersectionality as the most valid approach to analyze social stratification as a whole'. Intersectional analysis, she claims, 'does not prioritize one facet or category of social difference'. 'As to the question of how many facets of social difference and axes of power need to be analyzed', she clarifies her view of its fluidity:

> this is different in different historical locations and moments, and the decision on which ones to focus involve both empirical reality as well as political and especially ontological struggles. What is clear, however, is that when we carry out intersectional analysis, we cannot homogenize the ways any political project or claimings affect people who are differentially located within the same boundaries of belonging.[116]

Intersectionality can be merely an *academic* discipline, divorced from class struggle, or it can be a healthy counterbalance to what remains of reductionist Marxism, which views any consideration of oppression and exploitation beyond social class to be diversionary.[117] At its worst, intersectionality simply creates 'a list of naturalized identities, abstracted from their material and historical context',[118] of which the 'practical upshot ... is the perpetual articulation of *difference*, resulting in fragmentation and the stagnation of political activity'.[119] Intersectionality viewed thus, renders social class as non-axiomatic, not the crucial social relation on which depends the ability or otherwise of capitalism to sustain and reproduce itself.

At its best intersectionality is 'rooted in real material conditions structured by social class'.[120] As Sharon Smith concludes, as 'an *additive* to Marxist theory, intersectionality leads the way toward a much higher level of understanding of the character of oppression than that developed by classical Marxists'. Underlying the Marxist position that no academic political theory is valid if it is divorced from workers' struggles, Smith adds that intersectionality thus defined enables 'the further development of the ways in which *solidarity* can be built between all those who suffer oppression and exploitation under capitalism to forge a unified movement'.[121]

OUTLINE OF THE BOOK

Miles has argued that 'at a certain point it doesn't matter who you are, you can be ... racialized'.[122] Thus in this book, analyses range from the attempted annihilation of indigenous peoples of colour in pursuit of land and profit centuries ago, to the economic exploitation of (lower wages means more surplus value, hence more profit) and oppression of (blue-eyed blond haired) white Eastern Europeans today. In Chapter 1, I begin with a consideration of older colour-coded racism which had its origins in the British colonial era and still resonates today. I go on to argue that in the United Kingdom racism's parameters lie beyond skin colour, and that there are three long-existing forms of non-colour-coded racism, racializing the Irish, Jewish people, and the Gypsy Roma and Traveller communities. I also consider in the first chapter of this book, the existence of a newer form of non-colour-coded racism, xeno-racism, as well as what I refer to as hybridist racism: Islamophobia and anti-asylum-seeker racism. I conclude with some observations on (xeno-)racism in the run-up to the 2015 general election and on racism in the context of austerity/immiseration capitalism. In this chapter I also address the decline of multiculturalism at the level of the state. It is useful to differentiate multiculturalism and multicultural societies. Multiculturalism is a fundamentally liberal (in the sense of 'middle of the road politics' rather than the US interpretation of the more politically Left of centre position). While twenty-first-century socialists rebuff the ideology of multiculturalism, they are firm advocates of multicultural societies, and of interculturalism (pertaining to two or more cultures) and intraculturalism (variations within one culture) – key concepts in Latin American politics.

Racism in the United States needs to be seen, I argue in Chapter 2, in the context of 500 years of institutional racism, beginning with the 1492 Spanish invasion (Columbus's first 'voyage') and the subsequent attempted genocide of the indigenous people, the consequences of which reverberates piercingly in the twenty-first century. I then look at racism directed at Alaskan Natives both historically and today. In order to understand the racism experienced by African Americans today, it is necessary to know about slavery and segregation, both of which still exist as realities today, the former in the guise of the prison-industrial complex, the latter clearly visible in the major cities of the United States. In addition, in order to understand anti-Latina/o racism it is important to understand the history of Mexicans and Mexican Americans, and of Puerto Ricans and Puerto Rican Americans. In this chapter, I also consider racism facing Asian Americans, both historically and today. I conclude the chapter with a consideration of Islamophobia, antisemitism and the proliferation of hate groups. While the election of Barack Obama is to be welcomed as of great significance symbolically by all those who believe in multiculturalism, and in part reflects the fact that the 'white establishment' is becoming a minority, there is little else to celebrate.

The United States remains a deeply racist rather than a 'post-racial' society. White men still hold the power, and Obama has continued and reinforced US imperialism, which, it is pointed out in this chapter, has the effect of reinforcing and exacerbating racism.

As in the United Kingdom and the United States, racism and racialization in Australia is multifaceted. I begin Chapter 3 by examining older colour-coded racism. This means first, a consideration of settler colonialism, which entailed invasion and the attempted genocide of indigenous peoples, as well as the exploitation of Aboriginal labour, and the kidnapping of South Sea islanders for indentured labour. Anti-Asian racism is then examined both historically and contemporaneously. I next look at older non-colour-coded racism in the forms of anti-Irish racism and antisemitism. The 'white Australia' policy dominated Australian politics for much of the twentieth century, but immigration was mediated by Anglo-Celtic racism, resulting in a hierarchical racialized segmented labour market. Beneath this segmented market are Indigenous peoples, marginalized to permanently unemployed, fringe-dweller status. Racism in the latter part of the twentieth century and the beginning of the twenty-first cannot be understood, I suggest, without an examination of 'Hansonism' and the Howard government. All these forms of racism persist today. Newer colour-coded forms of racism are directed at migrant communities, and as in the United Kingdom, anti-asylum-seeker racism is a prominent element in Australian racism today. As in the United Kingdom and the United States, newer hybridist Islamophobia, I note, is ever-present in the contemporary context. Also as in the United Kingdom, there has been a decline of multiculturalism at the level of state policy. Like the United States, Australia has a number of hate groups.

In each of the chapters, I use neo-Marxist, Gramscian and Althusserian theory, as outlined in this Introduction, to try to make sense of the continuity of racism and the overwhelming acceptance by the populace of capitalism, including its current austerity/immiseration mode. One salient feature of capitalism is the massive and increasing disparity in wealth between the working class and the ruling class, with poverty among the working class being clearly racialized, as noted earlier. Citing the Durban Declaration of 2001, Mutuma Ruteere argues that poverty is closely associated with racism, and contributes to the persistence of racist attitudes and practices which in turn generate more poverty.[123] This connection was reinforced in 2009 when it was reported to the United Nations that minority 'racial' and ethnic groups are disproportionately affected by poverty, with lack of education, inadequate housing and health care transmitting poverty generationally, perpetuating racism and stereotypes.[124] As Ruteere argued in 2013, racialized groups are disproportionately affected by poverty in all regions of the world, where they are trapped in conditions of 'chronic deprivation of resources' with limited choices and vulnerable to multiple violations of their rights – they are discriminated against for being poor and on account of their 'race' and ethnicity.[125]

Readers will note the absence of a discussion of the myriad and massively important struggles against racism that began from the very beginnings of imperialism and colonialism, and which continue up to the present day. Space precludes a discussion of them in this book. The way the book veers strongly in the direction of analyses of the constraining structural features of capitalist societies, towards interpellation and hegemony (rather than counter-hegemony) is, of course, a reflection of this. Analysis of antiracism requires a book in its own right. Hence a companion volume[126] will trace the histories of, and contemporary manifestations of, antiracist struggles, which are not covered in this book.

1

The United Kingdom

INTRODUCTION

In the Introduction to this book, I referred to the close correlation between poverty and racism, and the way in which they reinforce each other. As Helen Barnard of the Joseph Rowntree Foundation points out, referring to a report on ethnicity by think tank Policy Exchange,[1] it 'does not highlight one of the most important facts about ethnicity in Britain: there is more poverty in every ethnic minority group than among the White British population'[2] (see Figure 1.1). The legacy of empire, therefore, still looms large in the United Kingdom. However, this by no means tells the whole story of racism there. In the Introduction, I argued for a wide-ranging definition of racism. Such a definition must include non-colour-coded racism. In many accounts of racism, assumptions are made that it is solely about skin colour. In reality, significant forms of racism in the United Kingdom are not colour-based. In the immediate post-war period of mass migration, white Irish workers were racialized, along with Asian and African-Caribbean migrants. As immigrants' children entered school, they too were on the receiving end of processes of racialization.[3] With the mechanization of farming, many English Gypsies moved from rural areas to cities and towns, encountering hostile reactions from the local population and from the authorities,[4] with similar consequences of racialization as their children entered the education system. Given the presence in England of Irish Travellers, anti-Gypsy, Roma and Traveller racism is compounded with anti-Irish racism.

Islamophobia became a major form of racism in Britain after the first Gulf War (1990–91),[5] intensifying after 9/11 and 7/7. This form of racism may be termed hybridist,[6] in that Muslims may or may not be subject to colour-coded racism and are often marked out not so much by their colour as by their beards and headscarves.[7]

These various and multifaceted forms of colour-coded, non-colour-coded and hybridist racism were made even more convoluted when in 1993 the Maastricht Treaty created the European Union. The integration of the United Kingdom into Europe and the disintegration of Eastern Europe has witnessed yet another form of racism directed at (predominantly) white Eastern European migrant workers and their

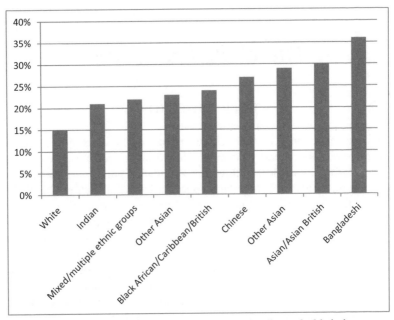

Figure 1.1 Poverty rates by ethnic group, HBAI (households below average income), June 2013

Source: Gov.UK, 'Households below average income (HBAI) statistics', 1 July 2014, www.gov.uk/government/collections/households-below-average-income-hbai–2

families: xeno-racism.[8] In addition, in the 1990s 'asylum seekers' became racialized as both centre-right and centre-left parties in Europe began to implement laws that criminalized them.[9] All these types of racism need to be contextualized alongside ongoing and continuing antisemitism, still a significant form of non-colour-coded racism in the second decade of the twenty-first century, with racialization dating back centuries. There can, of course, be permutations among these various forms of racism.

In this chapter, I begin by looking at what I call older colour-coded racism from the colonial era up to the present, concentrating on people of Asian, black African, black African Caribbean and Chinese origins. I go on to examine older non-colour-coded racism, focusing on anti-Irish racism, antisemitism and anti-Gypsy Roma and Traveller (GRT) racism, before turning to a consideration of newer forms of racism. Under this heading, I discuss both newer non-colour-coded racism, namely xeno-racism and newer hybridist racism, which can be either colour-coded or non-colour-coded. In this final categorization, I include both Islamophobia (in this section I refer to the decline of state multiculturalism) and anti-asylum-seeker racism.[10] Throughout, I relate (changes in) racism to (changes in) the requirements of capitalism, and the ways in which this is mediated by the apparatuses of the state: in particular, the political establishment and the media. I go to make some observations on racism in the run-up to the 2015 general election, before concluding with a discussion of racism in the context of austerity capitalism.

OLDER COLOUR-CODED RACISM: THE COLONIAL ERA AND ITS LEGACY

Empire, Nation and 'Race'

Racialization is of course historically and geographically specific. Thus, in the British colonial era, when Britain ruled vast territories in Africa, Asia, the Caribbean and elsewhere, implicit in the rhetoric of imperialism was a racialized concept of 'nation', whereby the British were 'destined' to rule the inferior 'races' in the colonies.

Biological racism at the time of the British Empire was considered a science. One example of scientific racism will suffice, here directed at Africans by a president of the Anthropological Society of London, James Hunt:

> there is as good a reason for classifying the Negro as a distinct species from the European as there is for making the ass a distinct species from the zebra; and if we take intelligence into consideration in classification, there is far greater difference between the Negro and the Anglo-Saxon than between the gorilla and chimpanzee … the analogies are more numerous between the Negro and apes than between the European and the ape. The Negro is inferior intellectually to the European … the Negro is more humanised when in his natural subordination to the European, than under any other circumstances … the Negro race can only be humanised and civilised by Europeans … European civilisation is not suited to the requirements and character of the Negro.[11]

The ongoing ferocious and relentless pursuit of expanding capital accumulation in the days of the British Empire in the nineteenth century has to be seen in the context of competition from other countries, and the need to regenerate British capitalism amid fears that sparsely settled British colonies might be overrun by other European 'races'.

On the affinity between 'race' and class in the European mind in general, but prescient of the attitudes of the Victorian ruling class in particular, V. G. Kieran writes:

> If there were martial races abroad, there were likewise martial classes at home: every man could be drilled to fight, but only the gentleman by birth could lead and command. In innumerable ways his attitude to his own 'lower orders' was identical with that of Europe to the 'lesser breeds'. Discontented native in the colonies, labour agitator in the mills, were the same serpent in alternate disguises. Much of the talk about the barbarians or darkness of the outside world, which it was Europe's mission to rout, was a transmuted fear of the masses at home.[12]

Bernard Semmel has developed Karl Renner's concept of social imperialism to describe the way in which the ruling class attempted to provide a mass base for imperialism. Social imperialism made the links between nation and empire:

> Social-imperialism was designed to draw all classes together in defence of the nation and empire and aimed to prove to the least well-to-do class that its interests were inseparable from those of the nation.[13]

The ideology of social imperialism, as Semmel points out, was presented to the working class by the Unionist Party in many millions of leaflets and in many thousands of street-corner speeches.[14] In addition, there were set up self-professed propaganda organizations, such as the Primrose League, established in 1883. The League was organized on medieval lines: its full members were described as knights and dames and imperial knights, whereas the working class were enrolled as 'associate members'. By 1891 it was claiming a million members; by 1901 1.5 million, of which 1.4 million were said to be working class.[15] Its very effective propaganda exploited each of the imperial highlights of the 1880s and 1890s, such as the death of Gordon at Khartoum and the Boer War. Its leaflets had direct and simple messages, and it dressed up its propaganda in the guise of popular entertainment, often taking the form of 'tableaux vivants', magic lantern displays, lectures and exhibitions.[16]

By the end of the nineteenth century, the ideology of the 'inferiority' of Britain's colonial subjects and the consequent 'superiority' of the British 'race' was, then, available to all. As far as popular culture in general is concerned, patriotism and Empire were highly marketable products from the late 1800s to 1914. There were a number of reasons for this. First, important social and economic changes had occurred, especially the transformation of Britain into a predominantly urban, industrial nation.[17] Basic state education, available after the 1870 Act, and underpinned by imperial themes,[18] and technical developments[19] facilitated the introduction of cheap popular imperialist fiction.[20] Britain's imperial 'adventures' were justified by institutional racism in popular culture: in music halls,[21] in juvenile fiction,[22] in popular art[23] and in the education system. For example, with respect to the educational ideological state apparatus (ISA), textbooks attempted to justify the continuance of 'the strong arm and brave spirit ... of the British Empire'.[24] An imperial 'race' was needed to defend the nation and the colonies.[25] Thus, the African subjects of the colonies were racialized, in school textbooks, as 'fierce savages' and 'brutal and stinking',[26] while freed Caribbean slaves were described as 'lazy, vicious and incapable of any serious improvement or of work except under compulsion'.[27] At the same time, references were made to 'the barbaric peoples of Asia',[28] and the most frequent impression conveyed about Indians and Afghans was that they were cruel and totally unfit to rule themselves.[29] Missionary work was seen as 'civilizing the natives'. Racism in all its manifestations had become collective 'common sense'.

John Hobson writes of the importance of 'hero-worship and sensational glory, adventure and the sporting spirit: current history/falsified in coarse flaring colours, for the direct stimulation of the combative instincts'.[30] Springhall states:

> that the 'little wars' of Empire, which took place in almost every year of Queen Victoria's reign after 1870, provided the most readily available source for magazine and newspaper editors of romantic adventure and heroism set in an exotic and alien environment.[31]

Such images, Springhall continues,[32] were also apparent in commercial advertising, school textbook illustrations, postcards, cigarette cards, cheap reproductions and other ephemera which appropriated and mediated the work of popular British artists of the time. Scientific biological racism had thus become institutionalized in popular culture in the British Imperial era in many ways.

The Empire and China

While imperialism did not take hold in mainland China as it did in other parts of Asia, Africa and the Caribbean, China was greatly affected by the

British Empire, and its political and cultural legacies are still apparent today in the ex-colony of Hong Kong, despite its now being back under control of (the People's Republic of) China.[33] As a result of a high demand in Britain for tea, silk and porcelain, the British bartered Indian opium in exchange for these goods.[34]

Opium for medicinal purposes was first manufactured in China toward the end of the fifteenth century, and was used to treat dysentery, cholera and other diseases. It was not until the eighteenth century that there were any accounts of opium smoking in China.[35] In 1729, concerned at its debilitating effect, the Chinese imperial government forbade the sale of opium mixed with tobacco and closed down opium-smoking houses.[36] Selling opium for smoking 'was classed with robbery and instigation to murder, and punished with banishment or death'.[37]

But, as Kristianna Tho'mas points out,[38] this did not stop the British, who had gradually been taking over the opium trade from their European capitalist rivals, Portugal and Holland. Much of the opium at this time was grown and manufactured in Britain's Indian Empire. As Marx put it, noting how the employees of the English East India Company exploited the Indians politically and economically, and facilitated drug addiction on the Chinese:

> The ... Company ... obtained, besides the political rule in India, the exclusive monopoly of the tea-trade, as well as of the Chinese trade in general, and of the transport of goods to and from Europe. ... The monopolies of salt, opium, betel and other commodities, were inexhaustible mines of wealth. The [employees] themselves fixed the price and plundered at will the unhappy Hindus.[39]

So, Tho'mas writes, 'while the Chinese government was taking stronger and stronger measures to end the opium trade, the British were doing all they could to increase it'.[40] This led to a rapid increase in opium in China between 1790 and 1832, and resulted in a generation of addicts and accompanying social instability.[41] Opium sales rose gradually from 2,330 chests in 1788 to 4,968 in 1810.[42] In 1830, Britain's governor-general of India wrote, '[w]e are taking measures for extending the cultivation of the poppy, with a view to a large increase in the supply of opium'.[43] Once the British got a monopoly, they forced up the sales to 17,257 chests in 1835,[44] which generated millions of British pounds in surplus value, and hence profits. Clashes between the Qing government and British merchants ultimately escalated into the infamous Opium Wars of 1839–42 and 1860–62. One military official at the time of the first war noted that a war 'undertaken against a nation so puerile in that art would better deserve the name of murder, and could certainly add no laurels to British valour'.[45] As Bernard Porter points out, murder:

> seems an apt word: tens of thousands of Chinese were killed (some killed themselves, out of shame), but the British (and Indian auxil- iaries) suffered only minor casualties. Julia Lovell describes it from eyewitness accounts: the 'brain-spattered walls' of the forts the British stormed; 'bent, blackened, smouldering, stinking' human remains; 'the bodies of the slain … found literally three and four deep'; the sea 'quite blackened with corpses' … as well as the excesses of the rampaging British troops.[46]

They were, Tho'mas suggests, the world's first drug wars, their sole purpose being 'to secure the importation of an addictive substance that provided a bountiful flow of profits'.[47] As Joshua Rowntree put it, the British were 'in a great hurry to make money out of the East, and the gunboats were found to clear the way quickly. All vestiges of compassion for mankind had been swept away by the silver stream of rupees which poured into the Calcutta Exchequer'.[48]

At the end of the 1839–42 Opium War, the British expanded its Empire only a little with the acquisition of the island of Hong Kong.[49] As Tho'mas concludes, this was:

> the bloody origin of Hong Kong's 155 years as a British colony. It paralleled imperialist conquest in Africa, Latin America, the Middle East and the rest of Asia – a heritage that in the 20th century has brought both great misery and great revolutionary movements for national liberation.[50]

According to Richard Klein,[51] from its inception colonial Hong Kong was unsurprisingly saturated with white supremacy. Klein describes how the British used the law as a tool to consolidate control of Hong Kong in the hands of a privileged minority. The British enacted legislation which insti- tuted two sets of laws, one for the Europeans and another for the Chinese. Laws were passed to ensure that no Chinese person would live in the most desirable areas. In a land in which 98 per cent of the population was Chinese, English was the official language, and Chinese was not permitted in government offices. Laws regulating conduct were written exclusively in English, which the vast majority of the population could not understand. The fact that Hong Kong remained a British colony until 1997 testifies to the success of these racist British laws.[52]

Carl H. Nightingale argues that segregation started with British rule in Madras (Chennai) and the East India Company's decision to split Calcutta (Kolkata) into 'White Town' and 'Black Town', while the word 'segregation' itself comes from techniques used in Hong Kong and Bombay (Mumbai) in the 1890s.[53] Elsewhere, Nightingale relates segregation to British imperialism and to the creation of 'Chinatowns':

> Urban segregation was central to the first modern empire's first big undertaking, the British conquest of India ... to the hundred and seventy five segregated 'stations' of the British Raj – scattered from Afghanistan to the Malay Peninsula, from the hot military outposts in the plains to the cool 'hill stations' in the uplands – racial segregation proved itself in an enormously diverse political, social, economic, religious and geographical terrain. The second surge, associated with the European 'opening' of China, brought segregation to places as diverse as Singapore, Shanghai, Hong Kong and Yokohama. From there the concept of the Chinatown sprang across the Pacific, adapting for the first time to the rawer racial politics of white settler colonies, such as those headquartered in San Francisco, Vancouver, Melbourne and Honolulu.[54]

In the nineteenth century, 'national efficiency' served as a convenient label under which a complex set of beliefs, assumptions and demands could be grouped – it completed the racist chain of Empire, nation and 'race'. One prominent current subscribed to the belief that the low level of efficiency of the army reflected the degeneration of the 'race', based on the belief that the British were a chosen race, destined for historic achievement: therefore, positive ways must be taken to 'improve the race', if necessary by controlling the rights of the more 'degenerate' sections of the population to breed, and engineering a stimulus to the birth rate, especially amongst the well-off sections of society. National efficiency thus provided a powerful stimulus to the 'social Darwinism' of people such as Benjamin Kidd and Karl Pearson, who advocated theories of the 'degeneration of certain national types' (for example the Jews and the Irish).[55]

As we shall see later in this chapter, the indigenous racism of the period was anti-Irish and antisemitic.

The Beveridge Report

It is in the context of these historical antecedents that the Beveridge Report of 1942, one of the key documents informing the founding of the welfare state, was written. As Gail Lewis explains, it was long accepted among all sections of the Left that the creation and administration of the Beveridge welfare state in Britain represented a 'settlement' between capital, organized labour and the state – reform not revolution. The components of this historic compromise were steady economic growth, sustained by Keynesian policies (a mixed economy of state ownership and spending on economic infrastructure, utilities and welfare alongside private businesses) with a commitment to full (male) employment. It was also established since the 1970s by feminists that a central additional component of this settlement was a normative family form of male breadwinner, dependent housewife and their children. However only since the 1980s has there has been a gradual, wider acceptance that deeply embedded in the conceptualization and practice of the Beveridge welfare reforms was also a notion of the nation, and with it one of 'race'.[56]

Indeed here, in the context of welfare, the links between 'race' and nation, and gender too, were made explicit. For example, the argument deployed in favour of introducing child allowances was that 'with its present rate of reproduction the British race cannot continue, means of reversing the recent course of the birth rate must he found'.[57] Women were assigned the role of baby-machines in the service of capitalism and British hegemony, and were told, 'In the next thirty years housewives as Mothers have vital work to do in ensuring the adequate continuance of the British Race and British Ideals in the world.'[58] The clearest example of the racism inherent in the Report can be seen in Beveridge's essay *Children's Allowances and the Race.* In it he stated:

> Pride of race is a reality for the British as for other peoples ... as in Britain today we look back with pride and gratitude to our ancestors, look back as a nation or as individuals two hundred years and more to the generations illuminated by Marlborough or Cromwell or Drake, are we not bound also to look forward, to plan society now so that there may be no lack of men or women of the quality of those earlier days, of the best of our breed, two hundred and three hundred years hence?[59]

The Post Second World War Period

The Empire came home to roost after the Second World War. The demands of an expanding post-war economy meant that Britain, like most other European countries, was faced with a major shortage of labour, with white 'indigenous' workers moving into jobs with higher rates of pay and conditions of work – light engineering, manufacturing of consumer durables and the service sector.[60] The overwhelming majority of migrants to Britain were from the Indian subcontinent and the Caribbean (these were British subjects and not initially subject to immigration control), as well as the Republic of Ireland (itself subject to British colonization in parts in the sixteenth and seventeenth centuries – see the next section of this chapter), who were given privileged access to the British labour market.[61] Those industries where the demand for labour was greatest actively recruited Asian, black and other minority ethnic workers in their home countries.[62] Despite the heterogeneous class structure of the migrating populations,[63] the vast majority arrived with little or no capital, and having no choice but to sell their labour power, these migrant workers came to occupy overwhelmingly semi-skilled and unskilled positions in the English labour market.[64] Furthermore, they found themselves disproportionately concentrated in certain types of manual work characterized by a shortage of labour, shift working, unsocial hours, low pay and an unpleasant working environment.[65]

Unlike contract labour, African Caribbean and Asian workers were theoretically free to compete with white British workers for higher-paid jobs with better conditions. However, unsurprisingly given the colonial history and its aftermath, employers believed or assumed that the labour market consisted of different 'races' with predetermined characteristics: Asians who were 'slow to learn', and African Caribbean people who were 'lazy, unresponsive to discipline and truculent', with 'coloured people' generally being more prone to accidents or requiring more supervision than white workers.[66] This racialization of workers led to their exclusion in two ways. First, Asian and African Caribbean workers were excluded when white labour was available. Second, where they were employed they were excluded from certain jobs, or their numbers were limited by a predetermined quota.[67] Elements of organized labour colluded with employers to exclude these workers.[68]

It was not only in the economic sphere that Asian, black and other minority ethnic workers were on the receiving end of racism. The state played a critical and formative role in restricting Commonwealth immigration. In the late 1950s, there was growing concern within Parliament, the media and the major political parties of the 'dangers of unrestricted immigration'. This contributed to an important shift in public policy from one of support for unrestricted immigration to one that 'stressed that the immigration of "non-whites" had to be curbed if the social fabric and cohesion of the country was not to be irreparably undermined'.[69] As a result the first of a number of Immigration Acts was passed in 1962. This restricted immigration from Asia and the Caribbean, but not from the Republic of Ireland. The consequences of these processes were clear. According to Robert Miles, these different racialized groups came to:

> occupy a structurally distinct position in the economic, political and ideological relations of British capitalism, but within the boundary of the working class. They therefore constitute a fraction of the working class, one that can be identified as a racialized fraction.[70]

In the post-Second World War period, not unexpectedly given these developments in racialization, and bearing in mind Britain's colonial history, the British Cabinet perceived many in the African-Caribbean community as 'accustomed to living in squalid conditions and have no desire to improve',[71] while their children were described by one local education authority (LEA) as 'physically robust and boisterous, yet mentally lethargic'. At the same time the same LEA perceived there to be 'very real problems' with the 'domestic habits and personal hygiene of the Asiatics' as well as 'the problem of [their] eating habits'.[72] Children from minority ethnic groups (not a source of cheap labour, as were their parents) were racialized as problems to be dealt with in schools in these post-war years.

Thatcherism

The election of Margaret Thatcher and the onset of Thatcherism in 1979 is notable, of course, for its championing of neoliberalism (the free rein of market capitalism with very minimal state regulation, accompanied by the privatization of production of goods and services) as the only viable way to run economies. Its concurrent triumphal discrediting of socialism was achieved by directly related socialism to the collapse of the Soviet Union, which was interpreted by many as meaning that Marx's theories and socialism were no longer viable. Thatcher was equally successful in falsely equating the Soviet Union with socialism, with the British Labour Party and militant trade unions, and urging their collective confinement to the dustbin of history. This was, of course, essential if Britain were to move in the direction of labour market compliance and labour flexibility. Following the late 1980s revolutions in Eastern Europe and the Soviet Union, Thatcher argued that Marxism was extinct. A majority response to Thatcher was, 'That's obvious! That's right! That's true!'[73]

In this scenario, class struggle, a fundamental tenet of Marxism, becomes outmoded. Therefore the Labour Party was also now extinct. It is precisely the success of this formulation that projected Tony Blair, a believer in the free market, to centre-stage – as a saviour of the Labour Party, but only if the Labour Party became reformulated as 'New Labour'. The term 'New Labour' was coined in 1994, when Blair become leader of the Labour Party, as part of an orchestrated campaign to distance the party from its socialist roots, to modernize it – in other words, to establish an unequivocal pro-capitalist base for the party. Thatcher was later to describe 'New Labour' as her greatest achievement. New Labour racism, as we shall see in this chapter, arguably exceeded that of the Thatcher years, and laid the foundations for the ConDem government of 2010.

The advent of Thatcherism also represents a decisive turning point in racialization in the last quarter of the twentieth century. In 1978 Margaret Thatcher, then leader of the opposition, told a television news programme that 'people are really rather afraid that this country might be swamped by people with a different culture'.[74] From the late 1960s, racism had begun to find a growing political expression, in the form of the National Front (NF), a fascist political party that also commanded the support of a section of disgruntled Tories and 'empire loyalists' who could not come to terms with Britain's post-war loss of power. In the 1970s, as economic crisis began to break up the post-war compact between capital and labour, the NF also attracted a layer of working-class support, receiving an unprecedented share of the vote (though no seats) in the Greater London Council elections of 1977.[75]

Thatcher's 1978 intervention had an immediate short-term effect on public opinion. After her 'swamping' interpellation, there was a dramatic surge in support for the Conservative Party, which jumped to an 11 per cent lead over the Labour Party in opinion polls (they had previously been trailing by 2 per cent). A year later Thatcher won the general election, while the NF, which had stood a record number of candidates, failed to win a single seat and collapsed amid bitter recriminations.[76]

As Daniel Trilling argues, Thatcher's 'swamping' comments reintroduced racist discourse to mainstream politics, after it had been confined to the far-right fringe for a decade. As he explains, the promise to drastically restrict the numbers of Commonwealth immigrants entering Britain was 'no dispassionate economic calculation', but rather founded on the premise that 'people' were 'threatened by the incursion of an unwanted – and, by the use of the pejorative "swamped", harmful – foreign culture'.[77]

In a less often quoted part of Thatcher's interview, we can see how a racist belief in British superiority is used to heighten the sense of threat:

The British character has done so much for democracy, for law and done so much throughout the world that if there is any fear that it might be swamped people are going to react and be rather hostile to those coming in.[78]

Thatcher is, of course, *not* referring to the white Commonwealth citizens of countries such as Australia, Canada and New Zealand. Most enduringly, Trilling concludes, Thatcher bequeathed us the idea that when confronted with a surge in support for racist or xenophobic parties, all a mainstream politician needs to do is take to the airwaves and adopt some of their rhetoric.[79] Later in this chapter, I discuss mainstream responses to the xeno-racism of the UK Independence Party (UKIP) in the run-up to the 2015 UK general election.

Racism Today: British Asians and Black British People

As was stressed at the beginning of this chapter, racism related to Britain's colonial past still has a significant presence. Today, while a number of descendants of migrant workers have moved up the social class ladder, racism continues unabated. Moreover, while factors other than social class such as gender, age, health, religion, history and neighbourhood impact on minority ethnic poverty rates, all minority ethnic groups are adversely affected by poverty[80] (see also Figure 1.1). With respect to employment, racism in recruitment adversely affects those whose 'names ... do not appear to be white British'. British Pakistani, Bangladeshi and black people are also paid less on average than those with similar qualifications from either white British or Indian backgrounds, the latter reflecting a social class advantage.[81]

Racism in the police service is a significant problem. The force was declared 'institutionally racist' by the Stephen Lawrence Inquiry Report (1999)[82] into the death of black teenager Stephen Lawrence in 1993, after a lengthy intense campaign by Stephen's parents, Doreen Lawrence and Neville Lawrence. The legacy of the Criminal Justice and Public Order Act (1994) has a major impact on black and Asian people today. Under Section 60, the police are able to stop and search people without suspecting involvement in crime. Statistics show that this is used up to 28 times more on average on black people than on white people, and 10 times more on Asian Britons. Underlining the racist way in which Section 60 is used, in England as a whole, only just over 2 per cent of stop-and-searches resulted in an arrest, with arrest rates being similar among black and white people.[83]

In a 2013 debate in parliament, black Labour Party MP Diane Abbott pointed out that the systematic use of stop-and-search powers by the police was a major factor behind the riots which broke out in the capital in 2011. As she put it:

> [N]o single police activity causes more unhappiness and antagonism between the police and young black people than stop and search. That goes all the way back to the 1980s and the Brixton riots. Even after the 2011 riots, when I spoke to young people in Hackney about what triggered the riots, they said, 'Stop and search'.[84]

If we look at mental health, members of black and minority ethnic communities are disproportionately represented in hospital statistics, with black African, black Caribbean and black/white mixed groups of adults three times more likely to be admitted to hospital than the population as a whole. In addition they are up to 44 per cent more likely to be sectioned (detained without their consent). Black and minority ethnic groups have three times the risk of psychosis, with seven times the risk in black African-Caribbean groups, and a two to threefold increased suicide risk. Black Caribbean, black African and white/black Caribbean mixed groups are 40–60 per cent more likely than average to be admitted to hospital from a criminal justice referral. This means that mental health problems are often only detected when they come into contact with law enforcement agencies. Black men are almost twice as likely as white men to be detained in police custody under Section 136 of the Mental Health Act. Finally, black African Caribbean and South Asian patients are less likely to have their mental health problems detected by a general medical practitioner (GP). At the same time, and paradoxically, they are more likely to have other problems wrongly attributed to mental health issues.[85]

Football matches have traditionally been a hotbed of racism, and provide a good example of spaces where racism can arise from or be accentuated by stimuli from others. The chair of the British Asian Football Forum referred to a comment from an opposition coach that there was no point in checking photos on players' registration cards before a match because 'they all look the same'. According to Colin King of the Black and Asian Coaches Association, there are at least three cases of racism a week 'from being called things like "Paki", to the "N-word"'. He concludes, 'we've still got the monkey-shouting that takes place from parents and other managers as well. I do park football every week and I see racial abuse consistently'.[86] During the 2014–15 season, the number of alleged racist incidents increased by over 200 per cent from the previous year. There were 677 allegations of discrimination, mostly alleged racism. Heather Rabbatts, chair of the Football Association's Inclusion Advisory Board, stated that black players currently feel excluded when they retire. She pointed to the lack of black football managers.[87]

The local and national pride invoked at football matches not only inflames racism, but plays a valuable ideological role for the ruling class by deflecting the pain of people's economic and social circumstances. This thought aversion is particular useful in the current climate of austerity/immiseration capitalism.

Racism Today: UK Chinese People

Sue Adamson from the University of Hull and her co-authors ended their 2009 report on racism directed at the United Kingdom's Chinese population as follows:

> The experience gained from the focus groups further confirms evidence of wide-ranging forms of racial harassment and violence experienced by UK Chinese people across a multiplicity of contexts including at primary and secondary school, in higher education, at home, at work, at leisure, on public transport and while shopping. All three groups, of younger students, catering business workers and older people, were able to substantiate the prevalence of racial harassment experienced in and around restaurants and takeaways. The role of children and young people as perpetrators and victims is a recurring theme.[88]

A study focusing on the North-East of England found that among 'all the (frequent) racial abuse against the Chinese community, general verbal abuse is the most serious', much of it perpetrated by teenagers.[89] This is because Chinese people in the North-East are quite isolated, with low incomes, less involvement in community organizations, and are particularly more exposed to racism in rural contexts.[90]

Some six years after the 2009 research by Adamson and her colleagues, Michael Wilkes from the British Chinese Project told BBC *Newsbeat* reporter Emily Thomas that people regularly contact the community group about physical and verbal abuse from all over the United Kingdom, pointing out that there is 'a lack of knowledge about the words Chinese people find offensive'.[91] Wilkes explained that the Chinese community is widely dispersed, meaning that many Chinese people are very isolated, stand out more and are therefore vulnerable. He went to note that a lot of racist attacks go unreported, because of widespread mistrust of the police. In the *Newsbeat* report one young British-born Chinese woman complained of a double standard: 'It's just become such a norm that the N-word or the P-word aren't allowed but people feel they can use the C-word. But I feel I die a little inside when some people say it.' Talking of her family's takeaway in a North-Eastern coastal town, she stated, 'Every night it would sound as if it was raining and it would be people throwing loads of chunks of rocks. We'd have windows smashed, they'd literally rip the tarmac off the roads and throw it at us, they'd shout at us, maybe spit.' She regularly reported the racist abuse her family experienced to the police. There were court cases but no one was ever convicted. 'It got to the point where we started losing faith in the police. We never had a life outside school because we daren't go outside.' She told Thomas that every member of her family has been physically assaulted for being Chinese, and cried when she described her mum being kicked unconscious on the doorstep of their home by a group of young men. Late in 2014, Chinese takeaway owner Jie Yu was stabbed during what police described as a racially aggravated attack in Edinburgh. Three men were charged with attempted murder. Simon Hu, a manager at Chinese restaurants in Wigan and Liverpool, said in the report that it is also common for takeaways to be vandalized. Another young Chinese man told *Newsbeat* that as a teenager, he experienced racist taunts every single day and had suffered one brutal physical attack: 'On my 18th birthday, at the station, three middle aged men came up to me and said, "Oi c…, what are you staring at?" before they beat me up.' 'I feel like I will never really escape from racism', he went on. 'I get the occasional verbal abuse on the street – you get "hey look, it's Jackie Chan" and they make Chinese sounds at me.'

During the 2014–15 football season, the chair of Wigan Athletic football club was fined £50,000 for antisemitism. Part of that fine was also for using an offensive word for people of Chinese origin.

OLDER NON-COLOUR-CODED RACISM

Anti-Irish Racism

While in the colonial era the biological 'inferiority' of Britain's imperial subjects was perceived in Britain itself mainly at second hand,[92] the indigenous racism of the period was antisemitic[93] and anti-Irish.

There has been a continuity of anti-Irish racism, often taking the form of anti-Catholicism – racism therefore based on religion as well as nationality – stemming back to the sixteenth and seventeenth centuries, which saw the first full colonization of the island with Protestant settlers from

Britain. Dennis O'Hearn has argued that at three separate times in modern history, the Irish people, or settlers in Ireland, have tried to industrialize, and each time their attempts have been thwarted. The first was when the Irish economy was brutally incorporated into the English colonial empire in the 1640s by Cromwell's army, when within a few years about 40 per cent of land was transferred to Cromwell's soldiers and sponsors. The second occurred at the end of the eighteenth century, as the profits from the Empire meant that Britain developed more sophisticated technology which led to the collapse of the Irish cotton industry and mass emigration from Ireland. The third attempt took place in the first half of the twentieth century, but failed as the Irish began to be incorporated into the American Atlantic economy.[94]

Traditionally male Irish workers in Britain have been associated with a narrow range of jobs: working on the canals or the docks, labouring on the roads, building sites and railways. Irish women have often worked as domestic servants, street traders, factory workers or nurses.[95] Male Irish workers on the canals, known originally by the arguably racist term 'navvies', earned relatively good money working on the canals, but many Irish immigrants were poor.[96] In 1836, the *Report on the State of the Irish Poor in Great Britain* claimed that unskilled and ill-educated Irish workers had 'possession of all the lowest departments of manual labour', and were an essential part of the workforce in England. The *Report* referred to Irish immigration into Britain as 'an example of a less civilised population spreading itself as a substratum beneath a more civilised community'.[97] These processes of 'divide and rule' were recognized by Marx some 145 years ago.

In Ireland itself about a million people died of starvation and epidemic disease between 1846 and 1851, as a result of the potato crop failures – nearly one-eighth of the population. These deaths were exacerbated by 'doctrines of inaction'[98] held by the British ruling class, which led them to fail to adopt relief measures. This inaction was guided by the ideologies of laissez-faire economics and the Protestant evangelical belief in divine Providence, and by anti-Irish racism.[99] During this period, almost a million Irish people emigrated to Britain.

The 1911 census found that 70 per cent of England's Irish-born males were unskilled labourers, and 8 per cent were working on the land.[100] Ireland became independent in 1922, following the 1919–21 Irish War of Independence, and after this, large numbers migrated as a result of harsh economic conditions between the 1930s and the 1960s, and to make up the United Kingdom's labour shortages following the Second World War. In 1951, nearly a third of Irish workers worked as labourers or in the building trade.[101] Emigration continued steadily throughout the twentieth century, often as a result of sectarian violence between Catholics and Protestants. It rose again during the 2008–11 Irish financial crisis.[102]

There were two notable public resurgences of anti-Irish racism in 2012. The first involved an anti-Irish 'joke'. Anyone who has lived in the United Kingdom will be familiar with the omnipresence of such 'jokes', which invariably depend on imagined notions of Irish lower 'intelligence' to justify their punch line. Daley Thompson, the former Olympic decathlete, was forced to apologize after commenting on a BBC programme about a photograph of a woman wearing a tattoo on her arm which was misspelled as 'OYLMPIC torch bearer' that 'the tattooist must have been Irish'.

The second incident involved a march in Liverpool by the James Larkin Society, which traces its roots back to Liverpool's Irish Catholic immigrant community, and is named in honour of the famous Irish trade unionist and socialist. Palash Ghosh described the event. The march, designed to protest against racism, fascism and economic inequality in Britain, was taunted and harassed by far-right British groups, including the English Defence League, which characterized the demonstration as an 'IRA march'.[103] The anti-march protesters shouted, 'IRA off our streets!' with one man screaming 'F...k off back to Ireland, ye murdering bastards', and others chanting, 'Rule Britannia' and 'No surrender to the IRA.' One poster carried by protesters read, 'Over the past several years the city of Liverpool and north-west England has seen the rise of anti-British feeling projected on them by immigrant families from the Republic of Ireland.' A leaflet proclaimed, 'These people [Irish] are much like Islamics [sic]. They take, take, take with one hand and abuse their host nation with the other. They openly support Sinn Féin and the Irish Republican Army and we are expected to stand by, smile and allow them to spread their hatred for Britain.'

In addition, between 2012 and 2014 there were a series of racist incidents related to two Scottish football teams, Glasgow Rangers and Glasgow Celtic. Rangers supporters are historically Scots with a long Scottish ancestry and also Ulster Scots who originate from Northern Ireland, while Celtic supporters are historically Irish-Scottish. An employee of Frontline Noir publishers, Angela Haggerty, who is descended from Irish immigrants to Scotland on both sides of her family, edited the book *Downfall: How Rangers FC Self-Destructed* for Irish author I Phil Mac Giolla Bhain. Following its publication in September 2012, some Rangers fans used social media and blogs to launch personal attacks on both Mac Giolla Bhain and Haggerty.[104] Roy Greenslade states that 'much of their bile exhibited both racial (anti-Irish) and religious (anti-Catholic) prejudice'. One of the fans, David Limond, referred to Haggerty in a podcast as 'Taig of the day', with several expletive-laden epithets and a call to his listeners to 'hit her with all you've got' (Taig is a racist term for an Irish Catholic, used mainly in Northern Ireland and Scotland). Within minutes, according to Greenslade, Haggerty 'began receiving abuse tweets calling her a Fenian and a Provo' (also derogatory words for Irish Republicans). Limond was eventually imprisoned for six months for 'sending a threatening communication aggravated by racial and religious prejudice'. In a *Sunday Herald* interview in January 2014, with the headline '"I am a victim of anti-Irish racism," says Scots writer', Haggerty stated:

> It was vicious. You suddenly feel very isolated and targeted, that there is a group of people out there that have a genuine hatred for you and that's quite intimidating. *Downfall* was the first real professional work I had done and I was really proud of it, and really excited about it, so to suddenly have all this was a shock to the system.[105]

She also pointed out that many fans refused to back down after Limond was sentenced, continued to call her names, and even started a 'Free Limmy' hashtag as if people thought there had been some great injustice done to him and she had played the victim card. Haggerty concluded:

> There's a reluctance in Scotland to talk about anti-Irish racism – everything gets lumped under the sectarian banner when it's not actually tackling the problem. I know this was a podcast called 'Rangers chat', but this wasn't about Celtic or Rangers. I don't think anything in that podcast was related to football other than the fact I'd edited the book on Rangers. It was about how I looked, it was about my religion, it was about my ethnic background – those kinds of things.

When Northern Irish Catholic Neil Lennon played for Leicester City in England, there was little trouble, but when he moved to play for Celtic, first as a player and later as a manager, he was the victim of nearly a dozen assaults and attempted assaults. There were websites set up with threats against him, including one with his address and pictures of his partner and child.[106] Between 2011 and his departure from Celtic in 2014, he and his family received round-the-clock police protection at home and at his children's school.[107] As Scottish journalist Kevin McKenna argues, in a clear reference to racism based on a combination of religion, cultural and biology, 'there is still a sizable remnant of Scots who cling stubbornly to old ideas of religious and cultural supremacy and who regard the Irish as an inferior race'.

Anti-Irish Traveller racism, which also has a continuous history, is referred to later in the chapter, under the heading of 'Anti-Gypsy, Roma and Traveller racism'.

Antisemitism

From the 1880s there was a sizeable immigration to Britain of destitute Jewish people from Eastern Europe, and this fuelled the preoccupation of politicians and commentators about the health of the nation, the fear of the degeneration of 'the race', and the subsequent threat to imperial and economic hegemony.[108] Jewish people were routinely referred to in the same contemptuous way as the people in Britain's vast colonial Empire, described by the media as 'semi-barbarous', unable or unwilling to 'use the latrine', depositing 'their filth' on 'the floor of their rooms'.[109] At the other end of the social class spectrum, Jews were said to be involved in world conspiracy (thus directly threatening British imperial hegemony).

Such attitudes were not confined to the ruling class and its spokespersons in the media. 'Whenever, there is trouble in Europe', the Independent Labour Party (ILP) paper *Labour Leader* put it, 'you may be sure a hook-nosed Rothschild is at his games'.[110] Such sentiments fed directly into accusations at the time of the First World War that Jews had started the war to ruin Europe financially and politically, thus rendering Europe susceptible to Jewish 'control', and that Jews exploited the misery of the war to enrich themselves and prolonged it in order to lead the Bolshevik Revolution and further the aim of world revolution and domination.[111] Between the First and Second World Wars – the second of which of course unleashed the Holocaust – many Jews changed their names in order to offset racism.[112]

While antisemitism is not generally acceptable in the public domain today, it comes readily to the surface in certain contexts. For example, the Community Security Trust (CST) noted 628 antisemitic incidents in the first half of 2009 – a record high – owing to antisemitic reactions to the conflict in Gaza in January of that year.[113] CST recorded 299 antisemitic incidents across the United Kingdom in the first six months of 2012, an increase of 2 per cent from the 294 in the first six months of the previous year. The most common single incident was 'random, spontaneous, verbal anti-semitic abuse, directed at people who look Jewish while they go about their business in public places'.[114]

Racism at football matches also has a significant antisemitic element. Antisemitic taunts include references to Adolf Hitler, such as chants of 'Hitler's coming to get you', as well as persistent hissing which, according to Anthony Clavane, is an allusion to the gas chambers.[115] One player was banned for five games for antisemitism during the 2014–15 season.

As noted earlier, during the 2014–15 season the chair of Wigan Athletic Football Club was fined £50,000 for antisemitism.

Antisemitic hate crime also increased by over a third in the first six months of 2014, and spiked to a five-year high in July of that year. The CST recorded a 36 per cent rise in the total number of antisemitic incidents (to 304) between January and June. This was followed by 130 incidents in July alone, which coincided with the Israeli military offensive in Gaza, which by August had left more than 1,400 Palestinians dead. In the first six months of 2014, the CST recorded 304 antisemitic incidents across the United Kingdom, including 22 violent assaults, 27 attacks on property, 19 antisemitic threats, 232 incidents of abusive behaviour and four cases of mass-produced antisemitic literature. The CST confirmed that many of those carrying out the antisemitic attacks in the United Kingdom after the Gaza offensive referenced the Israeli government's actions there.[116]

CST spokesperson Mark Gardner identifies a range of factors. As he puts it, successive conflicts in the Middle East have created 'a crush of trigger events' that has not allowed anger to cool: the second intifada in 2000, the Israel–Lebanon war of 2006, and the three Israel–Hamas conflicts in 2009, 2012 and 2014 have 'left no time for the situation to return to normal'. In such a climate, he concludes, three brutal antisemitic murders in the past eight years – all in mainland Europe, and none coinciding with Israeli military action – have served 'not to shock, but to encourage the antisemites', leaving them 'seeking more blood and intimidation, not less'.[117]

Contemporary antisemitism in the United Kingdom, like Islamophobia (discussed later in the chapter), needs to be seen in the context of hegemonic global US capitalism and imperialism, in which Israel is a key player. It is vital to make a distinction between antisemitism, and anti-Zionism and concern about the state of Israel's close relationship with the United States. This is particularly important for Marxists and other Left factions whose brief must be total and unremitting opposition to all forms of racism.[118] As Gardner said of the 2014 rise in antisemitism, 'There is no excuse for this wave of racist intimidation and violence and we call upon all good people to unequivocally condemn it.'[119] This was echoed by Nick Lowles, of the anti-fascist campaigning group Hope Not Hate, who said it was crucial to defend Jewish people. As he put it:

> Fear is gripping Britain's Jewish community but sadly few organisa-
> tions have stepped forward to offer support, and some of those who
> have made statements have only done so after they have been asked.
> Whatever one's views on the Gaza conflict, taking it out on Britain's

Jewish community is clearly wrong and more people need to start saying it.[120]

Like all forms of racism, antisemitism is not directed at people because of their political viewpoints, but because of their perceived 'race', ethnicity, nationality, culture or religion. People in the United Kingdom who identify as Jewish do so for a variety of reasons primarily based on religion, ethnicity or culture. Moreover, it should be stressed that many Jewish people are totally opposed to Israeli foreign policy and identify politically with the Palestinian cause. Thus, with respect to the hate incidents in July 2014, those who threw bricks through a synagogue in Belfast had no interest in the political views of those who attended the synagogue; the men who drove through a Jewish area of Greater Manchester shouting 'Heil Hitler' and hurling missiles at pedestrians were not protesting against the exploitation and oppression of Palestinians by the Israeli state, merely exhibiting their irrational hatred of Jewish people. The same may be said of the man who used Twitter to call for a Jewish neighbourhood in London to be bombed so that 'Jews feel the pain' of the Palestinians; and those who were part of the widespread postings on Twitter of the hashtags 'Hitlerwasright' and 'HitlerDidNothingWrong'.[121] In the same month, 'world conspiracy theory' (that Jewish people conspire to control the world) was invoked by a producer at the BBC who claimed that western politicians had failed to intervene in the Middle East because they had been 'bought' by the Jews.[122]

It is crucial, of course, to be vigilant against the rhetoric of racists and fascists who promote conspiracy theory and 'Holocaust denial', which have for so long been part of fascist ideology, with fascism reaching its apotheosis in that exceptional form of the capitalist state and associated mode of production in Nazi Germany.[123] Many world conspiracy theorists, holocaust deniers and up-front fascists presumably aim to reinstall similar exceptional forms of the capitalist state, and related modes of production.

Anti-Gypsy Roma and Traveller racism[124]

Anti-Gypsy Roma and Traveller racism, which has a long history in the United Kingdom, is based on perceived notions of 'race' and ethnicity. By the late nineteenth century, despite increased statutory controls, such as the 1822 General Turnpike Road Act which charged a 40 shilling fine for camping on the side of a turnpike road,[125] traditional stopping places were reasonably freely available,[126] and as Duffy and Tomlinson argue, always surviving on the margins of society, Gypsy people became a useful source of cheap labour seasonally in the fields, as blacksmiths and as entertainers.[127] A pattern of travelling on specific circuits continued until the Second World War, when with the need for intensive labour, members of the Gypsy Roma and Traveller communities were recruited into semi-permanent work on the land, in the mining industries, in the army, and in factory and munitions work.[128]

After the Second World War, with the mechanization of farming, the lifestyle of Gypsies changed drastically.[129] This mechanization of the traditional rural work started in the 1950s, and previous sources of livelihood in the rural areas were no longer sufficient. With industrialization began the migration from rural areas. The changes in society – the 'golden age of capitalism' – were also reflected in the Romany Gypsy population. No longer wanted for hop or strawberry picking and other traditional trades, they found that they had to adapt. Work was difficult to find for some families and the motorization of families also changed the travel patterns. Many Gypsies moved from the rural areas to cities and towns, often meeting hostile reactions from the local population and from the authorities.[130] Where caravans were visible to non-Gypsy Roma and Traveller people (for example, next to a roadside), this attracted the attention of the authorities, and thus began a cycle of rapid repeat eviction.[131]

The most notorious eviction occurred at Dale Farm, an 'unauthorized' Traveller site (without planning permission for that use), where police used tasers on unarmed protesters when storming the site while trying to clear it. One of the Travellers described the experience as 'terrifying'. Another returned from hospital in a wheelchair with a fractured spine, stating:

> [a] police officer pushed me against a wall. Then he got me on the ground. He kept kicking me and kicking me. Two officers dragged me along the ground, even though I kept saying I was in pain.

At times the police operation was absurd, with heavily armed riot police marching in military formation around the site for no apparent reason.[132]

In July 2012 it was estimated that the total number of Gypsy and Traveller caravans in England was approximately 19,400, about 700 more than the total in July 2011. Of these, 16 per cent were on 'unauthorized' land.[133] Families with young children, Duffy and Tomlinson point out, are evicted on a daily basis, under Section 62a of the Criminal Justice Act of 1994, which is used to hound homeless families from one district to another.[134]

Trevor Phillips, chair of the then Commission for Racial Equality (CRE) (now subsumed under the Equality and Human Rights Commission, EHRC) suggested in 2004 that discrimination against Gypsies and Travellers is the last 'respectable' form of racism,[135] and two years later the CRE concluded that

Gypsies and Irish Travellers are the most excluded groups in Britain today.[136] Gypsy/Roma pupils and pupils of Irish Traveller heritage (GRT) today are among the lowest-achieving groups at every key stage of education.[137] Duffy and Tomlinson note a lack of understanding by service providers. This is through lack of cultural awareness, racism, or just lack of awareness of the communities' requirements.[138]

With respect to health issues, despite a lack of national data on Gypsies and Travellers, as the Irish Traveller Movement in Britain puts it, 'studies have revealed their health outcomes to be much poorer than the general population and also poorer than others in socially deprived areas'. Even though Gypsies and Travellers have the lowest life expectancy of any group in the United Kingdom, and experience an infant mortality rate three times higher than the national average, the Department of Health (DoH) does not include Gypsies and Travellers as one of the 16 ethnic minority categories monitored by the National Health Service (NHS).[139]

As Colin Clark has argued, there has been a collective assumption that tabloid racism against Gypsy Roma and Traveller peoples is 'safe ground', since there is little response to this form of racism.[140] This has often taken a strident aggressive form, characteristic of such newspapers as the *Sun*, the most popular UK tabloid. For example, one of its reporters, using the standard rhetoric used to stoke up fear and hatred, claimed that Irish Travellers (mostly Catholics, who were merely wishing to see the head of their Church) had thrown a planned visit by the Pope in 2010 'into turmoil amid fears hordes of gipsies will gatecrash a mass'. He went on to suggest that '[w]aves' had already arrived,[141] then invoking 'common sense' (in the sense articulated by Gramsci),[142] added, 'of course we don't want hordes of gypsies messing up our beautiful countryside'.

In the same year the first edition of the television series *My Big Fat Gypsy Wedding* was broadcast on Channel 4, attracting around 6 million viewers. While it might appear that this programme was sympathetic and giving a voice to Irish Travellers, it actually presented 'an exoticised image of their lives: the horse-drawn wagons, extravagant dresses and flamboyant wedding arrangements seem to encapsulate how they remain the "other" of British society', with images of the communities 'polarised between vilification and the exotic'.[143] The series has been blamed for an increase in bullying and negative stereotyping of the Gypsy and Traveller communities. For example the second series was advertised by Channel 4 as being 'Bigger. Fatter. Gypsier'. According to Brian Foster, who chairs the advisory council for the education of Romanies and other Travellers, and is also a trustee of the Irish Traveller Movement in Britain (ITMB), this caused 'real, measurable and long-term harm'.

In a report for the Advertising Standards Authority (ASA). Foster stated:

> That harm is on a number of levels, including physical and sexual assault, racist abuse and bullying, misinformation and hostile questioning, resulting in damage to the self-esteem of children and withdrawal from school. Evidence drawn from practitioners across the country presents a consistent picture that the *Big Fat Gypsy Weddings* programmes have significantly contributed to racist bullying and abuse of Gypsy, Roma and Traveller children in schools.[144]

Families cite racist bullying as a major issue for removing children from schools.[145]

Arthur Ivatts, who specializes in the education of GRT communities, and worked as a senior policy adviser to the Department for Education for more than 30 years, also noted in the report: '[t]here is no doubt in my professional opinion that this advertising campaign has seriously damaged and harmed Gypsy, Roma and Traveller communities and caused harm (physical, mental and emotional) to very many GR&T children'. He went on, '[s]upposing the posters had said, "Bigger, Fatter, Blacker"? Hopefully this example illustrates the point being made here in this report.'[146] The Channel 4 ad campaign was criticised by the ASA, which ruled that it depicted a 15-year-old child in a sexualized way, reinforced negative stereotypes, and said Channel 4 had acted 'irresponsibly'.[147]

In the intervening years since Trevor Phillips's coining of the phrase 'the last respectable form of racism', and since the CRE concluded that Gypsies and Irish Travellers are the most excluded groups in Britain today, Phillip Brown has argued that it appears that 'very little has changed and some positive in-roads that were being made are now in reverse'.[148]

Research for the EHRC shows that the exclusion of Gypsies and Travellers is particularly acute in the areas of health, education and social care, with the lack of culturally appropriate accommodation – sites on which caravans can legally be located – a key driver of exclusion.[149] In September 2014, exclusion was exacerbated when the ConDem government put out for consultation new rules stating that councils will only have to provide sites for those who regularly move from place to place (the *Sun*'s headline on 14 September was 'GYPSY SITE BLITZ'). Moreover, such a move, according to Marc Willers, a barrister specializing in Gypsy and Traveller cases, challenges human rights legislation. As he argued:

> We would argue forcefully that a requirement to show [Gypsies and

Travellers] are continually travelling when there are no stopping sites available and draconian measures in place to force them to move on is a wholly disproportionate breach of their rights.[150]

NEWER NON-COLOUR-CODED RACISM: XENO-RACISM

Liz Fekete has written at length about newer forms of racism.[151] Her specific focus is on anti-asylum-seeker racism, xeno-racism and Islamophobia. Referring to the underlying economic dimension of these newer forms, Fekete argues that the combination of anti-immigration movements and an onslaught from the press became too much for mainstream parties. Politicians knew full well, she suggests, that because of Europe's declining birth rates, an ageing population and shortage of skilled workers in some areas, and semi-skilled and unskilled workers in others, the continent was in desperate need of migrant workers. But they also knew that to openly acknowledge this would be to antagonize the electorate. At the same time, she goes on, governments feared that the globalization-inspired irregular movements of people, resulting in migratory flows of labour surplus to Europe's economic needs, would derail a political strategy based on micro-managing the migration process quietly and behind the scenes.[152]

On 1 May 2004, ten more countries joined the European Union (EU): Cyprus, the Czech Republic, Estonia, Hungary, Latvia, Lithuania, Malta, Poland, Slovakia and Slovenia, bringing the total from 15 to 25 member states. On 1 January 2007 two more countries, Bulgaria and Romania, joined. Croatia became a member on 1 July 2013. This fact has given rise to a new form of non-colour-coded racism, based on nationality, and directed primarily at Eastern European workers: xeno-racism. Sivanandan has defined xeno-racism as:

> a racism that is not just directed at those with darker skins, from the former colonial countries, but at the newer categories of the displaced and dispossessed whites, who are beating at western Europe's doors, the Europe that displaced them in the first place. It is racism in substance but xeno in form – a racism that is meted out to impoverished strangers even if they are white. It is xeno-racism.[153]

Recognizing the salience of non-colour-coded racism is not new. Over 20 years ago, Miles identified individuals and communities not marked out by their skin colour from Ireland, Italy, Cyprus, Malta, Poland, and Jews from Russia and Germany.[154] The experiences of these communities highlighted for Miles that racism does not have to be based on skin colour. He states that:

> it is not only 'black' people that are the object of racism. Such an interpretation constitutes a strange perversion of European history, a history in which the concept of racism was generated to comprehend the use of 'race' theory by the Nazis in the course of formulating a 'final solution' to the 'Jewish question'.[155]

Eastern European workers have been racialized, exploited, oppressed and vilified in a number of ways since their arrival in the United Kingdom, in many senses similarly to migrant workers from the colonies and ex-colonies (discussed earlier in this chapter). Just as the structurally distinct position of those earlier workers meant that they constituted a racialized fraction of the working class,[156] so do their more recent counterparts.

Jon Burnett has argued that patterns of racial violence in the United Kingdom are shifting. Whereas before, attacks were often concentrated in impoverished inner and outer areas in large urban conurbations, there is now a significant increase in racist incidents in rural areas, towns and smaller cities. Such is the extent of violence in some of these areas, he goes on, that it appears almost routine. As he puts it:

> Vicious attacks against … migrant workers have become a regular occurrence in some areas. Radical transformations in local economies, relying on deregulated, unprotected and flexible labour forces, have pushed workers into jobs where they are isolated, vulnerable and exposed to a risk of violence. As particular forms of popular racism have formed nationally – such as anti-Muslim racism generated through the war on terror [see the section on Islamophobia in this chapter] – localised racisms have manifested themselves in abuse, harassment and brutality. Far-right organisations, in such climates, have been able to capitalise on emerging hostilities.[157]

Jane Hardy explains how legally employed migrant workers 'face huge problems at work'.[158] She describes the abuse of such workers over employment contracts and wages, and lists complaints of 'excessive working hours with inadequate breaks and no enhanced overtime'. She cites evidence of 'recruitment and temporary labour agencies' imposing 'high charges for finding employment, lower payment than promised and the withholding of wages'.[159] In East Anglia, workers from the new EU countries, she states, are widely used in agriculture, food processing, distribution and supermarkets, where 'there is evidence of terrible working conditions and bullying' and of 'gangmasters running some small towns'.[160] Truck drivers from the new EU countries working in supermarket distribution centres, she concludes, are often on zero-hour contracts (contracts that do not guarantee work, and pay only for work actually done), and Polish workers she interviewed in a fruit-packing factory were continually told to work faster to meet supermarket demands.[161]

Focusing on Peterborough, Burnett notes that migrant workers, mainly from Poland, Lithuania and Slovakia, are 'frequently employed in back-breaking jobs in the construction industries, in factories, in catering, as carers and in the agricultural hinterlands surrounding the locality'.[162]

As a direct result of the 2007–08 financial crisis, itself a symptom of another deeper crisis which is a systemic crisis of capitalism itself,[163] increasing numbers of people in Peterborough were forced to become homelessness, and resorted to squatting in back yards or setting up desperate makeshift camps, which were reminiscent of shanty towns, on roundabouts and in woods. By 2010 it was estimated that as many as 15 camps were scattered around the city.[164] In the same year, a project that was the first of its kind in the country was launched in Peterborough. It involved rounding up homeless migrants and attempting to force them to leave the United Kingdom.[165] The then immigration minister Phil Woolas stated:

> People have to be working, studying or self-sufficient and if they are not we expect them to return home .... This scheme to remove European nationals who aren't employed is getting them off the streets and back to their own country.[166]

Stewart Jackson, a local Conservative MP, described them as 'vagrants' and remarked:

> I don't know how these migrants are surviving sleeping rough on roundabouts and bushes but they are a drain on my constituents and taxpayers .... If they are not going to contribute to this country, then, as citizens of their home country, they should return there.[167]

With many people only permitted to stay in the United Kingdom 'legally' if they stayed in the job they had registered to work in, Jon Burnett explains, employers were given the green light 'to exploit their employees – paying poverty wages, withholding money, forcing ever longer hours of work and taking away reductions to pay for pre-arranged housing'.[168] Burnett notes that 'housing inspectors found ten men living in a tiny brick lock-up in the back of someone's garden. Their accommodation had no electricity and no heating, and filthy mattresses were crammed into whatever small space was available.'[169]

The role of the media in depicting Peterborough has been to blame Polish workers and to vilify the city: 'Britain's migrant squatter shambles' (*Daily Express*) and 'the town the Poles took over', 'a city crumbling under pressure from immigrants' and 'a symbol of the changing face of Britain' (*Daily Mail*).[170] Migrant workers are 'blamed for increasing unemployment, for undermining welfare, for higher levels of violence and crumbling public services, and the city is evocated as an example of the fault-line in successive governments' immigration policies'. As Burnett puts it, 'beneath these headlines (and fuelled, in part, by them) anti-foreigner and racist attacks have involved vicious beatings and firebombings'. However, it is not these physical abuses of migrant workers that the tabloids concentrate on, they prefer 'voyeuristically inspecting their living conditions', and in a similar fashion to the 'problem' of the 'Asiatics' perceived by the LEA in the post-Second World War period, their '(alleged) eating habits'.[171]

A 'beautiful and once quintessentially English city' is how the *Daily Mail* describes Peterborough.[172] Now, however, 'the city is depicted as a symbol of what happens when supposedly lax immigration policies and supposedly over-generous welfare policies converge'. Burnett concludes, '[w]hen journalists want a story about the perils of immigration, or when politicians seek a shot of political capital by claiming they will "solve" the same, they turn to Peterborough'.[173]

The 'common sense' reaction to all this is that 'it all makes sense'. It is not entrenched neoliberalism and austerity capitalism in the United Kingdom and in mainland Europe that is breaking up communities, causing unemployment, a declining welfare state and inadequate public services, not to mention lives of sheer misery for fellow human beings, but those fellow human beings themselves. The problem is not xeno-racism and xeno-racialization; it is not capitalism but Eastern European workers looking for jobs. It is unlikely that in the mid-1980s, before the collapse of 'communism',[174] anyone would have predicted that these workers would be subject to racism in the United Kingdom some 30 years hence, which points to the unpredictability of the (xeno-) racialization process. I return to a discussion of xeno-racism later in this chapter in a consideration of racism in the run-up to the 2015 General Election.

NEWER HYBRIDIST RACISM

Under this heading I am including Islamophobia and anti-asylum-seeker racism. My reason for using the term 'newer hybridist racism' is that unlike the forms of racism described above that are either essentially colour-coded or essentially non-colour-coded, Islamophobia and anti-asylum-seeker racism can be either colour-coded or non-colour-coded, or a combination of both. For example, the top ten countries of origin of asylum seekers to the United Kingdom in the first quarter of 2013 were Pakistan 883, Iran 630, Sri Lanka 412, Syria 330, Albania 305, India 257, Bangladesh 249, Afghanistan 244, Nigeria 234 and China 193.[175] The mixture, which includes ex-colonies and a majority of Muslim countries, can spawn both older colour-coded racism and Islamophobia, or an amalgam of the two.

Islamophobia

The first recorded use of the term 'Islamophobia' in English was in 1991,[176] which coincided with the first Gulf War (1990–91) and the upsurge of anti-Muslim racism and hate crime that accompanied it.[177] Islamophobia is a major form of racism in the modern world. It is important to stress that, while it may be sparked by skin colour, Islamophobia is not necessarily triggered by colour of skin. It can also be set off by religious markers, by one or more (perceived) symbols of the Muslim faith. As Sivanandan put it, as noted earlier, referring to British Muslims – 'the terrorist within' – 'the victims are marked out not so much by their colour as by their beards and headscarves'.[178]

The UK Terrorism Act of 2000 cemented institutional racism aimed at Muslims by creating new offences based on the circulation of information useful for terrorism.[179] The possession of certain books, for example, is an offence. Even accessing the internet, perhaps merely out of interest, for information on political or radical Islam can lead to imprisonment.[180] Finally, measures introduced not just in the United Kingdom but throughout Europe make it possible to remove citizenship from those with dual nationality who display symptoms of 'unacceptable behaviour' such as the glorification of terrorism.[181]

In 2006, New Labour introduced the Terrorism Act which made it a crime to 'glorify' terrorism, although such behaviour was already covered by the long-established offence of incitement.[182] In a similar vein, three years later, Liz Fekete discussed the growing trend whereby arrests and prosecutions are based not on material evidence but on 'crimes of association', that is, 'association with terrorists or with the associates of terrorists'.[183] Thus the trustees of mosques fall under suspicion if they have been fundraising for international causes, such as humanitarian relief for Palestinian refugees in the occupied territories, on the spurious ground that 'even though the emergency relief was not destined for terrorist organisations, some of it may have ended up in their hands'.[184]

As far as the media is concerned, Fekete points out how Muslim cultures are presented 'through the grossest of stereotypes and simplification,'[185] whereas in fact, such cultures are no more of a monolith than Christian ones.[186] Nevertheless they are treated as all the same, both in terms of the racism directed at them and in terms of being a threat – the 'repressive force [of] global Islam'.[187]

In February 2011, the British Prime Minister David Cameron stated:

> under the doctrine of state multiculturalism, we have encouraged different cultures to live separate lives, apart from each other and the mainstream. We have failed to provide a vision of society to which they feel they want to belong. We have even tolerated these segregated communities behaving in ways that run counter to our values.[188]

Cameron's target was Islamic extremism and the process of radicalization, and although he was careful not to lump all Muslims together, his contrasting of what 'they feel' and 'our values' serves to accentuate notions of 'us' and 'them'. He went on to state that 'we need a lot less of the passive tolerance of recent years and a much more active, muscular liberalism'. Partly in response, there emerged a call for 'integration' and for a 'community cohesion agenda' comprised of tougher immigration and asylum laws, citizenship tests, compulsory citizenship education, and new employment policies giving preference to British workers.

Multiculturalism has a long history in the United Kingdom, in its modern form dating back at least to the post Second World War period of immigration from the colonies and ex-colonies. It was reflected in the debates in the UK education system about monocultural (celebrating 'British values'), multicultural and antiracist education. While the former had the effect of rendering minority ethnic communities invisible or inferior, the latter tended to be superficial and patronising, and was often taught by white teachers, leading antiracist educators to parody it as 'saris, samosas and steel bands'. Given more recent advances in technology that allow racialized groups to speak for themselves, and to an infinitely large audience, many on the Left would now advocate multicultural antiracist education.[189]

In 2011, which began with Cameron's anti 'state multiculturalism' and pro 'muscular liberalism' speech, Copsey and colleagues documented 632 Islamophobic hate crimes, while in the year (1 April 2012–30 April 2013) leading up to the attack on Lee Rigby, a British soldier wearing a Help for Heroes T-shirt who was hacked to death by Islamists on a London street near a military barracks, there were 584 recorded incidents.[190] Of these latter figures, offline incidents that were reported were mainly street-based (55 per cent), with 18 per cent taking place at mosques or other Islamic institutions, and 13 per cent at work or school. Half the offline attacks involved low-level abuse and harassment, with under 10 per cent involving extreme violence. The major victims were female, and of these over 80 per cent were 'easily identifiable' as Muslim. Most perpetrators, Copsey and colleagues go on, were male (78 per cent) and under 40 years of age. A far-right link was apparent in a quarter of the offences.

Most offences, however, occurred online (74 per cent), and the majority of these did include threats of offline action. Most were male, and nearly 70 per cent were connected to the far right, with the English Defence League most implicated. Copsey and colleagues conclude that:

> The overall link to the far right reported by victims stood at 56 per cent for the period 1 April 2012 to 30 April 2013 – 300 online incidents reported a link to the far right; 29 offline cases reported such a link.[191]

They point out that all of these figures should be treated with caution, because Islamophobic attacks are seriously under-reported.

In December, 2012, the Institute of Race Relations reported nine Islamophobic insults and attacks in just over a month (November–December). These include a pig's head being placed outside a mosque; the ripping of a hijab from a Muslim woman's head, after which she and her pregnant friend were repeatedly punched; offensive graffiti daubed on the path of a Muslim family's home, the latest of a spate of racist incidents directed at them in the space of a few weeks, including a cross wrapped in ham being balanced by their front door; pieces of ham thrown at a mosque; graffiti sprayed on mosques; 'racial chanting' during a demonstration against the proposed opening of a mosque; offensive graffiti spray-painted in view of a mosque; the racial abuse of three Asian men who had escaped a house fire, followed by the hurling at them of a large metal sword; and racist abuse directed at three Muslim schoolgirls.[192]

Within hours of Rigby's killing in May 2013, a man entered a mosque in Gillingham and smashed up the inside.[193] At about the same time, someone was arrested outside an Islamic centre in Essex in possession of a knife and incendiary device. Later the same evening, a group of teenagers threw bricks through the windows of a mosque in Grimsby, damaging cars parked nearby. A few days later, two former soldiers threw petrol bombs inside the same building. A young family was inside at the time. By now, a swathe of Islamophobic incidents was being and continues to be reported. As of the end of May 2013 about 200 incidents had been recorded by Tell MAMA (Measuring Anti-Muslim Attacks), a tenfold increase, many by people associated with far right groups.[194] In June 2013, swastikas and the letters 'EDL', 'KKK' and 'NF' were sprayed on to the wall of a mosque in Redditch, and pigs' heads were left at Muslim families' homes.[195]

Islamophobia is also rampant on social media. Imran Awan found that the three most common phrases used to attack Twitter users were 'Muslim paedos', 'Muslim terrorists' and 'Muslim scum'.[196] The majority of tweets (72 per cent) were posted by males, and over 75 per cent of the tweets examined displayed a strong Islamophobic feeling. For example, on 11 September 2013 the hashtag #FuckMuslims was trending.

As Chris Marsden puts it, referring to the murder of Rigby, and succinctly connecting new imperialism, the effects of austerity/immiseration capitalism on the working class, and the corruption of the international ruling class:

> The murder of Lee Rigby is only one of many, many tragic manifestations of how decades of wars and other colonialist adventures have served to poison social and political life in Britain and internationally, pursuant to the predatory aims of the financial oligarchy. To secure control of vital resources such as oil, gas and minerals, large parts of the world have been despoiled, impoverished and subject to brutal intervention. Meanwhile, working people in Britain, Europe and America are forced to pay the trillions of dollars these wars cost through savage cuts aimed at enriching the criminal element that now dominates society. No one should be intimidated or confused by the 'patriotic' lies and crocodile tears emanating from the ruling class and its media. In the most fundamental sense it is they who are responsible for what happened at Woolwich. And it is they who should be politically held to account by the broad masses of working people.[197]

Unlike xeno-racism and anti-asylum-seeker racism, Islamophobia has less to do with migration and more, in its contemporary form, to do with US imperialism (aided by other 'western powers'), US hegemony and capitalist greed for oil and profit, and the consequences of the accompanying so-called 'war on terror', hyped up by politicians and the media.

Anti-asylum-seeker racism[198]

Given the 'discourse of derision'[199] surrounding the issue of 'asylum', emanating from sections of the media and from the mouths of some politicians, and the hysteria that this helps to generate, it is instructive to begin this section of the chapter with some definitions. According to Article 1 of the 1951 Convention Relating to the Status of Refugees, a refugee is someone who:

> owing to a well-founded fear of being persecuted for reasons of race, religion, nationality, membership of a particular social group, or political opinion, is outside the country of his [sic] nationality, and is unable to or, owing to such fear, is unwilling to avail himself of the protection of that country.[200]

An asylum seeker is a person:

> who has applied for asylum and is waiting for a decision as to whether or not they are a refugee. In other words, in the United Kingdom an asylum seeker is someone who has asked the Government for refugee status and is waiting to hear the outcome of their application.[201]

There is no such thing as a 'bogus' or 'illegal' asylum seeker:

> Everybody has a right to seek asylum in another country. People who don't qualify for protection as refugees will not receive refugee status and may be deported, but just because someone doesn't receive refugee status doesn't mean they are a bogus asylum seeker.[202]

In the words of Kofi Annan:

> Let us remember that a bogus asylum-seeker is not equivalent to a criminal; and that an unsuccessful asylum application is not equivalent to a bogus one.[203]

Thus, it needs to be stressed again and again that asylum seekers are simply people waiting for a decision on whether they have refugee status, and refugees are extremely vulnerable people who have left their country because of well-founded fears for their safety should they remain there. They are not criminals or illegal. Contrary to what you might assume from reading the *Sun* or the *Daily Mail*, as of the end of 2013, refugees, pending asylum cases and stateless persons made up just 0.23 per cent of the population.[204]

Fekete describes how from the 1990s, 'both centre-Right and centre-Left parties began to implement laws that criminalized asylum seekers'.[205] She provides painstaking documentation of the multifaceted horrors of anti-asylum-seeker racism in contemporary Europe. While no one can deny the exploitative nature of the smuggling networks that bring asylum seekers to Europe, she reminds us that it is the blocking of legal routes that 'throw them into the arms of smugglers and traffickers'.[206] Institutional racism directed at asylum seekers by governments is not only apparent in the United Kingdom, but exists throughout the continent. It is now an offence all over Europe, she notes, to assist anyone trying to cross a border 'illegally', whether they are in need of protection or not.[207]

'Dealing' with asylum seekers also entails the brute force of the state – in the form of detention. Institutional racism exists also in the form of a separate prison complex for asylum seekers, where the 'use of measures more germane to serious criminal investigation, such as the compulsory finger printing of all asylum seekers ... has become routine'.[208] Some immigration removal centres (IRCs), formerly known as detentions centres, are run by HM Prison Service but the majority are run by profit-making private companies. Mary Bosworth's fieldwork in five IRCs reveals that they are 'prison-like', given that they isolate, confine and impose institutional rules on inmates.[209] Often these inmates have a long history in the United Kingdom. Detainees tell of their attachment to the United Kingdom, thus challenging the logic of IRCs as 'sites of estrangement'.

The centres transform people into strangers who no longer belong in Britain and can be removed forcibly. They are frequently violent places, and people self-harm. Crucially, people are held for administrative purposes, and unlike prison sentences, there is no fixed period for incarceration. Asylum seekers can be detained indefinitely under the Immigration Acts, as long as they are being detained 'with a view to removal'.[210] The aim of detention is 'to break down the will of detainees, so as to make them compliant to their own removal'. Thus, Fekete concludes, those 'who challenge their proposed deportation may be asked to choose between lengthy detention in the host country or return to torture in their country of origin'. She quite rightly describes this as 'psychological torture'.[211]

Fekete explains that the motor that sets 'the brutal deportation machine' in motion is 'targets', initiated throughout Europe by governments. For example, in 2004, Tony Blair established a deportation formula based on the 'monthly rate of removals' exceeding 'the number of unfounded applications'. As Fekete argues, the imposition of such targets 'necessarily undermines the whole humanitarian principle of refugee policy – 'need not numbers' – and becomes its obverse, 'numbers not need', with failed asylum seekers being reduced to 'a statistic for removal, even when they have strong claims to remain on humanitarian grounds'. Forced removal involves 'officially sanctioned state violence' on both routine passenger flights and chartered special flights and military jets. The latter are increasingly favoured, since passengers, pilots and crew on commercial flights object to the violence, which can include:

> crying children frogmarched on to planes ... violent control and restraint methods against adult deportees, who may be bound head and foot, gagged (with special adhesive tape) or have their heads forced into the special deportation helmet (a chin strap prevents the deportee from moving [the] lower jaw, an additional strap covers the detainee's mouth).[212]

Sometimes the deportations are filmed to discourage attempts at seeking asylum. For example, the UK government sent a crew to film the deportation of about 24 Afghans from Gatwick airport, to be broadcast in Afghanistan as a warning to those considering coming to Britain.[213]

An asylum seeker with a five-month-old baby claims she was placed in a property by the private contractor G4S that was infested with cockroaches and slugs. G4S holds contracts to supply accommodation to asylum seekers across much of England as part of the UK Border Agency's (UKBA's) COMPASS (Commercial and Operational Managers Procuring Asylum Support Services project).[214] G4S describes itself as 'the world's leading international security solutions group',[215] and its employees have emblazoned on the back of their jackets, 'Here to assist you'.[216] The woman, trafficked to the United Kingdom and sold into prostitution before seeking asylum, said she and her baby were left in the house for weeks before the local council intervened to ensure they were rehoused. Leeds City Council's inspectors found the property was a 'Category 1 hazard', unfit for human habitation. She made repeated complaints to both G4S and its subcontractor, and was told by the firms that they had carried out their own inspections and were satisfied the accommodation was 'decent'. When she rang about the infestation, as she puts it, '[o]ne of the people said to me ... "slugs are not harmful, even if your baby eats one of them"'.

Charlotte Philby remarks that the 'case raises fresh concerns over the treatment of vulnerable people put in the care of G4S' – which was awarded a seven-year £211 million deal with UKBA in mid-2012.[217] Another company working for G4S in the same month removed a heavily pregnant asylum seeker from her house despite knowing that she was being induced to give birth on the same day.[218]

While those awaiting the results of asylum applications do not have to pay for NHS treatment, free treatment was removed from failed asylum seekers in 2004, except in the case of emergency, adversely affecting cancer sufferers, newly diagnosed HIV/AIDS patients and pregnant women. The DoH even tried (unsuccessfully) in 2007 to ban failed asylum seekers from obtaining primary care at doctors' surgeries.[219] Indeed from 1997 onwards, the New Labour governments' focus was on stopping foreign 'scroungers' draining the UK welfare state, which became a cornerstone of the politics of the market state.[220] New techniques of coercion and surveillance were applied to asylum seekers, including compulsory ID.[221] New Labour's Immigration and Asylum Act in 1999 rendered asylum seekers second-class citizens by providing support in the form of vouchers rather than cash, and introduced a policy of dispersing them around the country.[222]

In 2002, the Nationality, Immigration and Asylum Act contained the Section 55 rule which resulted in homelessness for thousands of asylum seekers who did not make their claims quickly enough on arriving in Britain,[223] while the Asylum and Immigration Act of 2004 threatened to take asylum seekers' children into care if the parents refused to leave Britain 'voluntarily' after their asylum claims had been rejected. The same Act required that claimants carry out forced labour in exchange for benefits.[224] Arund Kundnani explains how the ISAs around New Labour rationalized the process. He gives the example of a widely read article for *Prospect* magazine by David Goodhart, entitled 'Too diverse?', in which Goodhart argued that entitlement to welfare should be clearly aligned with a shared British culture, and that the survival of the welfare state depended on denying access to 'them' in favour of 'us'.[225]

New Labour greatly increased the numbers held in detention. When it took office in May 1997 there 733 detained, and by June 2006 there were some 2,285 in these centres, despite a lower rate of asylum claims than in 1997.[226]

In 2009 the Borders, Citizenship and Immigration Act came into force, designed to simplify immigration law, strengthen borders and extend the time it takes to gain citizenship. According to a report published by the Institute of Race Relations (IRR) in October 2010, racist asylum-seeker and immigration policies in the United Kingdom led to the deaths of 77 asylum seekers and migrants in the previous four years. Of these, seven are reported as having died after being denied health care for 'preventable medical problems'; more than a third are suspected or known suicides after asylum claims have been turned down; seven are said to have died in prison custody, and 15 to have died during 'highly risky' attempts to leave the country.[227]

Moral panics about asylum seekers, exacerbated by 'common sense' – 'everyone knows most are here illegally and are taking us for a ride' – serve to divert attention from the real reasons displaced persons are in the United Kingdom.[228] A quick glance at the top ten countries of origin of asylum seekers listed earlier in this chapter reveals that they are all developing countries. Marxist or world systems analysis regards migration pressure to the core of developed countries as a consequence of economic deprivation at the periphery.[229] Desperately poor people are also often fleeing state oppression because of their political views, as well as human rights abuses.

Jimmy Mubenga and his wife arrived in the United Kingdom in 1994, after he was forced to flee the Angolan regime (his wife's father had been killed and Mubenga's life was under threat), and was granted exceptional leave to remain.[230] Four of their five children were born and raised in the United Kingdom. In 2006 Mubenga was convicted of actual bodily harm and sentenced to two years in prison after a brawl in a nightclub. After serving his sentence he was transferred to an immigration removal centre, and was in and out of detention subsequently as his family fought to stop him being deported. When the state finally won in 2010, Mubenga was allowed one last phone conversation with his wife from his plane seat between two agents of the repressive apparatuses of the state in the form of private security guards.[231] His wife explained, '[h]e was so sad, he was saying: "I don't know what I am going to do, I don't know what I am going to do." Then he said: "OK, just hang up and I will call you back" … but he never did call back.' His lawyer explained that '[h]e was desperately worried about leaving his wife and family. He was a devoted family man and was extremely anxious about the impact his deportation would have on them all.' His wife stated that people still wanted to kill him in Angola and 'he was worried that if he went he would never see his children again.'[232]

Witnesses on the flight pointed out that Mubenga was forcibly restrained by three security guards, and was shouting that he could not breathe. One passenger said he heard him shout:

> They are going to kill me. You could hear the guy screaming at the back of the plane. He was saying 'they are going to kill me'. That's what he repeatedly said. He was saying that right from when I got on the plane. He just kept repeating that all the way through.[233]

The three guards forced Mubenga's head down, restricting his breathing for 36 minutes, as he sat handcuffed from behind in his seat. Mubenga collapsed and had a heart attack, dying later in hospital.[234] As July Hyland explains, the restraint technique, known as 'carpet karaoke', is known to create a risk of asphyxia.[235] Some 20 witnesses, passengers on board the flight, said that they had heard Mubenga cry out repeatedly, 'I can't breathe.' One of them testified, 'I could hear somebody being loud, like he did not want to be there. He was saying "All you people are watching them kill me. I can't breathe. They are going to kill me."'[236]

The three guards, who received a monthly retainer of £1,000 and £6 per hour for every deportation they completed, were acquitted of manslaughter in December 2014.[237] Just days later, it was revealed that racist text messages sent by two of them had been concealed from the jury. One of 100 or so messages read, referring to immigrants, 'F••• off and go home you free-loading, benefit-grabbing, kid-producing, violent, non-English-speaking, c••k suckers and take those hairy-faced, sandal-wearing, bomb-making, goat-f•••ing, smelly rag head b•••••ds with you.'[238] After Mubenga's death, one of them posted on Facebook an image of a man with dark skin on a plane, under the question, 'Come on then what's wrong with this pick [sic]???' to which one of his friends replied, 'He hasn't got two hairy arsed escorts either side of him, no cuffs and not shouting, "Kill me now I'm not a hanimal."'[239]

As Hyland points out, the case has obvious parallels with the chokehold killing of Eric Garner by New York police. His last words were also 'I can't breathe'[240] (see Chapter 2). Hyland succinctly concludes with respect to the repressive and ideological apparatuses of the state:

> A working environment in which misanthropy thrives, combined with financial incentives to ensure the 'easy' despatch of deportees is a recipe for cruelty. Moreover, the racism evidenced by the guards' text messages is one deliberately cultivated by the powers-that-be as they scapegoat foreign workers for the social crisis capitalism has created. The vile diatribe against immigrants cited above as being 'free-loading, benefit-grabbing' is repeated, in one form or another, by all the political parties and the media.[241]

Matt Carr's description of Calais in August 2014, when there were violent clashes between Sudanese and Eritrean migrants at the food distribution centre, suppressed by rubber bullets from the French police, succinctly encapsulates the horrors experienced by today's asylum seekers. As he puts it, while Calais is for millions of British tourists 'a gateway for continental driving holidays and the pleasures of the Summer', for others it is 'a trap and another of the world's border bottlenecks, where Europe's unwanted migrants come each year in the hope of getting onto a truck that can take them to the UK'. He continues:

> Most of them have endured astonishingly harsh and difficult journeys to escape poverty and political, religious or gender oppression, only to find themselves living in derelict squats, tent camps or on the streets, constantly watched, harrassed, arrested and often beaten by the contingents of the Republican Security Companies [the riot control forces and general reserve of the French National Police].[242]

The main reason migrants are trapped in Calais, Carr argues, 'is because they want to come to Britain, but Britain doesn't want them and won't acknowledge them and expects France to do the dirty work on its behalf':

> The result is an unacknowledged policy of deterrence in which both the British and French governments are complicit. It is intended to make life in Calais as harsh for migrants as possible, without actually killing them, in the hope that they will stop coming.[243]

In fact, however the numbers have increased over the last twelve years from the low hundreds to about 1,500. Referring to changing patterns of migration, Carr reminds us that until recently, 'Britain was preparing to bomb Syria in order to save its population from tyranny. In Calais, Syrians are no longer worthy of salvation but only of exclusion and the policeman's truncheon.' Carr concludes by indicting the political and communications ISAs in their interpellation of the populace that racialized capitalism is common sense:

> All this ought to shame and disgrace us, but politicians, the tabloid press and the public have managed to make it seem necessary and normal. And until that changes, and until we wake up to the poisonous politics and essential inhumanity that underpins contemporary 'migration management', Calais will remain one of the most brutal of Europe's 'hard borders' – and a microcosm of the twenty-first century's savage and racialised divisions of wealth, power, and lifestyle.[244]

In 2015, the UK Home Office instigated a change in procedures for submitting further submissions (new asylum claims by those who are 'appeal rights exhausted') on asylum and human rights applications. All submissions now have to be made in person, in Liverpool. As Right to Remain has explained, for a great many people, arranging and travelling to these appointments in Liverpool, rather than as at present making the submission in their local area, will be a very significant barrier to their pursuing their application for protection. Many are required to travel hundreds of miles, with no reimbursement of travel expenses, even for those who have no cash support at all.[245]

Asylum seekers are not scroungers or criminals, but some of the most desperate of the world-wide victims of capitalist exploitation. Moral panics about asylum seekers, like the other forms of racism discussed in this book, also direct people's thoughts away from their own exploitation and oppression.

RACISM AND THE RUN-UP TO THE 2015 GENERAL ELECTION

'Ask me my three main priorities for government and I tell you: education, education and education.' Tony Blair's famous mantra for a future Labour government pledged at the Labour Party Conference in Blackpool in October 1996, some seven months before his election victory, has been replaced in the current climate of austerity/immiseration capitalism by all mainstream parties in the run-up to the 2015 general election by 'immigration, immigration, immigration'.[246] As Nigel Farage stated at the 2014 UKIP Conference, the issue that would dominate the next election was open door immigration. He added, to a huge cheer, that we are 'borderless Britain'.[247] In the actual event, if anything was slightly more prominent in the election run-up, it was fears over the demise of the NHS.

In November 2013, ConDem Prime Minister David Cameron announced a raft of anti-immigrant measures ahead of new EU rules that came into effect on 1 January 2014 and ended restrictions on Bulgarians and Romanians entering the United Kingdom. While Eastern Europeans in general are xeno-racialized, the prime scapegoats were originally the Poles. While Polish people continue to be xeno-racialized, increasingly xeno-racist remarks are directed at Bulgarians and Romanians. The measures included no unemployment benefits for new migrants for the first three months of their stay; out-of-work welfare payments to end after six months, unless the claimant can prove they have a 'genuine prospect' of a job; new migrants not allowed to claim housing benefits immediately; and any migrant caught begging or sleeping rough to be deported and not allowed to return to the United Kingdom for a year. In addition migrants wishing to claim benefits are subject to more restrictions. This includes a new minimum earnings threshold. Failure to meet the requirements leads to the removal of welfare benefits, including Income Support.[248]

The ConDem government's Immigration Act of 2014 came into effect in May of that year. It contains 77 clauses and makes fundamental changes to the functioning of the immigration system. The Electric Immigration Network (EIN) summarizes its main provisions as follows:

- cutting the number of times immigration decisions can be appealed from 17 to 4, while allowing the government to return certain harmful individuals before their appeals are heard if there is no risk of serious irreversible harm
- ensuring that the courts have regard to Parliament's view of what the public interest requires when considering European Convention of Human Rights (ECHR) Article 8 claims in immigration cases – making clear the right to a family life is not to be regarded as absolute and unqualified
- clamping down on people who try to gain an immigration advantage by entering into a sham marriage or civil partnership
- requiring private landlords to check the immigration status of tenants, preventing those with no right to live in the United Kingdom from accessing private rented housing
- requiring temporary migrants with time-limited immigration status to make a financial contribution to the NHS.[249]

Saira Grant of the Joint Council for the Welfare of Immigrants (JCWI) has argued that the Act seeks to turn landlords, health workers and other public sector workers into border guards, while former EIN chair of trustees Keith Best, drawing parallels with the infamous 'sus laws', said he believed that the Immigration Act will be seen as so racist that it will become untenable.[250]

While 'sus laws' were targeted against young black men who bore the brunt of the crisis of capitalism and ideology in the 1970s, when there were moral panics about 'mugging' (analysed in detail in the book *Policing the Crisis*[251]), the 2014 Immigration Act needs to be seen in the light of austerity capitalism, xeno-racism, moral panics over so-called 'illegal immigration', and the accompanying rise of UKIP. It should be stressed that UKIP's racism is, in the official public sphere at least (its membership in general may be less exclusively racist), overtly 'xeno-'. (To underline this, Farage appointed mixed 'race' Steven Woolfe as migration spokesperson in July 2014, while on UKIP's official website, black member Winston McKenzie calls for withdrawal from the European Union and 'a free trade Commonwealth Market'.[252]) In the light of the defection of several Tories to UKIP, including one on the eve of the 2014 Tory Party Conference, as well as the switching of a major donation by one ex-Tory from the Conservatives to UKIP, and in the context of a concerted campaign of interpellation by the right-wing tabloids to demonize and criminalize Eastern Europeans, the main parties have been desperately trying to outbid each other to establish their xeno-racist credentials.

Thus Shadow Home Secretary Yvette Cooper, at the 2014 Labour Party Conference, stated that Labour 'got things wrong on immigration – on transitional controls for Eastern Europe, on the impact on jobs'. Castigating the Tories for not reducing net immigration and interpellating that 'people are more worried than ever' because things have got worse, Cooper pledged that 'a Labour Government will bring in stronger border controls to tackle illegal immigration', with proper 'entry and exit checks, so visas can be enforced and criminals stopped'. She went on:

> And we need radical reform when it comes to Europe. To stop the growing crisis at Calais, strengthen restrictions on new countries, change benefit rules so people can't claim when they first arrive, change deportation rules to make it easier to send home EU citizens who commit crimes and to change employment rules to stop employers exploiting cheap migrant labour to undercut wages and jobs. Not free movement, but fair movement.[253]

She insisted that 'it is not racist to be worried about immigration or to want stronger controls', and in an attempt to restrict racism to prejudice based on skin colour, concluded that 'when a UKIP candidate says [black entertainer] Lenny Henry should leave the country because of the colour of his skin, that is racist. We will never let racism go unchallenged.'[254]

In his speech to the Conservative Party Conference in 2014, Cameron's mantra was 'A Britain that everyone is proud to call home'. Relating this to controlling immigration, he went on to refer to 'getting our own people fit to work ... controlled borders and an immigration system that puts the British people first'. He went on to interpellate his audience: 'But we know the bigger issue today is migration from within the EU.' Cameron continued with a number of sound bites:

> Immediate access to our welfare system. Paying benefits to families back home. Employment agencies signing people up from overseas and not recruiting here. Numbers that have increased faster than

we in this country wanted ... at a level that was too much for our communities, for our labour markets.

'All of this', he went on, 'has to change – and it will be at the very heart of my renegotiation strategy for Europe.' The interpellation continued: 'Britain, I know you want this sorted so I will go to Brussels, I will not take no for an answer and when it comes to free movement – I will get what Britain needs.' He concluded with his promise on a referendum on the European Union, and to abolish the UK Human Rights Act enacted by the Labour Party in 1998, and to replace it with a new British Bill of Rights 'rooted in our values'.[255]

As Jonathan Freedland argued:

> From now until May, the Tories will seek daily to blunt Ukip's bayonets .... Ukip wants out of the EU, so Cameron promises a referendum. And Ukip slams 'human rights', damned as the co-conspirator of 'political correctness' in sending the country to the dogs, so the Tories promise to crack down on them too – and forget the pesky details.[256]

Freedland concluded that this is 'the pool of fury Ukip drinks from and which the Tories want to channel their way'. It is not about constitutional reform and legal jurisdictions, but an outlet 'for a much more visceral rage, the furious sense that the world is not as it should be – and that someone faraway must be to blame'. Freedland referred to the real problem, not Brussels or the European courts, but the 'borderless forces of globalisation that have upended economic life everywhere'.[257] These forces he failed to name are those of local, regional and international global neoliberal capital, and he did not point out that if Brussels and Strasbourg comprise the distant threat, the 'enemies' on British streets emanate from Sofia and Bucharest.

There is disturbing evidence that xeno-racism against Bulgarians and Romanians extends to schools. ChildLine in 2013 recorded a 69 per cent increase on the previous year of young people contacting them for counselling about racist bullying.[258] Dugan suggests that this coincided 'with rising political hostility to immigration – especially in the lead-up to [January 2014's] lifting of restrictions on Romanians and Bulgarians entering the UK'.[259] As Sue Minto, head of ChildLine explains, there is 'so much more of a focus in the news at the moment about immigrants ... it's a real discussion topic and children aren't immune to the conversations that happen around them'.[260]

Here is a timeline of announcements and events from the communications and political ISAs from about six months before election until this book went to press, in order of being announced or reported in the media. Two interpellative devices that were particularly noticeable in the speeches of all the mainstream Westminster politicians were a constant referral to 'our country', rather than 'the country', and a persistent reference to 'working people'. The former worked to reinforce a sense of 'us' and 'them' and to exclude 'foreigners', while the latter was useful to the ruling class on at least two levels. First, it served to render social class obsolete (since the term was working people, not the working class); second, it conveyed the message that there are just two groups of people: those who work and those who do not, thus denigrating those unable to find work and people receiving welfare. It also reinforced the myth of the Eastern European worker, just in the United Kingdom for benefits and free health and education.

9 October 2014: UKIP gained its first elected MP. Douglas Carswell, a defector from the Conservatives, won Clacton in a by-election. Farage said Carswell had 'shaken up British politics'.[261]

10 October 2014: emphasizing the essentially xeno-racist complexion of UKIP, Farage stated that skilled non-EU citizens 'are discriminated against because we have an open door into Europe. Today, if you're an Indian engineer, say, your chances of admission are limited. Ukip want to control the quantity and quality of people who come'.[262]

11 October 2014: Leader of the Opposition, Ed Miliband pledged a raft of hard-headed measures to ensure that migrants 'earn the right' to state benefits and face stiff English language tests before taking up jobs. Sources close to Miliband made clear that the announcements would go further than Labour's existing plans to extend the period EU migrants need to be in the United Kingdom before claiming out-of-work benefits to six months, and to prevent benefits from being sent back to families in other countries. Shadow home secretary Yvette Cooper stated, '[w]e should talk more about immigration and the things people are worried about'.[263]

16 October 2014: echoing Farage's xeno-racist remarks about a week before, prospective Conservative candidate Anna Firth said she supported the idea of blocking low-skilled European immigrants with an Australian-style points based system, a policy put forward by UKIP: '[o]nce we have that system in place then I think we will have a sensible immigration policy. One that says if you come to this country with skills we really need – say you're a brain surgeon or something in Australia as opposed to someone who has no skills, a fruit picker in Romania – then we say yes'.[264]

19 October 2014: a report revealed that undocumented immigrants suffering ill health are failing to seek treatment over fears that it could alert the authorities to their presence in the United Kingdom. Over 90 per cent were not registered with a GP and a fifth of those – over 100,000 – said it was because they were too scared to come forward. Dr Clare Shortall, who volunteers for Doctors of the World, stated, 'we are talking about vulnerable people who are victims of trafficking, children, victims of domestic violence, pregnant women. We are talking about them not being able to access health care.'[265]

22 October 2014: former Radio 1 DJ Mike Read apologized for his UKIP-supporting calypso song, which Farage had urged supporters to get to number 1 in the charts, and asked for it to be withdrawn from sale following criticism that it was racist. Sung in a fake Caribbean accent, it contains the lyrics: '[l]eaders committed a cardinal sin, open the borders let them all come in, illegal immigrants in every town, stand up and be counted Blair and Brown'.[266] Read said the UKIP anthem was just 'a bit of fun', adding, 'I don't have a racist bone in my body. I work across all cultures and creeds, I travel the world. I've got so many chums out in the Caribbean. I've spent a lot of time out there.'[267] A UKIP spokesperson said, '[i]t's a pity those so concerned with political correctness have trodden all over this'.[268]

23 October 2014: Miliband promised he would introduce an immigration reform bill within a month of winning the next election that offers 'clear, credible and concrete' measures to deal with the concerns of voters. The measures would include: strong borders to make sure migrants are counted in and out of the country; a specific criminal offence of exploiting workers by bringing people into the country to undercut wages; measures to stop recruitment agencies hiring only from abroad; requiring large employers who hire skilled workers from abroad to train local apprentices; and making sure all public sector workers in public-facing roles have minimum standards of English. He also said he would press for reforms in Europe, including longer restrictions on immigrants from new EU countries; stopping child benefit and tax credits being paid for children who live abroad; and doubling the period before new arrivals are entitled to benefits.[269]

25 October 2014: an Opinium/Observer poll revealed nearly one-third of voters would be prepared to vote for UKIP if they believed it could win in their own constituency.[270]

26 October 2014: after a reported comment that Angela Merkel would block Cameron's attempts to restrict EU migration, Defence Secretary Michael Fallon talked on the Sky News TV channel about preventing 'whole towns and communities being swamped by huge numbers of migrant workers … in some areas … towns do feel under siege from large numbers of migrant workers and people claiming benefits.'

27 October 2014: it was reported in the *Guardian* that a recent House of Lords written answer by Foreign Office minister Lady Anelay said that the government does not 'support planned search and rescue operations in the Mediterranean' believing that there was 'an unintended 'pull factor', encouraging more migrants to attempt the dangerous sea crossing and thereby leading to more 'tragic and unnecessary deaths'. More than 2,500 people were known to have drowned or gone missing in the Mediterranean sea since the start of 2014. British Refugee Council chief executive Maurice Wren commented, '[p]eople fleeing atrocities will not stop coming if we stop throwing them life-rings; boarding a rickety boat in Libya will remain a seemingly rational decision if you're running for your life and your country is in flames. The only outcome of withdrawing help will be to witness more people needlessly and shamefully dying on Europe's doorstep.'[271]

28 October 2014: the major of the French city of Calais, Natacha Bouchart, told MPs that 'illegal' migrants see the United Kingdom as a 'soft touch' and its benefits system acts as a 'magnet' to them. Cameron had urged 'action right across the board' and 'full-hearted cooperation between the British and French authorities to make sure we can stop people getting on to trains, getting on to container lorries or other vehicles and coming across the Channel'. UKIP's response was that the United Kingdom should send a message that 'its streets are not paved with gold. Welfare in the United Kingdom should be there for our own citizens, who have paid in, or whose family have paid in. It is not something for anybody turning up at our borders to be able to access.'[272]

10 November 2014: Cameron was urged to keep Britain in the European Union by the Confederation of British Industry (CBI), who told him immigration was part of the solution, not the problem. As pointed out in the Introduction, the interests of politicians and capitalists do not always correspond, nor do they coalesce around racialization. This because of capitalists' need for labour market flexibility, cheap labour and enhanced surplus value and hence profit; and politicians' desire to get elected.[273] While Cameron personally wishes to stay in the European Union, he realized the electoral gains from promising a referendum, thereby retaining hegemonic control of the ('British') workforce by the ongoing xeno-racialization of Eastern European workers.

12 November 2014: asked by the *New Statesman* if UKIP could support a minority Labour government, Farage replied 'I'd do a deal with the Devil if he got me what I wanted.' When pressed on whether he was ruling a coalition out, he replied, '[o]f course not.' He went on, 'I'd be very comfortable supporting anybody that gave me an opportunity to get my country back.'[274]

14 November 2014: ex-Conservative prime minister John Major intervened to warn that the United Kingdom is likely to leave the European

Union unless it permits the country to restrict immigration. He stated, 'our small island cannot absorb' the huge numbers moving here each year. He said that while the country welcomed hard-working migrants, the 'sheer scale of the influx' had put 'strains on our health, welfare, housing and education services'. He went on to argue that the United Kingdom had taken in 'one of, if not the largest population movement in peacetime European history', adding that failure to tackle the trend would result in 'huge public disquiet'. Lest we should not be fully aware who Major was talking about, Mail Online reporter James Chapman then made the point that more than 'a million people have entered Britain from Poland and seven other former Eastern bloc countries since 2004, when temporary restrictions on migrants from those nations were dropped by Labour'. Major's comments were discussed with the prime minister's office in advance.[275]

14 November 2014: following the story of 'a skint scrap worker from Romania' enthusing about having a better life for his family in the United Kingdom, which as he points out is his right as an EU citizen, and is 'a dream new start' for his family, Brian Flynn, writing in the *Sun*, decided to get a quote from Conservative MP Philip Hollobone, tipped at the time as the next defector to UKIP, who described it as a 'flagrant abuse of the system', adding that 'Sun readers will be appalled'. Another Conservative MP, Philip Davies, said 'EU rules are a farce', while the anti-immigration organization MigrationWatch said it 'comes as no surprise'.[276]

16 November 2014: Louise Mensch, *Sun on Sunday* columnist, in celebratory mood following the decision by the European Court of Justice (ECJ) to restrict benefits for three months, wrote about European migrants coming to Britain for 'life on the dole', a 14-year-old Romanian 'begging on the streets', whose aunt 'lives in a comfy four-bedroom house, and she's got benefits of £2,500 per month on top'. 'The aunt', she insisted, 'should go home – and take the niece with her.' The ECJ went further, ruling that those who have no job and no money have no right to live in an EU country other than their own. For Mensch this meant 'one moment of sanity' as opposed to 'all those Brussels bureaucrats trying to flood our island with the no-hopers clogging the lorry parks in Calais'.[277]

19 November 2014: Conservative defector Mark Reckless, at the time a UKIP candidate in the Rochester and Strood by-election caused by his defection, suggested Polish plumbers and other EU migrants could be asked to leave Britain if his party were in government, adding that those who had lived in the United Kingdom for a long time would be looked at sympathetically while others might only be allowed to stay for a transitional period. When asked again whether this would mean a Polish plumber could be deported, Reckless said, '[p]eople who have been here a long time and integrated in that way I think we'd want to look sympathetically at'. UKIP emphatically denied the claims. A Conservative leaflet for the same by-election referred to 'uncontrolled immigration' and not feeling 'safe walking down the high street of our town'.[278]

18 November 2014: The Labour Party pledged to pay for 1,000 extra border guards by imposing a charge on visitors from the United States and 55 other countries. Yvette Cooper was said to accept that the opposition 'needs to talk more' about public concerns and would say action to restore public confidence that illegal entrants are being caught and dealt with is 'vital for a progressive approach'.[279]

21 November 2014: the *Daily Telegraph* reported that Miliband was forced to say he felt a sense of 'respect' whenever he saw a white van (often seen as a symbol of a patriotic working-class small tradesperson, usually male, and in certain parts of the country in danger – from Labour's point of view – of voting UKIP) or a house draped in the flag of St George (ditto). This was an attempt to defuse allegations that North London-based professional sections of the Labour Party deride working-class voters. This followed a post on Twitter during the Rochester and Strood by-election from the then shadow attorney general, Emily Thornberry, with a photo of a house with three St George's flags and a white van parked outside, and the caption 'image from Rochester'. Thornberry was sacked by Miliband, who was 'more angry than he has ever been in his life'. Cameron waded in, accusing the Labour Party of 'sneering' at people who 'work hard, are patriotic and love their country. I think that's completely appalling'. Meanwhile some Labour MPs warned that Thornberry's tweet was further evidence that the party had lost touch with the working class and would lose the general election if it did not learn to speak the language of voters. The by-election was subsequently won by Reckless for UKIP, who became the party's second MP. The front page of the first edition of the *Sun* referred to 'Snob Labour MP's dig at white van man England flags'. According to the author of the *Telegraph* article, Steven Swinford, one Labour insider said, '[t]he whole party is incredibly depressed. We're being run by a group of North London MPs who are totally detached from reality, who have never worked in the real world and have more in common with the Liberal Democrats than working-class voters'. Swinford pointed out that Dan Ware, the owner of the house featured on Twitter, 'who works in the motor trade and is also a cage fighter', had visited both Thornberry's and Miliband's homes 'clutching a flag and demanding an apology'.[280]

21 November 2014: referring to Thornberry's tweet, Labour backbencher John Mann told Radio 4, '[i]t was horrendous. It insults people like me, it insults the people I know – my friends and family – Labour voters across the country because white vans, England flags, they're Labour values and actually pretty routine Labour values for most of us.'[281]

27 November 2014: Sky News reported that net migration to the United Kingdom had 'rocketed to 260,000' in the year to June – a hike of 43 per cent, thus derailing Cameron's 'no ifs, no buts' speech in 2011 about getting immigration to below 100,000 per year. According to Sky News, the latest figures also revealed a 'statistically significant increase' in Romanian and Bulgarian citizens arriving in the United Kingdom over the period, up to 32,000 from 18,000 in the previous year.[282] On the same day on the Sky News TV channel, Miliband said there would be no benefits for EU migrants for two years.

28 November 2014: It was reported by BBC News that, in an attempt to outdo Labour and the Liberal Democrats, Cameron had urged other EU leaders to support his 'reasonable' proposals for far-reaching curbs on welfare benefits for migrants, a priority in future negotiations over the United Kingdom's membership. Under his plans, migrants would have to wait four years for certain benefits. These measures would include stopping EU migrants from claiming in-work benefits, such as tax credits, and getting access to social housing for four years; stopping migrants claiming child benefit for dependants living outside the United Kingdom; removing migrants from the United Kingdom after six months if they had not found work; restricting the right of migrants to bring non-EU family members into the United Kingdom; stopping EU jobseekers claiming Universal Credit; speeding up deportation of convicted criminals; longer re-entry bans for beggars and fraudsters removed from the United Kingdom; stopping citizens from new EU entrants working in the United Kingdom until their economies had 'converged more closely'; and extra money for communities with high levels of migrants.[283]

7 December 2014: Farage blamed his late arrival at an event on immigration: '[i]t took me six hours and 15 minutes in the car to get here. It should have taken three and a half to four. That has nothing to do with professionalism. What is does have to do with is a country in which the population is going through the roof, chiefly because of open-door immigration, and the fact the M4 is not as navigable as it used to be.'[284]

2 December 2014: François Crépeau, the UN special rapporteur for migrants' rights, criticized the British government's decision not to support search and rescue missions in the Mediterranean, saying there could be terrible consequences for the tens of thousands of people in ramshackle boats in search of a better life. He also attacked the ongoing narrative against immigration in the United Kingdom, describing the fantasy that there is a core British culture. Referring to the idea of 'Cool Britannia' of the 1990s, he stated: '[i]fBritannia is ruled by the Ukip, or with Ukip-type policies, it is not going to be cool.'[285]

12 December 2014: owner of the right-wing tabloids the *Daily Express, Sunday Express, Daily Star* and *Daily Star Sunday,* Richard Desmond pledged £300,000 to UKIP, indicating that these newspapers would support UKIP in the election.[286]

13 December 2014: the president of the European Commission, Jean-Claude Juncker, said there had to be an end to discrimination against Poles, Romanians and Bulgarians, but that he would not 'shoot down' Cameron's reform plans. As he put it, '[e]specially in Great Britain, which always fought for the enlargement of the European Union, there has to be an end to discrimination against countries just because it goes down well topically when you beat up others'. He went on, 'I am utterly against behaving as if all Poles, all Romanians, all Bulgarians in the European labour market are of a basic mentality that is criminal. These are people who are working and earning their wages.'[287]

19 December 2014: defending UKIP general election candidate Kerry Smith's calling a Chinese woman a 'chinky bird', Farage explained that it was because Smith grew up in a council house in East London. Farage asked, '[i]f you and your mates are going out for a Chinese, what do you say you're going for?'[288]

21 December 2014: Sky News reported that Home Secretary Theresa May wanted the Conservative Party's next manifesto to include a pledge to make non-EU graduates return home and apply for a work visa from overseas if they want to continue living in the United Kingdom, according to the *Sunday Times*, in order for Cameron to reach his target for cutting migration.[289]

8 January 2015: *The Times* reported that the reason UKIP councillor Rozanne Duncan was expelled from the party was that she has a problem with 'negroes' because there's 'something about their faces'.[290]

19 January 2015: the Muslim Council of Britain (MCB) raised objections to a letter from ConDem Communities Secretary Eric Pickles and under-secretary, Muslim peer Tariq Ahmad, asking more than 1,000 Muslim leaders to 'explain and demonstrate how faith in Islam can be part of British identity'. While Pickles said he was proud of the way British Muslims had responded to the Paris terrorist attacks in January 2015, he stated that there was 'more work to do' in rooting out extremists and preventing the radicalization of young people. He went on say that faith leaders 'an important responsibility, in explaining and demonstrating how faith in Islam can be part of British identity ... proud of your faith and proud of your country'. Radicalization, he argued, 'cannot be solved from

Whitehall alone.'[291] Harun Khan, deputy secretary general of the MCB, asked, 'Is Mr Pickles seriously suggesting, as do members of the far right, that Muslims and Islam are inherently apart from British society?' As Lord Sacks, the former chief rabbi, pointed out, radicalized Islam is a global phenomenon transmitted by the internet and social media.[292]

23 January 2015: More than half of UKIP's supporters would not accept a Jewish prime minister, according to a poll conducted by YouGov for Tim Bale at Queen Mary, University of London. Among Conservative supports, 65 per cent would find a Jewish prime minister acceptable, as would 72 per cent of Labour supporters and 73 per cent of Liberal Democrats. Miliband if elected would have been the first Jewish prime minister since Benjamin Disraeli, who was last prime minister in 1880.[293]

4 March 2015: Appearing on the stage with a black member behind him at the UKIP annual conference, Nigel Farage promised a 'common sense' approach to immigration. He said he would restore 'sanity' by introducing an Australian-style points-based system to control who would be allowed to settle in the United Kingdom, and take back control of the borders by leaving the European Union. He stated that 'We as a party hold no prejudice against anyone on the grounds of their nationality, their religion or their race.'[294]

6 March 2015: the Migration Observatory unit at the University of Oxford announced that the migrant population of England had risen by 565,000 since 2011, with two-thirds coming from the European Union. These were projections suggesting that the foreign-born population of every local authority in the country might have risen, because similar official data would not be available before the general election.[295]

11 March 2015: Cameron said of presenter Jeremy Clarkson, suspended following an alleged fracas with a producer on his television motoring show, 'He's a constituent of mine, he's a friend of mine, he's a huge talent. I see that he said he regrets some of what happened. Because he is a talent and he does amuse and entertain so many people, including my children who'll be heartbroken if *Top Gear* is taken off air, I hope this can be sorted out because it is a great programme.' Clarkson had been involved in a number of racist incidents. Here are some examples:

- During one show, he and his co-presenters built a bridge over a Burmese river, and as a man walked across it, Clarkson said: 'That's a proud moment but there's a s•••• [racist term for an Asian] on it.'
- He was accused by the tabloid Daily *Mirror* of using the 'N-word' when chanting the rhyme 'Eeny, meeny, miny, moe'.
- In India, he built a toilet at the back of his car, claiming it would be

'perfect' for tourists because 'everyone' who visits the country gets diarrhoea.

- In another episode, the presenters tried to squeeze an overweight Albanian man, who had ostensibly been murdered, into the boots of their cars, having pretended to have been sent to the country to test drive cars for a mafia boss.
- He described Mexicans as 'lazy, feckless and flatulent' and branded Mexican food as 'refried sick'. The programme claimed the Mexican ambassador to the United Kingdom would not complain as he was likely to be asleep. The ambassador did in fact complain.
- He made a mock Nazi salute during a segment discussing a new Mini, claiming the car's in-built navigation system 'only goes to Poland'.[296]
- He physically attacked a Malaysian car with sledgehammer, likened the name of the car to a disease, and implied it was built by 'jungle people who wear leaves as shoes'.[297]

Deputy Prime Minister Nick Clegg added that he thought the show was 'great television', that he liked to watch it with his kids, and it made him laugh.[298]

12 March 2015: the *Guardian* reported that on a forthcoming television programme, Farage stated that 'race' and other anti-discrimination legislation should be abolished, arguing that it was no longer needed in the United Kingdom. Pressed on which discrimination laws he would get rid of, he said, 'Much of it. I think the employer should be much freer to make decisions on who he or she employs.' Asked whether there would be a law against discrimination on the grounds of 'race' or colour under UKIP, Farage added, 'No … because we take the view, we are colour-blind. We as a party are colour-blind.'[299] Farage later backtracked and said in an interview on Sky News on the same day that he was not talking about getting rid of race relations legislation, but that he wanted employers to be able to choose to employ black and white Britons rather than East Europeans.

14 March 2015: Miliband promised to stop migrants from claiming benefits for at least two years, as one of five election pledges.

14 March 2015: According to the *Daily Mirror*'s TV editor, Nicola Methven, during the fracas involving Jeremy Clarkson and a producer (see above), Clarkson called the producer a 'lazy Irish c•••' before splitting his lip with a punch.[300]

17 March 2015: It was revealed that during a television programme in February 2014, Clarkson was seen erecting a sign with the words 'Pikey's Peak'. The BBC cleared him of being racist. A spokesperson for the Traveller movement said he was 'horrified' the BBC had done so.[301] Clarkson also wrote in *Top Gear* magazine, referring to London taxi drivers, 'You have a chap who has just arrived from a country you've never heard of, whose car smells faintly of lavender oil and sick, who doesn't know where he's going and can't get there anyway because he never puts more than £2 worth of fuel in the tank of his car'.[302]

20 March 2015: Jonathan Stanley, a surgeon, stood down as a UKIP parliamentary candidate. He stated, 'I have given my full resignation to the party because of issues happening in Scotland: open racism and sanctimonious bullying within the party'. He went on, 'This sectarian racist filth in Scotland needs cleaning up. It is a great threat to the Eurosceptic cause and civil society'. He indicated that party turmoil in Scotland and Farage's pledge to restrict migrants' access to the NHS and schools were behind his decision to leave the party.[303]

21 March 2015: the ConDem government introduced an upfront Migrant Health Surcharge for migrants from outside the European Economic Area (EEA) coming to the United Kingdom for longer than six months at a fee of £200 a year. The DoH said the move would ensure those coming into the United Kingdom make an 'appropriate financial contribution to the cost of the health services they may use'. No other EU country has such a structural link between immigration applications and access to health services.[304]

23 March 2015: Anti-UKIP protesters in fancy dress forced Farage to flee his local pub where he was dining with his family on Sunday afternoon. The UKIP leader called the demonstrators 'scum', claiming they had caused his children distress. The group, however, said they were holding a 'cabaret of diversity' in support of those UKIP was seeking to marginalize, such as migrants, HIV activists, gay people, disabled people and breastfeeding mothers. The demonstrators, who formed a conga line, claimed their demonstration was good-natured throughout.[305]

31 March 2015: Farage declared immigration has left towns and cities in Britain almost unrecognizable for many people over the last decade, as he unveiled UKIP's first general election poster, an image of the white cliffs of Dover with three escalators running up them. He said he was making immigration the central plank of his campaign. Farage moved beyond making a case that immigration puts pressure on wages, schools and hospitals to a more emotional argument that it is changing the culture of the United Kingdom. He also emphasized the party's policy of requiring migrants to have health insurance for the first five years, and refusing entry to those with life-threatening diseases.

4 April 2015: Farage defended his controversial remarks about the treatment of foreign-born HIV sufferers: 'it is a sensible Christian thing to look after your family and your own community first'. He claimed 7,000 people are diagnosed as HIV positive in the United Kingdom every year – and 60 per cent of them are foreign nationals. 'We need', he went on, 'to put the National Health Service there for British people and families':

> What good Christian would say to an 85-year-old woman you can't have breast cancer treatment because we can't afford it, whilst at the same time shovelling billions of pounds on foreign aid, allowing people from all over the world to fly into Britain as health tourists to get a HIV test and drugs over £20,000 a year?[306]

16 April 2015: Farage said, 'We want our country back and then and only then can we actually control our borders.'[307]

17 April 2015: Farage was accused of 'insulting' the audience of the final election debate by saying they had failed to understand the issues and were too left wing: 'There is a total lack of comprehension amongst this panel and the audience, which is a remarkable.'[308] He went on to blame the housing problem on immigration: 'I just wonder, I'm curious can I get any recognition from any of you that the demand side of this equation is that a rapidly rising population due to open-door immigration, started by Ed Miliband's Labour parties in the 1990s, has directly contributed towards the housing crisis?'

19 April 2015: As many as 700 migrants were feared to have drowned just outside Libyan waters, in what could prove to be the worst disaster yet involving migrants being smuggled to Europe. If confirmed, this meant that at least 1,500 migrants had died up to then in 2015 while on route to Europe – at least 30 times higher than the previous year's equivalent figure, which was itself a record. This came just days after 400 others were drowned.[309]

19 April 2015: Simon Usborne commented on a piece by right-wing columnist Katie Hopkins in the previous day's *Sun*. The headline was 'Rescue boats? I'd use gunships to stop migrants.' She then referred to migrants in Calais who try to board trucks heading to Britain as 'a plague of feral humans'. She added, 'Some of our towns are festering sores, plagued by swarms of migrants and asylum seekers, shelling out benefits like Monopoly money.' Hopkins concluded, 'Make no mistake, these migrants are like cockroaches. They might look a bit "Bob Geldof's Ethiopia circa 1984", but they are built to survive a nuclear bomb. They are survivors.' As Usborne pointed out, in the environment 'that led to creation of the Third Reich in Germany, Polish people were seen as "an East European species of cockroach", while Jews were rats. When Hutu extremists used radio propaganda to incite violence against the Tutsis during the Rwandan Genocide, they called on people to "weed out the cockroaches."[310]

18 April 2015: Miliband said a future Labour government would pass laws to ensure all health workers spoke English well enough to care for patients before they could start work, and regulators would be given powers to enforce the rules. He also said he would introduce rules to stop immigrants claiming benefits for at least two years, and would stop child benefit and child tax credit payments for children living in other countries. Don Flynn, the chief executive of Migrants Rights Network, said the issue of immigrants learning English was a red herring, because most newcomers to the United Kingdom are keen to learn the world's most widely used language.[311]

22 April 2015: Commenting on the refugees fleeing across the Mediterranean in boats, Farage said it was 'fine' to accept a few thousand Christians, but no more:

> [If] we have to give some Christians refugee status given that with Iraq and Libya there's almost nowhere for them to go then fine but Europe can't send the message that everyone who comes will be accepted.

The remaining refugees should be sailed back to Libya: 'I am suggesting they should make sure that those who are coming in vessels which are not seaworthy are put on vessels that are.'[312]

5 May 2015: It was reported in the *Mirror* that during the election campaign Robert Blay, UKIP parliamentary candidate for North East Hampshire, was seen in a video apparently threatening to shoot his Conservative rival for the seat, Ranil Jayawardena, tipped as likely one day to become Britain's first Asian prime minister. In the video, Mr Blay reportedly said:

> If he is I will personally put a bullet between his eyes. If this lad turns up to be our Prime Minister I will personally put a bullet in him. That's how strong I feel about it. I won't have this f••••• as our prime minister. I absolutely loathe him.

Blay also questioned Jayawardena's background: 'His family have only been here since the Seventies. You are not British enough to be in our Parliament. I've got 400 years of ancestry where I live. He hasn't got that.' He went on, 'I said to his dad about two months ago – "When did you come to Britain?" He said "In the 'Seventies." I said "Why did you come?" He said "Things weren't very good politically in Sri Lanka and I came here and I could train as an accountant." So he's come here and ponced off us hasn't he like all the East Europeans are? That's what is happening. Continually.'

During his chat with the *Daily Mirror*, Blay also described how he called the police following a heated row after he stuck a UKIP election leaflet through an East European's door. 'He's in my country,' Blay fumed, 'He's a f•••••• immigrant and I'm not putting up with that s•••, because that was abuse.'[313]

CONCLUSION

I conclude the first chapter of this book with some further observations on the decline of multiculturalism at the level of the state, and some comments on racism in the context of austerity capitalism. Despite suggestions from a number of academics, politicians and media pundits that neoliberal capitalism or even capitalism itself was dealt a mortal blow after the Lehman bank demise of September 2008, it is clear that the international ruling classes have not forsaken neoliberalism. Indeed, as Dave Hill argues, neoliberalism is being ruthlessly reinforced to make sure that first, the capitalist system is saved, and second, workers pay for the current capitalist crisis.[314] Ha-Joon Chang has highlighted the similarities between the structural adjustment programmes (SAPs) imposed on governments in Latin America and Africa in the 1980s and 1990s by the International Monetary Fund (IMF), and the infliction by European governments of IMF-style programmes on their own populations.[315] The result of what Hill describes as 'immiseration capitalism' is that welfare is slashed, the poor live more precariously, more unhealthily, and die earlier. 'The low paid strata of the working class are duped and failed by the ideological apparatuses of the state, and repressed and kept in line and in prison, and (in some cases) in the ghetto, by the repressive apparatuses of the state.'[316] Moreover, capitalists and pro-capitalist politicians are using austerity capitalism to (attempt to) push through major structural changes, which they hope will be irreversible.

Robert Stevens has described this process as a counter-revolution. As he puts it, 'the capitalist class everywhere is seeking to extricate itself from its crisis through a social counterrevolution, aimed at a fundamental restructuring of economic and class relations'.[317] 'Every social gain ever won by the working class, including each and every basic welfare state provision,' he goes on, 'is being destroyed.' In the United Kingdom the ConDem government used the crisis to drastically diminish workers' rights and living standards, the latter having been pushed back 30 years,[318] and to undermine the very basis of the welfare state. Given that many (though not all) on the receiving end of racism are in a worse and more precarious social and economic position, they are more vulnerable and fare worse in this ongoing assault than the rest of the population.

Part of the counter-revolution in the United Kingdom is a direct assault on equality and human rights. The ConDem government slashed the budget of the EHRC by 62 per cent from £70 million in 2007 to £26.8 million for 2014–15, with some insiders claiming that the figure may be reduced further to £18 million. At the same time, the outgoing full-time chair of the commission has been replaced by a part-timer who will work only two days a week. Furthermore, the only two Asian and black commissioners, unlike their white counterparts, have not been automatically reappointed for a further term of office. African-Caribbean MP Diane Abbott, the shadow public health minister, commented, 'It seems to me that race is slipping off the agenda at the commission.'[319]

This view is corroborated by Lady (Doreen) Lawrence. Alarmed by moves to water down a key protection arising from the Macpherson Report, she wrote to the prime minister, the deputy prime minister and the other major party leaders. The letter was ignored, as were earlier communications seeking to establish relations with the government.[320]

Also part of the counter-revolution is the aforementioned attack on multiculturalism, a clear example of fragmenting the working class. As Ahmed argues, racialized groups become the focus of blame for the social ills of society, and all pillars of the capitalist state from the tabloid press to judges and politicians fall over each other to denigrate and scapegoat minority ethnic groups.[321] This is the real divide and rule: not a tactic of white people but a process rooted in the mechanics of capitalism itself. As noted earlier in this chapter, these tactics were identified by Marx some 140 years ago.

Divide and rule is accompanied by a ratcheting up of social control. As Thomas Scripps argues, after the extremely questionable Trojan Horse investigation of an Islamist take-over of academy schools in Birmingham, to counter the supposed threat of religious radicalization, schools are now required to 'actively promote' British values. These include:

- an appreciation that living under the rule of law protects individual citizens
- how citizens can influence decision making through the democratic process
- an understanding that bodies such as the police and the army can

be held to account by the people, through the democratic organs of government

- an understanding that the freedom to hold other faiths and beliefs is protected in law
- an understanding of the problems of identifying and combating discrimination.

As Scripps puts it:

> The government and media repeatedly claim that these proposals represent the 'depoliticisation' of education, as if the active promotion of bourgeois law, corrupt parliamentary democracy and their defenders in the form of the police and armed forces is a politically neutral act. Behind all the talk of democratic values, the British bourgeoisie – like its counterparts the world over – are developing more and more repressive measures to police working people. Any opinion considered threatening to the ruling strata is to be quashed. The practical implications of this policy make a mockery of the supposed 'freedom to hold other faiths and beliefs' listed in the core values.

'The indoctrination of youth into bourgeois society through the education system,' he goes on, 'is not news to Marxists, but rarely in history is the process so deliberate and clear. These proposals are a reflection of deepening social and political antagonisms.'[322]

It is three-quarters of a century since Beveridge instructed 'housewives as Mothers' to ensure 'an adequate continuance of the British Race' to produce 'the best of our breed'. Conservative MP Brian Binley, who is critical of ConDem leader and fellow Conservative David Cameron because Cameron fails 'consistently to chime with the natural instincts of [Conservative] supporters',[323] stated in an interview about his hostility to same-sex marriage (which Cameron supported):

> I think we need to keep marriage a little bit special as the building block of our society for the procreation of the race and the development of children. All the proof lies with the fact that married couples bring up children who make better citizens.[324]

The context is, of course, very different. As noted earlier, Beveridge was promising welfare as part of a historic compromise between capital and labour – reform not revolution. Binley's intervention comes at a time when neoliberalism, implemented with a vengeance after the election of Margaret

Thatcher in 1979 and consolidated under the Tony Blair governments, is firmly entrenched, and as part of the relentless pursuit of austerity/immiseration capitalism, the very existence of the welfare state is under threat. While the settings are very different, the continuity and similarity of racist and sexist thinking is stark. It should be pointed out in conclusion that Beveridge's and Binley's comments do not represent racist remarks in their own minds. While politicians often deliberately play the 'race card', particularly during election campaigns, competing with each other, as we have seen, to take the 'better stance' on immigration for example, Beveridge's and Binley's views on 'race' are part of their everyday thinking, 'just common sense' to them. As Talat Ahmed concludes:

> Individual attitudes and actions do not exist in a vacuum. The way racism operates is not a question of individual behaviour, much less individual psychology. Racism is structured into the very heart of the world we live in. It is a world that is organised on the basis of vast social and economic inequalities which are designed to pit groups of people against each other, while our rulers remain parasitic on our labour and suffering.[325]

In this chapter I have dealt with a sizeable array of different forms of racism, and have tried to be as comprehensive as possible. I can only apologize if I have left any groups out. In the next two chapters I tell a similar story about the United States and Australia. As we have seen, and will see in the next two chapters, a central function of racism in capitalist countries is to undermine threats to the capitalist mode of production, and in the case of the three 'developed' countries under discussion in this book, to justify imperialism, whether old or new.

2

The United States

INTRODUCTION

As in the United Kingdom, in the United States white people experience less poverty than every other ethnic group. At the last US Census, the poverty rate for 'White, non-Hispanic' people was 9.9 per cent, for Asian Americans 12.1 per cent, those of 'Hispanic origin' 26.6 per cent and for black Americans 27.4 per cent.[1] Data from a Census Bureau American Community Survey reveals that poverty rates for Native Americans vary from a high 16.6 per cent to a staggering 50.9 per cent (see Figure 2.1).

In order to understand contemporary racism in the United States, it is necessary to give a brief historical overview of institutional racism.[2] There are three reasons. First, there is a tendency to restrict racism to the experiences of African Americans, what some critics (such as Delgado and Stefancic[3]) have referred to as the 'black–white binary', which 'considers the black–white relation as central to racial analysis', or 'black exceptionalism',[4] which holds that black people's history 'is so distinctive that placing it at the center of analysis is … warranted'. While, as we shall see, anti-black racism was and continues to be a prominent and abhorrent reality for African Americans, horrific institutional racism existed before enslaved Africans were brought to the Americas, and continues to oppress a wide constituency.

This brings me to the second reason. Institutional racism has existed on what is now US soil for half a millennium, starting with the racialization, exploitation and pillage of America's indigenous peoples.

Third, the repressive and ideological apparatuses of the state (RSAs and ISAs) have been applied excessively, unremittingly and mercilessly to maintain hegemony, to uphold and reproduce different forms of institutional racism. A variety of forms of intense counter-hegemonic antiracist resistance have been apparent for 500 years, too.[5]

In this chapter, I begin by looking at the legacy of Christopher Columbus, addressing myself to the situation of Native Americans and Alaskan Natives, both historically and contemporaneously. Next I move on to a consideration of a brief history of slavery in the United States, followed by some issues connected to the lives of African Americans, post-slavery and today. After that I look at racism experienced historically and currently

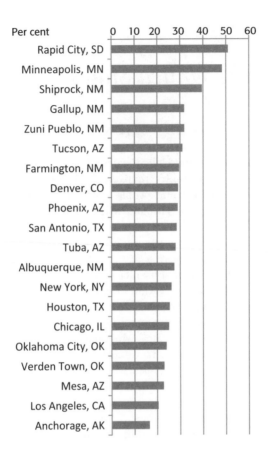

Figure 2.1 Poverty rates for the American Indian and Alaska Native Alone population in the 20 cities most populated by these groups, 2007–11

Source: US Census Bureau American Community Survey.

by Latina/o Americans, before moving on to trace the history of and the current realities for Asian Americans. I conclude with a consideration of Islamophobia, which I have referred to as newer hybridist racism, and which has been particularly rampant since 9/11.

NATIVE AMERICANS: A BRIEF HISTORY

In an attempt to find a new trade route to India, in 1492, funded by the Catholic Church in the context of deep economic crisis in feudalism with the Italian ruling class desperate for wealth,[6] Christopher Columbus 'discovered' America, which at first he assumed was part of the coast of Asia. Marx and Engels described how (unknown, of course, to Columbus at the time) the 'discovery of America paved the way' for the establishment by European modern industry of the world market.[7] As they put it:

> The discovery of America, the rounding of the Cape, opened up fresh ground for the rising bourgeoisie. The East-Indian and Chinese markets, the colonisation of America, trade with the colonies, the increase in the means of exchange and in commodities generally, gave to commerce, to navigation, to industry, an impulse never before known, and thereby, to the revolutionary element in the tottering feudal society, a rapid development.[8]

After landing in the 'new world', Columbus wrote in his log that the indigenous people were 'utterly convinced that I and all my people came from Heaven',[9] prompting Gary Okihiro to describe Columbus's venture as 'Christian imperialism'.[10] It has been estimated that at the time of Columbus's arrival, there were between 43 million and 65 million indigenous peoples in the Americas as a whole, and about 3.8 million indigenous peoples in North America alone.[11] Of these, about 3.3 million were in what is now the United States.[12] Following on from Columbus's assessment of the potential of this new category of people for exploitation, there then ensued, in the words of the Marxist organization Permanent Revolution, 'force; pillage conquest, mass murder, torture and religious bigotry'. As they put it, '[t]hat was how the "civilised" Europeans stamped their authority on the peoples of what came to be called 'the Americas'.[13]

In 1565, Don Pedro Menendez de Aviles and 600 Spanish soldiers and settlers colonized St Augustine, Florida, and by 1570 the continent had been named 'America'.[14]

From the 1590s through the seventeenth century, the Americas then experienced what has been described as 'the manipulation period' in indigenous white relations, where the imperialist powers of Spain, Britain and France struck alliances with indigenous peoples for colonial trade gains, in which the indigenous peoples took part.[15]

From the late seventeenth century to the end of the eighteenth century, the main issue was land rather than trade. This was a period in which, with England in control of the Atlantic seaboard, the French entrenched in Canada and along the Mississippi river, and Spain in Florida and the southwest, 'the Indians in the east found themselves surrounded by white men'.[16]

The next period saw the settlers angry with the British Crown over the proclamation of 1763, which, along with Crown taxes on tea and other goods, precipitated the American War of Independence of 1775 (and the founding of the United States of America in 1783). Not a single major Native American tribe joined the colonists in the war. This was because the Native Americans knew they could expect nothing from the colonists, and since 'Anglo-Saxon hegemony was secure', the 'politics of playing off European rivals against one another and against rival tribes no longer worked'.[17] Following the success of the American Revolution, Native Americans, after 300 years of dealing with rival European powers, faced a single enemy: the United States of America.

The strategy of the US government was to turn Native Americans from hunters into agriculturalists, so they would not need so much land. Tactics included getting chiefs into debt at state trading houses so that they were forced to sell off land, and exterminating the economic base of the hunting tribes, the buffalo. In addition to economic warfare through trade and debt, RSAs were used in military campaigns, and in attempts to annihilate the buffalo, while RSAs and ISAs combined to try to terminate the Native American traditional way of life with 'germ warfare, psychological warfare using alcohol ... ecological warfare using the reservation system [and] cultural warfare prohibiting Indian ceremonies'.[18]

The next period identified by Nederveen Pieterse witnessed the Indian Removal Act of 1830, when, under the presidency of Andrew Jackson, the 'West' was opened up for the 'American way of life'. Pieterse notes that 'Jacksonian Democracy' excluded both Native Americans and black Americans. The US military crushed the resistance, planters occupied Native lands, and their occupants were moved to Oklahoma territory, heralding the 'wars of the plains'.[19]

According to Perea and colleagues, the 'single most destructive achievement of the nineteenth century movement to break the structure and sovereignty of Indian tribes was Congress's passage of the General Allotment Act of 1887'. This act, also known as the Dawes Act, allowed the president of the United States to break up lands held jointly by tribes and reallocate them in separate parcels to individual tribal members, effectively converting indigenous peoples from hunters to farmers.[20]

David Getches and colleagues have argued that the Act had two goals: 'to open up more land for white settlement and to end Indian tribalism'. As they explain, the aim of the act was:

> to turn reservations into campuses for training Indians in the 'arts of civilization'. The Bureau of Indian Affairs took unprecedented control of everyday Indian life, seeking to squeeze out Indian government,

religion, and culture …. 'Surplus' lands were sold for non-Indian settlement; the result was a loss of about two-thirds of all the Indians' lands.[21]

President Theodore Roosevelt was brutally honest about the intentions of the Act, describing it as 'a mighty pulverizing engine to break up the tribal mass'.[22] The 1880s to the 1920s was a period of poverty and demoralization, during which time a number of other acts were passed that successively institutionalized the hegemony of US neo-colonialism.[23] In response to the decimation of tribal lands and culture caused by the General Allotment Act, attempts were made to restore tribal governance and sovereignty. The Meriam Report (1928) described in great detail Indian poverty, ill health and poor education.

As a result, in 1934 the Indian Reorganization Act (IRA) was passed, which sought to negate the General Allotment Act.[24] However, as Perea and colleagues point out, while the IRA represented an improvement, the improvement was merely partial.[25] Vine Deloria Jr. and Lytle argue that '[m]any of the old customs and traditions … had vanished …. The experience of self-government according to Indian traditions had eroded and, while the new constitutions were akin to the traditions of some tribes, they were completely foreign to others.' In general, they point out, traditional Indians of almost every tribe objected strongly to 'the Anglo-American system of organizing people'.[26]

It was perhaps the boarding school project that crystallized how racism was institutionalized for Native Americans. It was organized by Captain Richard Henry Pratt, who declared in 1892, 'a great general [General Phil Sheridan] has said that the only good Indian is a dead one …. In a sense, I agree with the sentiment, but only in this: that all the Indian there is in the race should be dead. Kill the Indian in him, and save the man'.[27] Citing Ward Churchill, Curry Malott lists 129 Indian boarding schools operating in the United States between 1880 and 1980.[28] Malott describes how the RSAs combined with the ISAs dealt with children as young as four years old, who were:

> forcibly removed from resistant parents and taken sometimes thousands of miles from home for years on end and prohibited from speaking their native tongue or practicing any of their other cultural traditions. In other words, they were prohibited from being 'Indian' and made, sometimes with deadly force, to be something else, that is, a low-level, manual laborer with white values and worldview.[29]

Ward Churchill estimated that between the late 1800s and the mid-1900s more than half of all Native American children were removed from their homes in this way.[30] Schooling socialized them into thinking that 'white society in general represented everything good and civilized and that "Indian" ways were shameful and savage'. Colonization and genocide was rarely discussed, and if it was, it was 'contrasted with the superior future that is now within their grasp thanks to the generous gift of "Western civilization"'. Native children's dress and hairstyles were changed, cultural materials brought from home were destroyed, cultural practices were banned, and Native languages were forbidden, even out of class. [31]

As Andrea Smith points out, mainstream churches and government were directly responsible for the deaths of at least 50,000 children as a result of this process of compulsory assimilation. The crimes that these institutions were guilty of included 'murder through beating, poisoning, hanging, starvation, strangulation, medical experimentation and forced sterilization' and paedophilia.[32] Moreover, as Malott explains, Native students had to 'contribute to the funding of their own cultural destruction through their collective labor power' in sweatshops, laundries and bakeries. While, as we shall see later in the chapter, African Americans were denied integration, American Indians faced a history of forced assimilation.[33]

The second half of the twentieth century witnessed the largest movement of Native Americans in US history. In 1952, the federal government initiated the Urban Indian Relocation Program, designed to entice reservation dwellers to seven major urban cities: Chicago, Denver, Los Angeles, San Francisco, San Jose, St Louis, Cincinnati, Cleveland and Dallas, cities where jobs were supposedly plentiful.[34] It is estimated that 750,000 Native Americans migrated to the cities between 1950 and 1980. Some came through the Relocation Program; others came on their own. In 1940 only around 8 per cent of Indians were living in cities, while in the 2000 Census, 64 per cent were urban dwellers.[35] Today, it is over 70 per cent.[36]

ALASKAN NATIVES: A BRIEF HISTORY

A major study in 2002 of the forgotten peoples of Alaska by the Alaska Advisory Committee to the US Commission on Civil Rights pointed out that the histories of Alaska Natives and American Indian groups have many similarities.[37] Their history is also marked by 'conquest, genocide, forced cultural and land loss, and the subsequent evolution of alcohol use, violence, and chronic disease'.[38] Racism in Alaska dates back to long before statehood to an era of Russian occupation and settlement, which began in the 1740s.[39] Russian settlers came to Alaska to establish the seal fur trade, and forced Native Peoples into enslavement. The tribal lives of Native Alaskans were disrupted for nearly 100 years.[40]

American whalers and traders later followed, and the land was bought from Russia in 1867 for 2 cents an acre, at a total cost of $7.2 million. Afterwards, the territory was soon forgotten, and it fell into a state of neglect, until the 1890s when a great Gold Rush era ensued, with the white settlers having little regard for the Native traditions, taking from the Native Alaskans, and providing little or nothing in return.[41] After the decline of gold production, Alaska was neglected until the Second World War, when the United States recognized the military potential of the region.

In 1935, top US General Billy Mitchell told the US Congress, 'I believe that in the future, whoever holds Alaska will hold the world. I think it is the most important strategic place in the world.'[42] As the Alaska Public Lands Information Centers explain, whoever controlled Alaska's Aleutian Islands, which run to the south-east of Alaska, controlled transportation routes in the Pacific during the Second World War. From June 1942, two of these islands were occupied by the Japanese for nearly a year.[43]

Eventually, in 1959, Alaska became the 49th state in the Union. The two decades following statehood witnessed:

> turmoil for Native Alaskans as they witnessed a dramatic shift in livelihood, land ownership, political power, and cultural domination. The traditional frontier and public domain of the land shifted toward multiple ownerships, and in the process many were left struggling to determine their place.[44]

As part of the 2002 submission by the Alaska Advisory Committee to the US Commission on Civil Rights, one local participant commented in 2001:

> Apartheid is a very real thing here in Alaska. It runs deep, it's covert, it's different than outright killing, but the net effects are the same. You manage to separate a people from their lands and from their resources. You manage to take away the customary rights of people that are very ancient rights.[45]

NATIVE AMERICANS AND ALASKA NATIVES TODAY

With respect to the reduced numbers of Native Americans living on reservations today, staff at the Indian Country Today Media Network (ICTMN) have elaborated on the poverty figures noted at the beginning of this chapter: the number of American Indians and Alaska Natives living below the federal poverty line was highest in Rapid City, South Dakota, home of the Pine Ridge Indian Reservation, at 50.9 per cent.[46] On that reservation, 'unemployment is 80 percent, and per capita income fluctuates between $4,000 and $6,000. Out of the estimated 400 to 500 homes on reservation, 150 houses and trailers are without running water or electricity.' Like other reservations, Pine Ridge is much too geographically isolated to attract industry.[47]

Moreover, data show that in a number of metropolitan areas, Native Americans have levels of impoverishment that rival some of the poorest reservations. Denver, Phoenix and Tucson, for example, have poverty rates approaching 30 per cent. In Chicago, Oklahoma City, Houston and New York – where more Native Americans live than in any other city – about 25 per cent live in poverty, while in Rapid City the poverty level stands at more than 50 per cent, and in Minneapolis, more than 45 per cent.[48]

Anti-Native American racism saturates US society. Commenting on the racist name of the US football team, the Washington Redskins, which its billionaire owner Dan Snyder has vowed never to change, DaShanne Stokes of the Lakota nation (indigenous people of the Great Plains) argues that 'while the primary blame for the continued use of a slur as a team name remains with Snyder, the responsibility is far from his alone'. Anti-Indian racism, he goes on, is institutionalized in US society, as taken for granted and an 'every day' occurrence. Many people, he goes on, 'don't bat an eye when it happens – because they see it every day'. As he puts it:

> Hardly a word is said, for example, about the wooden Indian statues that can be found at the liquor stores, bars, and tobacco shops that many people frequent, or about the stereotypical images depicted on every day products ranging from Native American Spirit cigarettes and Cherikee Red soda pop to Land O'Lakes butter and cheese.
>
> These are things people see every day. And when a person sees something all the time, the mind has a way of becoming accustomed to it. Over time, it's like it's not even there. That's one of the reasons why so many people, including some Native Americans, remain in favor of retaining the team name. It also explains why Snyder has been able to resist years of mounting protest for change. People have become so accustomed to the stereotypes and romanticized images – the Indian costumes at Halloween, the Hiawatha pageants, the face paint and feathered headbands many children make in Cub Scouts, take your pick – that they don't recognize them for what they are.[49]

That's also why, Stokes argues, 'Snyder's carefully calculated string of PR moves has been so convincing to his supporters'. He give the examples of Snyder's company having given winter coats to tribes across the Plains as well as shoes to children's basketball teams, and notes how the team's website, 'RedskinsFacts.com':

> presents an image of the team as warriors on the battlefield of righteousness and decency, fighting for 'tradition', a team whose name, they say, 'epitomizes all the noble qualities we admire about Native Americans – the same intangibles we expect from Washington's gridiron heroes on game day'.[50]

He concludes:

> It's a heroic image they're selling, one that simultaneously activates the classic stereotype of the 'noble savage' while also framing the team – not the people who are the object of the racial slur they are perpetuating – as the ones who are under attack.[51]

As Stokes points out elsewhere, studies have shown that Native American mascots, nicknames and logos perpetuate stereotypes; that having the power to 'play the Indian' without Native American consent negatively affects relationships between the two groups; and that Native Americans may experience significantly higher levels of psychological distress when viewing even neutral images of American Indian nicknames and logos.[52] One study concludes that in the context of college sporting events, the scripted form of white people 'becoming' Native American renders invisible the history of attempted genocide of indigenous peoples, which I outlined earlier in this chapter, replacing it with a culturally comforting myth of the 'American Indian warrior'.[53] In this way, a false unity is forged between Native Americans and European Americans based on the assumption that the former feel honoured and respected by racialized mascotry.[54]

Stokes concludes:

> Cumulatively, these studies show in horrific clarity what supporters of the Redskins – Native and non-Native alike – seem not to realize: that ethnic mascots are integrally intertwined with their offensive team names, and together they have the effect of perpetuating institutionalized racism. Institutionalized racism contributes to high rates of unemployment, poverty, health problems, and inadequate education for many Native Americans. In short, Native team names

and mascots contribute to the very problems we should be focused on solving. That's why ethnic team names and mascots aren't just silly words and images we can afford to ignore. They have a real, measurable impact, and they hurt us all – no matter where we live, what our backgrounds are, and whether we are personally offended or not.[55]

There is no doubt that institutional racism (shown by contemporary rates of poverty on and off the reservations as outlined earlier, lack of health care, education and housing guaranteed but not delivered in treaties dating back to the nineteenth century) is a major factor in suicide rates among young Native Americans, a problem that is especially acute on reservations. Byron Dorgan, a former Democratic senator from North Dakota who chaired the Senate Committee on Indian Affairs, said that the high number of young people on reservations who commit suicide is directly related to a 'trail of broken promises to American Indians'.[56] The number taking their own lives on reservations is more than three times the national average, and on some reservations, up to ten times the average.[57]

Sari Horwitz attributes this to a 'toxic collection of pathologies – poverty, unemployment, domestic violence, sexual assault, alcoholism and drug addiction' that has seeped into the lives of the 566 tribes in the United States.[58] Theresa M. Pouley, the chief judge of the Tulalip Tribal Court in Washington, points out that Indian young people graduate from high school at a rate 17 per cent lower than the national average, their substance abuse rates are higher, they are twice as likely as any other ethnic group to die before the age of 24, and they have twice the rate of abuse and neglect. She concludes that their 'experience with post-traumatic stress disorder rivals the rates of returning veterans from Afghanistan'.[59]

On Gila River Indian reservation eight young people ended their lives in just one year, and on Spirit Lake Nation a 14-year-old killed herself after lying in bed for three months following her father's and sister's suicides.[60] Sarah Kastelic, a member of the native village of Ouzinkie in Alaska, and deputy director of the National Indian Child Welfare Association, refers to 'historical trauma'. 'Youth suicide', she points out, 'was once virtually unheard of in Indian tribes', since there was in place a system of child protection which was sustained by tribal child-rearing practices and beliefs, where everyone in a community was responsible for the safeguarding of young people, providing 'a natural safety net', which was lost in the assimilation processes described earlier in this chapter. In many cases, Kastelic explains, echoing Andrea Smith above, 'the schools, mostly located off reservations, were centers of widespread sexual, emotional and physical abuse'.[61]

Racism is still rampant in Alaska. As Native Alaskan Eric Huntington points out, it manifests itself 'through social media ... [in] schools, in businesses, in churches, in law enforcement'.[62]

Anti-Native American racism, of course, exists outside of the United States. When I was a child in the 1950s in the United Kingdom, playing 'cowboys and Indians' and watching 'cowboy and Indian' films at the cinema and on television was the norm. There were also 'cowgirls' and 'squaws', playing a subsidiary role. In both play and on the screen, the cowboy (with a mandatory 'cowboy hat' and gun in a holster) was always the good guy, and the Indian (obligatory 'tomahawk' and feathered headdress) the bad guy, often referred to as 'a savage' by the man in the cowboy outfit. A Google search for 'children's cowboy and Indian outfits' threw up over a million results in less than a second, suggesting that 'cowboys and Indians' is still a popular childhood 'game'. At the same time, old racist movies are still regularly run on numerous TV channels throughout the world, thus reinforcing a global institutional racism with respect to the indigenous peoples of America.

AFRICAN AMERICANS: A BRIEF HISTORY

Although enslaved Africans were first brought to Spanish Florida as early as the 1560s, the origins of mass slavery in the United States were in the first English colonization of North America in Jamestown Island, Virginia in 1607.[63] The first enslaved Africans were brought there in 1619, and thereafter slavery spread like a cancer, as the English colonists realized its vast financial returns.[64] The slave trade was triangular, in that the ships first departed from Europe to Africa, after which enslaved Africans were taken to the Americas (the 'Middle Passage'), followed by the return of the ships to Europe. It is estimated that between the sixteenth and nineteenth centuries, about 12.5 million Africans were shipped from Africa to the Americas, of whom approximately 10.7 million actually arrived, the rest having perished on the way.[65] Of these, some 390,000 arrived directly from Africa in what is now the United States.[66]

Peter Kolchin describes graphically the transit to the 'new world':

Marched in chains to points of embarkation, sold to strange-looking men who spoke an incomprehensible language, branded, dragged struggling into long canoes that took them to ships waiting offshore, Africans began their voyage to America in despondency and often in panic. Some had never before seen giant ships, the ocean, or white men ... many ... feared [they were] about to be eaten.[67]

This was followed by the transatlantic voyage, where enslaved Africans were usually kept in chains in holds, sometimes so cramped they could hardly move.[68] A doctor refers to conditions in bad weather when they were in temperatures 'so extremely hot as to be only bearable for a very short time', when the floors were 'so covered with the blood and mucus which had proceeded from them ... that it resembled a slaughterhouse'.[69]

Those that survived the journey faced further terror, either with prospective buyers rushing on to the ship, or a public auction where they would be poked, prodded and examined. As Kolchin puts it, '[o]nce again, anger, humiliation, and fear of impending doom gripped them'.[70]

Such blatantly inhuman treatment required that African peoples be rendered subhuman. This facilitated the embedding of institutional racism, as decrees by the Southern colonies in the 1660s ensured that all imported 'negroes' should be slaves, while whites should be indentured servants (contracted legally for a fixed period in return for transportation, food, clothing, lodging and other necessities).[71] Following on from this, a series of laws, primarily in the eighteenth century, established that slaves and the children of slave women would be slaves for life. Such legislation also limited the rights of slaves and of free blacks – they were not allowed to vote, to testify in court against whites or marry whites. In addition, slaves were forbidden from carrying arms or leaving home without written permission. Severe corporal punishment was introduced for those who challenged white authority. Slaves were interpellated 'to be awed by the power of their master', to merge their interests with his, thus 'destroying their own individual needs'.[72]

This was accompanied by the deployment of both RSAs and ISAs. As Howard Zinn states, all this was accomplished by hard labour, the break-up of the slave family, the creation of disunity by separating 'field slaves' from the more privileged 'house slaves', and 'the lulling effects of religion'. The ultimate power was that of the overseer to 'invoke whipping, burning, mutilation, and death'.[73] Women were often raped, not merely for reasons of sexual gratification and vilification, but to boost slave numbers and thereby increase profits.

The period from the American Revolution of 1776 to the Civil War of 1850 has been described by Ira Berlin as the 'Second Middle Passage', a 'central event' in the life of a slave between the American Revolution and the Civil War, where they were uprooted or lived in fear of being uprooted.[74] The cause of this total disruption to the lives of slaves was the growing demand for cotton, and the resultant move west in search of suitable land. As Kolchin explains, slave owners moved hundreds of thousands of 'surplus' slaves west. With the break-up of families and the forcible removal of slaves to distant parts, the Second Middle Passage replicated many of the horrors, if on a reduced scale, of the international slave trade which was coming to an end. Kolchin estimates that about twice as many slaves were moved west between 1790 and 1860 as had crossed the Atlantic from Africa to what is now the United States.[75]

While the slave trade was, of course, of great benefit to the colonizers, it also fuelled capitalism in the homeland. Marx and Engels argued that slavery was as crucial to English capitalism as the growth of machinery:

> Direct slavery is as much the pivot of our industrialism today as machinery, credit, etc. Without slavery no cotton; without cotton no modern industry.
>
> Slavery has given value to the colonies; the colonies have created world trade; world trade is the necessary condition of large-scale machine industry. Thus, before the traffic in Negroes began, the colonies supplied the Old World with only very few products that made no visible change in the face of the earth. Slavery is therefore an economic category of the highest importance.[76]

The American Civil War, which began in 1861, saw the beginnings of the end of slavery. The Republican president, Abraham Lincoln, although overtly racist (he once said, 'I ... am in favor of the race to which I belong, having the superior position'[77]), consistently reiterated his belief that slavery was wrong. Although opposed to the expansion of slavery, he initially promised that his administration posed no threat to already-existing slavery. As the war dragged on, however, Lincoln faced mounting pressure to aim for the freedom of the slaves.[78]

At the same time Southern blacks were showing their determination to be free by slave rebellions, escaping to the Northern states, and to the swamps, mountains and forests of the South, public opinion in the North was also warming to the idea, and by the autumn of 1862, Lincoln decided to move against slavery. At that time he warned the Confederates that unless they ceased their rebellion, he would do just that. On 1 January 1863 the first slaves were freed, and in 1865, the Thirteenth Amendment banned slavery throughout the United States.[79] This was followed a year later by the Civil Rights Act of 1866, which gave equal rights to all American citizens – that is, all people born in the United States – and in 1869 (ratified in 1870) by the Fifteenth Amendment to the Constitution, which gave the right to vote regardless of 'race, color, or previous condition of servitude'.[80]

Despite these measures, inequality remained rampant. As Kolchin explains, the South continued to lag behind the North in terms of industrialization and urbanization, and remained much poorer, with white racism limiting the opportunities of black people, and the latter continuing to work for white planters with a considerable degree of coercion characterizing the relationships. As Kolchin puts it:

> Intense class struggle marked the spread of capitalist relations throughout the rural South, as freed people strove to secure what they considered their rightful fruits of freedom and planters endeavored to maintain as much control as possible over their 'free' laborers.[81]

Thus exploitation, poverty and hardship continued, sometimes under a system of 'sharecropping', whereby agricultural workers were paid an agreed share of the crop, often as little as one-sixth or one-eighth in 1865, and typically one-quarter in 1866 and 1867. The workers also got food, shelter, livestock and agricultural implements.[82] To assist in the transition from the ownership of slaves to wage labour, or as Malott puts it, 'from chattel slavery to wage slavery',[83] the federal government created rudimentary education and social services' for African Americans.[84]

Segregation between black and white became the norm throughout the United States. Between 1876 and 1965, a number of Jim Crow segregation laws were passed that enforced segregation in all public places.[85] The North, of course, lacked a history of slavery, but not of institutional racism. As C. Vann Woodward explains, the North was 'a race-conscious segregated society devoted to the doctrine of white supremacy and [black] inferiority'.[86] As a result, segregation developed there early and extensively.[87] Leon Litwack describes the effects of Jim Crow laws in the North as follows:

> In virtually every phase of existence ... Negroes found themselves systematically separated from whites. They were either excluded from railway cars, omnibuses, stagecoaches, and steamboats or assigned to special 'Jim Crow' sections; they sat, when permitted, in secluded and remote corners of theaters and lecture halls; they could not enter most hotels, restaurants, and resorts, except as servants; they prayed in 'Negro pews' in white churches, and if partaking of the sacrament of the Lord's Supper, they waited until the whites had been served the bread and wine. Moreover, they were often educated in segregated schools, punished in segregated prisons, nursed in segregated hospitals, and buried in segregated cemeteries.[88]

The period of the late nineteenth to the mid-twentieth century was a time of great poverty, as well as educational and political deprivation, for African

Americans.[89] Throughout the South, racist violence erupted. This included threats and warnings, burnings, whippings, and lynchings.[90] Mob violence was inflicted freely on black people, and between 1882 and 1968 the Tuskegee Institute (a historically black university) recorded 4,743 people lynched, of whom nearly 73 per cent were black. As Perea and colleagues stress, this cannot be the full total, since the figure includes only those lynchings recorded.[91]

Echoing the preceding analysis in this chapter, Frank Chapman has noted that contemporary institutionalized racism in the United States 'is rooted in the historical reality of 250 years of slavery followed, after a brief period of Civil War and democratic reconstruction, by over seventy years of Jim Crow terror and state sanctioned racist discrimination'. African American communist Claude Lightfoot was right, Chapman goes on, 'when he said that present day racist practices and attitudes carry the stench of the slave market'. 'Ever since the great powers of Europe turned Africa into a commercial warren for hunting and enslaving Black people', he continues, 'racism has been an instrument of capitalist exploitation for super profits.'[92]

Chapman gives the example of the prison-industrial complex, which had its origins in the incarceration of African Americans in the era of repression initiated by the Federal Bureau of Investigation (FBI) and Central Intelligence Agency (CIA) against the black liberation and civil rights movements. The prison-industrial complex encompasses the contractors that built the prisons along with the hundreds of subcontractors that make specialized prison beds, toilets, window bars, locks and so on. It also includes food services that unload hundreds of tons of inferior food products, and clothing manufacturers who manufacture not only guard uniforms but prison uniforms as well, plus the garb that is given to convicts upon release. Other profiteers include gun manufacturers, those who make the chemicals used to kill those on death row, coffin makers for the bodies, the medical profession who are tasked with keeping the condemned alive until they can officially be put to death, and the public relations (PR) personnel who liaise with the media, sanitizing the whole system.[93]

AFRICAN AMERICANS TODAY

Manning Marable has used the neo-Marxist concept of racialization to trace historic changes in the mode of production, with respect to African Americans. Writing shortly before the onset of the 2007/08 financial crisis, he described the then era in the United States as the 'New Racial Domain' (NRD). This NRD, he argued, is 'different from other earlier forms of racial domination, such as slavery, Jim Crow segregation, and ghettoization, or strict residential segregation, in several critical respects.[94] These early forms of racialization, he goes on, were based primarily, if not exclusively, in the political economy of US capitalism. 'Meaningful social reforms such as the Civil Rights Act of 1964 and the Voting Rights Act of 1965 were debated almost entirely within the context of America's expanding, domestic economy, and a background of Keynesian, welfare state public policies.' The political economy of the NRD, on the other hand, is driven and largely determined by the forces of transnational capitalism, and the public policies of state neoliberalism, which rests on an unholy trinity, or deadly triad, of structural barriers to a decent life.

'These oppressive structures', he argues, 'are mass unemployment, mass incarceration, and mass disfranchisement', with each factor directly feeding and accelerating the others, creating an ever-widening circle of social disadvantage, poverty, and civil death, touching the lives of tens of millions of U.S. people.' For Marable, '[t]he process begins at the point of production. For decades, U.S. corporations have been outsourcing millions of better-paying jobs outside the country. The class warfare against unions has led to a steep decline in the percentage of U.S. workers.' As Marable concludes:

> Within whole U.S. urban neighborhoods losing virtually their entire economic manufacturing and industrial employment, and with neoliberal social policies in place cutting job training programs, welfare, and public housing, millions of Americans now exist in conditions that exceed the devastation of the Great Depression of the 1930s.[95]

As noted earlier, the poverty rate among African Americans is 27.4 per cent, nearly three times that of 'White, non-Hispanic' Americans. Philip Bump has analysed three possible explanations: that there is something about black culture that prevents African Americans from escaping poverty; there is something about the culture of being poor that prevents all the poor from escaping poverty; and that there are no internal cultural forces at play, and racism causes poverty. If the first explanation is correct, then it suggests trying to change the behaviour of black Americans is the answer; if the second provides the answer, then the solution is 'a broader cultural realignment among all poor people'. The first explanation involves blaming black people and the second blaming poor people. These represent the two common responses in the United States.[96] The preceding analysis in this chapter, of course, indicates that institutional and structural racism in US society is the most plausible explanation. Nowhere is this more apparent than in the prison-industrial complex.

On 31 December 2013, a staggering 1,574,700 people were in state and federal prisons, an increase of 0.3 per cent from year-end 2012, the rise being the first reported since a peak of 1,615,500 prisoners in 2009.[97] As Kate Randall points out, the figures suggest that the tendency toward a slight reduction in the US prison population in the years since the official end of the recession appears to have been short-lived. While the imprisonment rate for all prisoners decreased marginally from 480 prisoners per 100,000 US residents in 2012 to 478 per 100,000 in 2013, the statistics do not include the more than 850,000 prisoners held at local jails across the country. Taking these figures into account, the incarceration rate rose to 716 per 100,000 US residents as of October 2013. Although the United States makes up only 5 per cent of the world's population, it incarcerates about one-quarter of all prisoners on the planet.[98]

While white females comprised 49 per cent of the female prison population, compared with 22 per cent for black females, the imprisonment rate for black females – 113 per 100,000 – was twice the rate for white females. The number of male inmates increased by 0.1 per cent in 2013, and compared with the US population, the male prison population continued to be disproportionately represented by black people (37 per cent) and Latina/o people (22 per cent), rather than whites (32 per cent).[99]

Almost 3 per cent of black males, Randall points out, were imprisoned as of 31 December 2013, and more than 550,000 black men and women were incarcerated nationwide. In the age range that has the highest imprisonment rate for males, 25–39, black males were imprisoned at rates at least two and a half times greater than Latino males and six times higher than white males.[100]

A significant amount of incarceration is related to drug offences. A 2013 report by the American Civil Liberties Union (ACLU) found that, on average, a black person is 3.73 times more likely to be arrested for marijuana possession than a white person, even though blacks and whites use marijuana at similar rates.[101]

Randall concludes her analysis by attributing all this to the role of the police RSA in the context of austerity/immiseration capitalism:

> The rise of the number of US citizens incarcerated in the nation's prisons is more evidence of the police-state apparatus being built up by government at both the federal and state level to confront the rising social anger being produced by growing income inequality, austerity measures and police violence.[102]

A Report from Center on Budget and Policy Priorities (CBPP) shows a polarized society where the RSAs (prison and police-military apparatuses) are being continually expanded while vital social programmes are starved of funds. CBPP estimates that if state corrections spending had been held at mid-1980s levels, adjusted for inflation today, the 50 US states would have about $28 billion more each year between them to allocate to non-prison-related expenditures.[103]

As Randall explains, summarizing the report and underlining the devastating effects of austerity/immiseration capitalism, at least 30 states spent less in general funding per student in 2014 for K-12 schools than before the recession hit in 2008; 14 states have reduced funding by more than 10 per cent. Spending cuts for higher education have been even deeper, with the average state spending 23 per cent less per student since the recession. There is also a direct correlation, Randall goes on, between increased prison spending and education cuts, with many states with the highest incarceration rates making the deepest education cuts.[104]

Violence and harassment by the police

On 17 July 2014, black New Yorker Eric Garner died of a heart attack in police custody, hours after being put in an illegal (because it can be fatal) chokehold by police. In published footage, Garner is seen being approached by police and questioned about selling untaxed cigarettes.[105] He denies it, and police ask him for his hands so he can be handcuffed. When Garner resists arrest, he is put into a chokehold by one officer who is subsequently assisted by others, after which Garner can be heard telling police that he can't breathe. The video then shows Garner unconscious on the floor. The officer in question was not indicted.

On 9 August 2014, unarmed black teenager Michael Brown, a participant in the robbery of a convenience store the same day, was shot multiple times in broad daylight by a white police officer in Ferguson, St Louis County, Missouri as he knelt with his hands up. As Patrick Martin puts it, referring to the police response to the shooting, even if 'the photographs and testimony were conclusive evidence – and they are not – there is no death penalty for grabbing a few packs of candy-flavored cigars, priced at two for 99 cents'. Moreover the police later admitted that Darren Wilson, the police officer who shot Brown, had no knowledge of his alleged participation in a petty theft minutes earlier.[106] Brown's friend Dorian Johnson stated that he and Brown were walking in the street when Wilson pulled up next to them, yelling 'Get the f•ck on the sidewalk.' Next, according to witnesses, Wilson pulled his sports-utility vehicle in front of the two young men and attempted to choke Brown through the open window of his vehicle. As Brown tried to escape, according to Johnson, even though Brown 'did not reach for the officer's weapon at all', Wilson shot him. After the first gunshot, Brown ran away. Wilson left the vehicle and continued to shoot at Brown, according to Johnson. After Brown was hit again, he turned around, raised his hands in the air and said, 'I don't have a gun. Stop shooting.' At that point, Wilson resumed shooting, killing Brown. Multiple eyewitness accounts collaborate Johnson's claim that Brown was surrendering and had his hands up as he was gunned down.[107] No charges were levelled at Wilson.

Two months after Michael Brown was killed, another St Louis black teenager, Vonderrit D. Myers, was gunned down by an off-duty white police officer. The results of a private autopsy indicated that he was running away when he was shot, and subsequently killed execution-style with a bullet to the head.[108]

According to an Amnesty International report, 'On the streets of America: human rights abuses in Ferguson', the crackdown on peaceful protesters by police following the death of Michael Brown 'violated numerous US and international laws'. The report extensively documents systematic acts of police violence against peaceful protesters, and the arrest and assault of media and international observers. As the report observed, police confronted protesters while 'armed with semi-automatic weapons and leashed police dogs'. They 'moved among the protesters using armored vehicles which are more commonly seen in a conflict zone rather than the streets of a suburban town in the United States' it went on, and some of the officers 'had ... no names, badges, other identifying information visible'.[109]

'There are no jobs', is the first reason Denzil Dean, a small business owner, told reporter Rose Hackman when she asked him why he had joined in protests in Ferguson following the shooting of Brown, the consensus among African Americans being that racial profiling and police brutality are tightly intertwined with a lack of equal access to jobs. Latest figures for black unemployment in St Louis County show it is three times higher than for white people.[110] Nationally, it is just over double: 11 per cent compared with 5.1 per cent.[111]

Pedro Hall, a 33-year-old black person, described how he was driving to a gas station when a police car started following him. He had received a warrant for his arrest associated with his number plate after he missed a court date for driving without a licence – a misdemeanor offense. By the time he had reached the gas station and got out of his car, the police officer tailing him had drawn his gun and ordered him to the ground, ready to shoot. After this gas station encounter, Hall was later stopped by police as he walked down the street and accused of minor drug possession, something he disputes. But he was forced into a plea bargain by his appointed lawyer, who told him an all-white jury in Iowa would be unsympathetic to his case. Hall spent 32 days in jail. 'Now I am stopped all the time and I am treated like a drug dealer', Hall pointed out.[112]

Maulana Karenga argues that police violence is:

> *systemically based* and *socially sanctioned* as a legitimate, legal and necessary way to deal with Black people, other people of color, the poor, the mentally disabled and any others who are vulnerable, stereotyped, stigmatized and posed as a real or potential threat and deemed unworthy of due respect.[113]

Just over a month before the shooting of Michael Brown, Marlene Pinnock, a black woman, who was homeless, unarmed and apparently mentally disoriented, was severely beaten by a white police officer after she wandered about on a busy freeway in broad daylight. As Karenga points out, she was obviously in need of caring assistance, not a cold-blooded attack. As he puts it, this:

> increasing police violence which extends nationwide offers evidence that the attacking officer is not a rogue cop or an 'officer gone wild', but a representative of a definite system, a protector of the established order with its race and class determined rights, privileges and preferred people.[114]

'It is', he concludes, 'a reaffirmation of society's racist classification of her as racially and socially unworthy':

> Thus, she is tackled, pinned down, straddled, punched and pummeled in the head and face repeatedly and mercilessly. It is a violence rooted not only in general racist ideology, but also in racialized police perceptions of and approaches to the Black community as an occupied and hostile territory. It is also reinforced by the increasing militarization of police departments in training and weaponry and by the increased hiring of ex-soldiers from recent wars with little or no rules and restraints on things done to the 'enemy'.[115]

Other black people killed by the police in the United States in 2014 included Tamir Rice, a 12-year-old boy who pulled a replica gun from the waistband of his trousers in a playground; Akai Gurley, a 28-year-old unarmed African American man in the Louis Pink public housing projects of Brooklyn; and Rumain Brisbon, shot when the police officer mistook a bottle of oxycodone for the handle of a gun.

In March 2015, a Department of Justice Investigation of the Ferguson Police Department found:

Racial bias
At each juncture in the criminal process, the law is enforced more harshly against black people than others.
- Substantial evidence of intentional discrimination.
- Explicit racial bias in communications between police and court.
- While about two-thirds of Ferguson's residents are African American, only four of Ferguson's 54 police officers are.
- Historical hostility to African Americans living in Ferguson lingers among some police officers.

Emphasis on revenue
Ferguson's police practices are shaped by a focus on maximizing revenue rather than improving public safety.
- City officials put pressure on police to issue fines to raise revenue.
- Many officers appear to see some residents, especially those who live in Ferguson's predominantly African American areas, less as constituents to be protected than as potential offenders and sources of revenue.
- For example, police accused a black man sitting in his parked car cooling off after playing basketball of being a paedophile. He was eventually charged with eight violations, including 'making a false declaration' because he had given his name as Mike instead of Michael.

Unlawful court practices
The court's practices impose unnecessary harm, overwhelmingly on African Americans.
- Arrest warrants are issued if fines are not paid, instead of only being issued on the basis of public safety.
- Until recently, Ferguson added fines for missed court appearance and payment.
- Minor offences such as parking or driving violations can generate crippling debts, resulting in jail time because of an inability to pay.

Excessive force
Many officers are quick to escalate encounters with subjects they perceive to be disobeying their orders or resisting arrest.

- They have come to rely on weapons such as tasers where less force – or no force at all – would do.
- An officer used an electronic weapon against an African American woman in the Ferguson City Jail because she would not go to her cell.
- Police dogs have been released on unarmed people before attempting to use force less likely to cause injury.
- African-Americans accounted for 90 per cent of officers' use of force.[116]

LATINA AND LATINO AMERICANS: A BRIEF HISTORY

Currently people of Mexican origin (64.2 per cent) and Puerto Rican origin (9.3 per cent) make up nearly three-quarters of the total number of Latina/o peoples in the United States.[117] Like Native Americans and African Americans, Latina/o Americans have long history of colonization, capitalist exploitation, racialization and racist oppression.

Mexicans and Mexican Americans

As a result of a peaceful revolution in 1821, Mexico became independent from Spain.[118] At the time Mexico was about twice the size it is today, and included Texas, California, Arizona, New Mexico, Nevada and parts of Utah, Colorado and Kansas. After independence, American settlers began arriving in the Texas region, and in 1836 Texas claimed independence from Mexico, a claim not recognized by the latter. In 1845 the United States annexed Texas, and as a result of this, and of a dispute over where Texas ended, war ensued between the United States and Mexico between 1846 and 1848. The war was underpinned by a white supremacist belief in the superiority of the Anglo-Saxon 'race', which was ideologically fuelled from the mid-1830s to the mid-1840s. Mexicans were racialized as 'a mixed, inferior race with considerable Indian and some black blood',[119] 'an idle, thriftless people', as Richard Dana described them.[120] T. J. Farnham in 1840 viewed Mexicans as 'an imbecile, pusillanimous, race of men [sic], and unfit to control the destinies of that beautiful country'. 'The old Saxon blood,' he insisted, 'must stride the continent.' To take lands from such 'inferior barbarians' was thus no crime; on the contrary, it was God's work.[121] Indeed, according to George Kendall, most Mexicans were content if they could satisfy their animal wants, and 'will continue to be until the race becomes extinct or amalgamated with Anglo-Saxon stock'.[122]

For Rufus Sage, there are 'no people on the continent of America, whether civilized or uncivilized, with one or two exceptions, more miserable in condition or despicable in morals than the mongrel race inhabiting New Mexico'.[123] One government minister, Waddy Thompson, described the general Mexican population as 'lazy, ignorant, and, of course, vicious and dishonest'.[124] This 'Anglo-Saxon' racialization of Mexican peoples in many ways paralleled the 'Anglo-Saxon' racialization of African and Asian peoples during and after the demise of the British Empire (see Chapter 1). The US–Mexican war, in which the US forces were consistently victorious, resulted in the US acquisition of more than 500,000 square miles of Mexican territory, extending westward from the Rio Grande to the Pacific Ocean.[125]

Henceforth, while the Treaty of Guadalupe Hidalgo (1848) that ended the war granted federal citizenship to all Mexicans who remained in the 500,000 square miles, *darker skinned* Mestiza/o Mexicans residing in this area were denied citizenship and meaningful political participation by state and territorial legislatures.[126] The history of Mexican Americans is one of back-breaking farm labour. Given that the border between the United States and Mexico is 2,000 miles long, with the two countries separating by Rio Grande, a fence or merely an imaginary line in the sand, cheap Mexican labour, both 'legal' and 'illegal', came to fill the requirements of US businesses.[127] As Gilbert Paul Carrasco puts it, 'Mexican laborers have become the U.S's disposable labor force, brought in when needed, only to fulfill their use and be unceremoniously discarded, a trend that has been recurring for over 150 years', starting with the Gold Rush to California in 1848.[128] From then until the 1930s and the Great Depression, which lasted from the stock market crash in 1929 to about 1941, Mexican workers were generally welcome in the United States as cheap labour. (Prior to then, US immigration restrictions applied mainly to Asians and southern and eastern Europeans.[129]) During the Depression, many Mexican migrant workers returned to Mexico, often driven from the United States by racist violence, and also by reduced welfare payments. By the end of the Great Depression, over 400,000 Latina/os, including thousands of US citizens, had been 'repatriated' to Mexico, without any formal deportation procedures.[130]

After the entry of the United States into the Second World War in 1941, and Mexico's entry in 1942, the US and Mexican governments signed the Bracero Program, which laid down basic conditions, and allowed Mexican citizens to work in the United States for temporary renewable periods. Both the US government and the employers, however, ignored the stipulated conditions and exploited and oppressed the workers in the most brutal way:

Braceros across the country were compelled to endure poor food, excessive charges for board, substandard housing, discrimination, physical mistreatment, inappropriate deductions from their wages, and exposure to pesticides and other dangerous chemicals.[131]

The Bracero Program provided cheap labour in two senses: first, it freed employers from the constraints of supply and demand or collective bargaining agreements; second, unlike Americans who tended to have their families with them, *braceros* were often males travelling alone, making it easier to provide transportation and housing.[132] The Bracero Program came to an end in 1947, after the end of the Second World War, as US troops returned to work. However, this did not end the use of cheap Mexican labour, and a new Bracero agreement was signed in 1949, and another in 1951, in response to the start of the Korean War. As a result of labour union complaints about undocumented workers revealed by immigration authorities, a crackdown on 'illegal immigration' ensued in 1954. The commissioner of immigration and reputed 'longtime Mexican hater' coordinated border patrols and organized roundups and deportations between 1954 and 1959. 'Operation Wetback', named because many 'illegal immigrants' had entered the United States by crossing the Rio Grande, deported over 3.7 million Latinas/os, almost totally without formal proceedings, and accompanied by the violation of human rights.[133] The Bracero Program, however, continued during this period, to be followed by the McCarran–Walter Immigration Act in 1952, which allowed permanent admission to the United States. By 1977, there were about one million Mexican resident aliens in the United States, and many crossing the border backwards and forwards to get work.[134] Carrasco explains the ongoing nature of the exploitation and oppression of Mexican migrants:

Due to intense exploitation [of] migrant workers, their productive capacities are used up early in their lives and they have to be replaced by ... younger workers. For the United States, employment of migrant workers represents a significant savings in producing and reproducing 'human capital' because they stay in the United States only temporarily. Even though the United States needs Mexican labor, migrant workers arrive to face more than exploitation and brutal working conditions. They face racism.[135]

Mexicans, like the black slaves, were the victims of lynchings and killings throughout the nineteenth century. Language-based subordination and segregation was a major feature of the twentieth century for Mexican

Americans. Attempted assimilation into whiteness and English mono-lingualism was also a dominant feature.[136] So was schooling Mexican American children for their future roles in society. Juan F. Perea cites one Texas school superintendent who shows full awareness of the importance to capitalism of cheap Mexican American labour:

> Most of our Mexicans are of the lower class. They transplant onions, harvest them, etc. The less they know about everything else the better contented they are .... If a man [sic] has very much sense or education either, he is not going to stick to this kind of work.[137]

As Perea notes, Anglo farmers, many of them on school boards, were keen to keep Mexican Americans uneducated, 'guaranteeing a plentiful labor supply for their cotton fields'.[138]

Puerto Ricans and Puerto Rican Americans

In 1898 the United States expelled Spain from Puerto Rico, and annexed the island. Puerto Rico was seen as important to US hegemony for both military and economic reasons. Militarily, it was in an important location to control the Gulf of Mexico and the Panama Canal linking the Gulf to the Pacific Ocean; and economically, Puerto Rico provided a welcome market for US surpluses of goods. Subsequent debates on whether to grant full US citizenship to Puerto Ricans were, as usual, racialized. Thus one member of the House of Representatives, anxious about conferring US citizenship, claimed that '75 or 80 percent of those people are mixed blood in part and are not the equal of the full-blooded Spaniard and not equal, in my judgement, to the unmixed African, and yet they were to be made citizens of the United States'. Another member, also exalting biological rather than cultural racism,[139] believed that the problem was not in language but in colour, and that the climate and geography of Puerto Rico were not conducive to Anglo-Saxon government since 'the Tropics seem to heat the blood while enervating the people who inhabit them'. He felt that 'many people in this country who want to sever the tie that binds us to tropical and alien people take that position, because they see in it danger for us'. Just to underline the biological and genetic nature of his racialized view of people living in the tropics, he concluded that the 'many people' to whom he was referring, agreed as those living in lands within 20 degrees of the equator, could 'neither comprehend nor support representative government on the Anglo-Saxon plan'.[140]

The United States gave Puerto Rica's residents citizenship in 1917, because they were needed to fight as soldiers in the First World War. Currently, Puerto Ricans are US citizens by birth, but because the island is only a territory, its residents can vote for a president only if they move to a state. Florida is home to nearly 1 million of Americans of Puerto Rican descent, and is fast gaining on New York, which has around 1.2 million, according to the latest US Census. The 3.6 million residents of Puerto Rico pay only Social Security and Medicare taxes to the federal government. They have one member of Congress, but they do not get a vote on the House floor. They also have no say in most federal laws and regulations that govern them. In a non-binding referendum in 2012, just over half of voters rejected the island's territorial status for the first time, and in a follow-up question, over 60 per cent of those who answered said they favoured statehood (that is, becoming a state of the United States) over partial or outright independence.[141] As one marine veteran put it, 'How is it I can't vote for the person who will send me to war?'[142]

LATINA AND LATINO AMERICANS TODAY

At 26.6 per cent, like that of African Americans, the poverty rate of Latina/o Americans is nearly three times that of whites. The three possible causes of poverty among African Americans posited by Philip Bump earlier in this chapter might also apply to Latina/o people. However our analysis above suggests that institutional and structural racism in US society is again the cause of this poverty, rather than a generalized culture of poverty, or something pathological about Latina/o culture.

In 2013, something occurred that is reminiscent of the near 100 years of segregation discussed earlier in this chapter, an era when there were signs enforcing 'whites only' facilities. Similar signs that had been allegedly been in place for about a year were removed from a number of playgrounds in Milford, Delaware, where 16 per cent of the population is Latina/o, after protests. While the signs in English repeated the familiar warnings that parental or guardian supervision is needed and that children play at their own risk, the accompanying signs in Spanish read, 'You must have a permit to play in this field. Violators will be subject to police action.'[143]

Susana G. Bauman has suggested some key economic issues for the Latina/o communities in 2014: legalize undocumented workers, which among other benefits would lead to a boost in the housing market; make it known to immigrant families that as well as poor US-born families they too are eligible for food stamps; provide healthcare for all Latina/o people; and extend the minimum wage to those jobs currently exempted, many of whom employ Latina/o labour, such as 'tipped workers, many domestic workers, workers on small farms, some seasonal workers, full-time students, and certain disabled workers'.[144]

Much of the racism directed at Latina/o communities is related to the possibility that individuals might be undocumented. Kirk Semple describes a familiar racist action by one of the RSAs:

> A Latino immigrant is driving a car with out-of-state license plates, and a police officer pulls him over and asks for his driver's license. The driver, because he is an illegal immigrant, does not have a license, so the officer tells him to step out of the car and face the other way. The officer may ask to see the driver's wallet; then he starts to search the car. After a few minutes, he hands the wallet back to the driver, tells him that everything is fine and sends him on his way. Soon afterward, the driver discovers that money is missing from his wallet.[145]

Such incidents are not reported because the drivers fear police reprisals or even deportation. Immigrants' advocates, Semple points out, said that 'most of the incidents … occurred after the Justice Department had begun investigating allegations of discriminatory policing'. There were 'claims that the police not only discouraged Latino crime victims from filing complaints but also failed to investigate crimes involving Latinos'.[146] The Justice Department Inquiry, which began in 2009, was spurred on by the killing of Marcelo Lucero, an Ecuadorean immigrant who was attacked by a group of teenagers and stabbed to death. Following the incident, other Latina/o residents said they too had been victims of racist attacks, but that the police had failed to thoroughly investigate many of their claims. Juan Cartagena, president of and general counsel for LatinoJustice PRLDEF, an advocacy group that helped to spur the federal investigation in Suffolk County, stated, 'We're concerned about how forceful and comprehensive this investigation really is. This is the same police department that has demonstrated an inability to protect Latinos for years now'.[147]

In 2013 the number of deportations of immigrants reached a record high of 438,421, bringing the total deported under the Obama administration to more than 2 million.[148] Gonzalez-Barrera and Krogstad claim some immigrant advocates have dubbed Obama the 'deporter in chief', given that his administration had deported about the same number of immigrants in five years as the George W. Bush administration did in eight years. A new shift in migration patterns emerged between 2011 and 2013: the number of Mexican immigrants apprehended at the border and the interior continued to decline from a high of 1.1 million in 2005 to 425,000 in 2013, while more Central American and unaccompanied children were crossing the border.[149] Moreover, as the number of unaccompanied children trying to cross the US–Mexico border has surged, the increase in apprehensions among children aged 12 and younger was far greater than among teens.[150]

If geographical origins and ages have changed, the racism of the state apparatuses remains a constant. As Bill Van Auken puts it, comparing their treatment with the hostility invoked against the American working class as a whole:

> the Obama administration, the Republican Party, the corporate media and the entire political establishment have treated the recent increase in the number of immigrant families and unaccompanied minors arriving on the southern border of the United States as a criminal matter to be resolved with stepped-up enforcement and repression.[151]

Norisa Diaz points out that appalling conditions have been documented within the Immigration and Customs Enforcement (ICE) facilities throughout the South-West, where those who have arrived recently – mostly children – are processed and held:

> For up to nine days, families are packed into warehouse-like holding centers surrounded by razor-wire fences. Mothers are separated from their children, brothers from their sisters. Immigrants are kept in crowded pens and allowed outside only 45 minutes a day.[152]

These prison-like conditions are sometimes without adequate sanitation and medical care.[153] Diaz reminds us that many of many of the Central American immigrants are fleeing violence and extortion from gangs as a result of drug trafficking and the US-backed 'war on drugs', and that it is 'decades of US imperialist intervention in Central and Latin American countries, along with austerity policies' demanded by the International Monetary Fund and World Bank that 'have created the horrific conditions that make the thousand-mile-long, potentially deadly crossing a desirable alternative to trying to survive at home'.[154]

Most immigration experts, according to Van Auken, believe that the majority are entitled to refugee status or political asylum under both international and US law. Based on interviews with several hundred of the children, she says 'the United Nations High Commissioner for Refugees estimated that some 60 percent would qualify for such status'. While the government demands that the children be sent 'home', 'an estimated

80 percent have crossed the border to reunite with their fathers, mothers or other close relatives who are living in the US'.[155]

At the same time the government has made wide use of the unconstitutional method of immigration 'holds', asking local police and jails to hold people without warrants based on suspected civil immigration violations. In addition, since 2008, ICE has conducted more than 12,000 'silent raids' – involving the seizure from employers of I-9 forms that affirm the right of employees to work. This has resulted in more than 300,000 people losing their jobs. Despite all this, Van Auken concludes, the Republican Party exacerbates racism (he uses the term 'xenophobia') by attacking the Obama administration from the right on immigration, seeking to 'exploit concerns over disappearing jobs and falling wages by scapegoating immigrants, one of the most oppressed sections of the working class'.[156]

Late in 2014, Obama announced that some 5 million undocumented immigrant workers will qualify for non-deportation and 'be able to stay temporarily'. The bulk of these, however, must have lived in the United States for more than five years and have children who are US citizens or legal residents. They must also register with the Department of Homeland Security (DHS), pass a criminal background check, and pay any back taxes. The programme, moreover, includes less than half the 11–12 million undocumented immigrant workers and children now in the United States, who are subject to immediate detention and deportation as 'illegals'.[157]

As Patrick Martin explains, Obama spent a large part of his speech specifying how limited the changes will be, with no Medicaid, food stamps or other benefits to immigrants who get work permits. As Obama stressed:

> This deal does not apply to anyone who has come to this country recently. It does not apply to anyone who might come to America illegally in the future. It does not grant citizenship, or the right to stay here permanently, or offer the same benefits that citizens receive – only Congress can do that. All we're saying is we're not going to deport you.[158]

All undocumented immigrant workers, Obama stated, must 'play by the rules' and be held 'accountable'. Martin concluded:

> Obama's speech was entirely within the right-wing framework of official American politics, in which workers who come to the United States fleeing poverty and dictatorship – for which American imperialism is principally responsible – and take the hardest and worst-paid jobs are demonized as criminals who must be 'held accountable.'

Meanwhile, the true criminal class in America, the financial aristocracy that controls both the Democratic and Republican parties, amasses untold and unearned wealth.[159]

ASIAN AMERICANS: A BRIEF HISTORY

The total number of Asian Americans is small in comparison with Latina/o Americans. According to the 2010 Census the three largest Asian constituencies in the United States were Chinese (4,010,114), Filipana/os (3,416,840) and Asian Indians (3,183.063), followed by Vietnamese Americans (1,737,433), Korean Americans (1,706,822) and Japanese Americans (1,304,286). (The total population of the United States was 318,892,103.[160])

Chinese Americans

In January 1848, gold was discovered north-east of present-day Sacramento. As the news spread, among the thousands flocking to California in 1849 were 325 'forty-niners' from China. In 1852 over 20,000 Chinese arrived, and by 1870 there were over 60,000 Chinese in the United States.[161]

In the 1860s Chinese migrants served as a source of cheap and exploited labour in the construction of the Central Pacific Railroad. A report to President Andrew Johnson racialized Chinese workers via a 'seemingly positive attribute':[162]

As a class they are quiet, peaceable, patient, industrious and economical. Ready and apt to learn all the different kinds of work required in railroad building, they soon become as efficient as white laborers. More prudent and economical, they are contented with less wages.[163]

In a similar vein, Central Pacific's legal counsel judge put it to a California Congress member:

A large part of our force are Chinese, and they prove nearly equal to white men, in the amount of labor they perform, and are far more reliable. No danger of strikes among them.[164]

Min Zhou points out that few realized their dreams of becoming wealthy as a result of the gold rush, and many found themselves on the receiving end of exclusion and racism, both institutionalized and personal.[165] In

1852 and 1855, California statutes imposed licence fees on all foreign miners. California also enacted a 'commutation tax' intended to discourage Chinese migration to the state. The Chinese district associations protested against these racist forms of legislation, but met with legislative hostility and increasing violence in the mining districts.[166]

By the mid-1870s racist hatred of the Chinese had spread throughout California, and had generated anti-Chinese hate groups and an 'Anti-Chinese Union' pledged 'to unite, centralize and direct the anti-Chinese strength of our country'. Members of anti-Chinese clubs pledged not to employ Chinese people, not to purchase goods from the employers of Chinese people, and not to sustain the Chinese or employers of the Chinese.[167]

Responding to a complex set of economic hardships caused by economic distress, labour market uncertainty and sheer capitalist exploitation, organized labour also took part in this racialization process.[168] As the leader of the California Workingmen's Party put it:

> We have made no secret of our intentions ... we declare that the Chinaman must leave our shores. We declare that white men, and women, and boys and girls, cannot live as the people of the great republic should and compete with the single Chinese coolie in the labor market .... To an American, death is preferable to life on a par with the Chinaman.[169]

In 1882, the US Congress passed the Chinese Exclusion Act, later extended to all Asian potential immigrants up until the Second World War.[170] The number of new Chinese immigrants dropped from 123,000 in the 1870s to 14,800 in the 1890s, to a historically low number of 5,000 in the 1930s.[171] Zhou graphically explains the overall effects of massive institutionalized and personal racism directed at the Chinese migrant workers:

> Legal exclusion, augmented by extralegal persecution and anti-Chinese violence, effectively drove the Chinese out of the mines, farms, woolen mills, and factories on the West Coast. As a result, many Chinese laborers already in the United States ... returned permanently to China. Others, who could not afford or were too ashamed to return home, gravitated toward San Francisco's Chinatown for self-protection.[172]

Others travelled eastward in the search of alternative means of earning a living, and Chinatowns in the North-East of the United States, in particular

New York, and the Midwest, grew to accommodate those fleeing from the intense racialization and racism that they had experienced in California.[173] Up until the Second World War, the Chinese American community was predominantly male. However, after the 1950s hundreds of refugees and their families arrived in the United States from the People's Republic of China.[174] In addition, in 1965 the Hart–Cellar Act abolished the national origins quota system that had structured American immigration policy since the 1920s, and replaced it with a preference system that focused on immigrants' skills and family relationships with citizens or residents of the United States, thus further changing Chinese (and other minority ethnic) communities from being primarily male to family communities.[175]

Throughout the 1960s and 1970s, Chinatown in San Francisco had the highest tuberculosis and suicide rates in the Unites States, and as a result of high unemployment and underemployment, thousands of new immigrants were subject to intense exploitation in sweatshops and restaurants.[176] However, health and mental health problems do not only exist in Chinatowns. The overwhelming majority of Chinese Americans no longer live in Chinatowns. The rapid growth of the Chinese American population in the last three decades has been accompanied by further racism. Ling-chi Wang gives the example of San Francisco and Monterey Park in California, which tried to restrict Chinese American population growth by 'restrictive zoning of residential housing'. In addition, Chinese American achievements in education have led to the use of racist attempts to slow down or reverse their enrolment in select schools and colleges. Since the early 1980s, there has been a steady increase in incidents of reported racist violence.[177]

Filipina and Filipino Americans

Following the Spanish-American War of 1898, the Philippines became a territory of the United States. This meant that, while Filipina/os were not granted citizenship, they were classified as 'American nationals' with the right of entry to the United States.[178] Migrant workers arrived as labourers, mainly in agriculture and domestic service.[179] In 1910 there were just over 400 Filipina/os on the US mainland, and by 1930 there were over 45,000.[180] From the early days, Filipinos were racialized and sexualized. For example, in December 1929 in Watsonville, California, the local newspaper published a photograph of a Filipino embracing his white fiancée (he had previously been arrested for being with her, and was released when her mother explained that they were engaged and that the relationship had her approval).[181] A month later, the local chamber of commerce passed a resolution declaring that Filipinos were 'a moral and sanitary' threat and 'a menace to white labor'.[182] In the following month, about 200 Americans hunted Filipinos on the streets, and a dance hall where Filipinos were dancing with local women was raided. Two days later, a number of Filipinos were beaten, and one was killed, by a mob of 500 white Americans who also destroyed the Filipino quarters. Concerns of 'racial purity' and 'mixed race' offspring prompted changes in the anti-miscegenation laws to include Filipinos.[183]

The Philippines was granted independence in 1935, and Filipina/os were reclassified as 'aliens', with immigration becoming limited to 50 individuals per year. However, after the United States had entered the Second World War, thousands of Philippine-born Filipinos were recruited to the military, and this population comprised a second phase of immigration.[184] After the 1965 Hart–Cellar Act, Filipina/os began arriving in the United States for education and work, but also to get away from the repressive political regime of President Ferdinand Marcos.

Indian Americans

Indians came to the United States as early as 1820, the majority coming from the Punjab region.[185] From the early 1900s until 1922, small male Sikh worker communities emerged all along the West Coast.[186] Indians experienced racism from the early days. For example, in 1907 in Washington state, a mob of about 500 attacked boarding houses and mills, compelling about 300 Indians to flee.[187] More recent examples of racism occurred during the late 1980s. In New Jersey, a group known as the 'Dotbusters' – the name referring to the decorative bindi many Hindu women wear on their foreheads – violently assaulted several South Asian Americans and created a climate of hostility that eventually resulted in the murder of an Indian American in 1987.[188] In 1998, an American-born Indian was attacked with baseball bats by three white men and was racially abused. When his uncle ran to his assistance, he too was beaten.[189]

Vietnamese Americans

The first major phase of Vietnamese immigration to the United States began in 1975. Most were military personnel and their families, fleeing from North Vietnamese troops after North Vietnam had defeated South Vietnam, which the United States had supported in the Vietnam War (1955–75).[190] The second phase occurred in 1978, with those leaving becoming known as Vietnamese 'boat people'. Refugee families left in crowded leaky boats, risking death from storms, robbery, and rape of the women by pirates. It has been estimated that two-thirds of the boats were attacked by pirates, each boat on average more than twice.[191]

Like other Asian immigrants, Vietnamese Americans were subject to racism by white workers, as well as by the white supremacist Ku Klux Klan.[192] For example, the late 1970s and early 1980s coincided with poor shrimp fishing in the Gulf of Mexico. Car bumper stickers began to appear along the coast, stating 'Save Your Shrimp Industry? Get Rid of Vietnamese.' The Ku Klux Klan staged demonstrations calling for blood, and US fisherman started carrying guns on their boats.[193] In 1983, in Davis, California, a 17-year-old Vietnamese student was stabbed to death by a white student in a high school with a history of racial harassment against South-East Asian students.[194] Around the same time, in Lansing, Michigan, a Vietnamese American man and his European American wife were harassed and repeatedly shot at by white men shouting racist abuse.[195]

Korean Americans

After a series of laws barring the immigration of Chinese workers (see earlier in this chapter), between 1903 and 1905 some 7,000 Koreans were recruited and brought to Hawaii as plantation labourers. Before the Immigration Act of 1924 which effectively ended the immigration of Asians, about 1,100 Korean 'picture brides' entered the United States.[196] The term refers to the matchmaking of brides in Korea with Korean migrant workers via photographs and family recommendations. As Sonia Shinn Sunoo argues, the women were eager to escape the constricted Confucian society that was early twentieth-century Korea, and the tightening Japanese grip over the country.[197] Students and political exiles also migrated to the United States during this period.[198] Racist incidents began in 1909. One that drew significant attention was when an orchard owner arranged to hire 15 Korean fruit pickers. On arrival they were met by several hundred unemployed Euro-Americans who surrounded them, threatening them with physical violence, forcing them to leave on the next train.[199]

The second phase of Korean immigration was triggered by the Korean War (1950–53), after which US soldiers who had been stationed in Korea brought home Korean wives and adopted war orphans, and sponsored students to come to the United States.

Korean Americans were on the receiving end of the 1992 Los Angeles riots. The riots were precipitated by the acquittal of four white police officers who had badly beaten African American Rodney King. Over 50 people died and over 2,400 were injured.[200] Juan F. Perea identifies three media images: 'the horrifying image of organized police brutality and violence' meted out to Rodney King, resonating with centuries of similar violence; the horrible violence inflicted on white American Reginald Denny by African Americans; and armed Korean or Korean American merchants protecting their stores, many of which were barely profitable and uninsured.[201] Zia describes how, as stores were burned and looted, Korean Americans called 911 (the emergency services). But the Los Angeles Police Department did little to stop the violence; Korean Americans suspected that the police were relieved to have the intense anger over police brutality redirected.[202]

As Perea points out, the media portrayed the events as if they were the outcome of some simmering tensions between Korean Americans and African Americans, with the familiar theme, as we shall see, of the Asian (in this case Korean) Americans cast as 'good', and the other (the African Americans) labelled 'bad'.[203] Perea explains how the communications ISA served to obscure racist realities: Koreans were the good ethnics, 'model minority members' – hardworking, quiet, law-abiding property owners striving to climb the ladder of the American dream. Blacks were the bad – violent, criminal and out of control. The good minority versus bad minority oppositional pairing disguises our traditional racial hierarchy and racism by displacing it onto two oppressed minority groups.

Japanese Americans

Japanese people began entering the United States in significant numbers in 1885, when the Japanese government legalized emigration. In 1907, a so-called 'Gentlemen's Agreement' with Japan kept out the Japanese working class. This was the result of efforts by the Japanese and Korean League, formed in 1905, which sought to forbid entry to Japanese and Korean labourers but allowed entry to certain categories of business and professional people.[204] Following the 1924 Immigration Act, protests were made by the Japanese government, and a Japanese citizen committed ritual suicide outside the US embassy in Tokyo. On the day the law became effective, Japan declared a day of 'national humiliation'.[205]

Racism restricted the employment prospects of second-generation Japanese young people. A study of 161 graduating from the University of California between 1925 and 1935 reported that only 25 per cent were employed in professional occupations for which the university had prepared them.[206] As Perea and colleagues explain, for Japanese immigrants and their citizen children, their sense of being abandoned was deepened by the events of the Second World War. They describe the attack on the US naval base in Hawaii (annexed to the United States in 1898, and an 'official' territory' since 1900) that brought the United States into the war as follows:

The bombing of Pearl Harbor on December 7, 1941 plunged the United States into a declared war against Japanese combatants, and an undeclared war against citizens and aliens of Japanese ancestry resident in the United States.[207]

Between February 1942 and December 1944, 120,000 Japanese Americans were excluded from designated areas, removed by the Army, and detained in 'relocation centers' – barracks mostly in desolate areas of the West. Most spent the war years behind barbed wire guarded by military police.[208] A Congressional Record of the Senate in 1988 reported that the internment of individuals of Japanese ancestry was carried out without any military or security reason, and that the internment of the individuals of Japanese ancestry was caused by racism (the Record uses the term 'racial prejudice'), war hysteria, and a failure of political leadership.[209]

Looking back on these events 20 years on, in an attempt to find an explanation how Japanese Americans had survived it all, sociologist William Petersen, in an article in the *New York Times* in 1966, ascribed to Japanese Americans 'seemingly positive' attributes, thus laying the foundations for the racist 'model minority' myth. Petersen argued that racism can lead to a downward spiral that can create 'problem minorities'. Unlike, the American 'negro', he suggested, whose links to negritude in Africa are 'artificial', Japanese Americans 'could climb over the highest barriers our racists were able to fashion in part because of their meaningful links with an alien culture'. This means, Petersen goes on, that their connections with Japan gives them '"an achievement orientation" … in sharp contrast to lower-class Americans, whether white or Negro'.[210] The 'model minority' myth has become generalized for all Asian Americans, homogenizing the rich and diverse culture of Asian American peoples. The myth constitutes a classic example of my submission in the Introduction to this book that the ascription of 'seemingly positive attributes' will probably ultimately have a number of racist consequences.

ASIAN AMERICANS TODAY

The 'model minority' myth has been defined by Delgado and Stefancic as the '[i]dea that Asian Americans are hard-working, intelligent, and successful and that other groups should emulate them'.[211] They explain that exalting Asian Americans as 'the perfect minority group – quiet, industrious, with intact families and high educational aspiration and achievement' is not only untrue, but is 'injurious' to the many Asian American subgroups who are poor and need assistance[212] (as was demonstrated by the history of Asian Americans outlined in this chapter). The myth causes a backlash for Asian Americans in general. Describing Asian Americans as hard working very quickly becomes 'unfair competition'.[213] Frank Wu notes that when Asian Americans are praised for having strong families and strong family values – nuclear families that stay together – they are then criticized for being 'too clannish, too ethnic, too insular, not mixing enough, self-segregating'.[214]

Robert Chang notes another negative response that results from the 'model minority' myth: 'when we try to make our problems known, our complaints of discrimination or calls for remedial action are seen as unwarranted and inappropriate'.[215] Benji Chang and Wayne Au summarize the racism inherent in the 'model minority' myth, giving a number of examples, most of which have been demonstrated earlier in this chapter. The myth masks the diversity and ethnic inequity within the Asian American communities; the class divide, sometimes rooted in specific immigration histories; economic circumstance, such as larger household size and residence in high-cost parts of the United States; racism and class exploitation; and attributing success and failure of other minority ethnic groups to cultural or 'racial' weaknesses.[216] With respect to this last point, other minority ethnic groups are interpellated on the lines of 'Asian Americans made it, why can't you?'[217]

What then is the current reality? The poverty rate for Asian Americans of 12.1 per cent cited at the beginning of this chapter conceals much higher rates among specific constituencies. For example the rate among Hmongs is 37.8 per cent, among Cambodians 29.3 per cent, Laotians 18.5 per cent and Vietnamese 16.6 per cent.[218] Moreover, nearly 2 million Asian Americans and Pacific Islanders (AAPIs collectively – AAs for the category of Asian Americans and NHPIs for the subcategory of Native Hawaiians and other Pacific Islanders[219]) live in poverty. AAPI poor are one of the fastest-growing poverty populations in the wake of the on the onset of the recession and the enactment of austerity/immiseration capitalism.[220] From 2007 to 2011, the number of AAPI poor increased by more than half a million, an increase of 38 per cent (37 per cent increase for AAs in poverty and a 60 per cent increase for NHOPIs in poverty). The general poverty population grew by 27 per cent. The only other ethnic group with a larger percentage increase was Latina/o, with a 42 per cent increase.[221] All this is rendered invisible by the myth of 'model minority', and provides a major reason to dispense with it.

So is any of this discussed in the media? ChangeLab, 'a grassroots political lab that explores how U.S. demographic change is affecting racial justice politics, with a strategic focus on Asian American identity',[222] conducted two studies (January to June 2012 and January to June 2013) focusing on the TV channel MSNBC, which in the view of Scot Nakagawa is 'the undisputed leader' when 'it comes to racial diversity among the Sunday political talk shows'.[223] Two of its anchor weekend talk programmes included more guests of colour and hosted more discussion of issues of 'race' than all of the other networks offering similar programming combined. Nakagawa argues that the 'difference is not just in quantity but in the depth and quality of the discourse'. However, even on MSNBC, Asian Americans are generally mentioned incidentally. When a substantive point is made, out comes the 'model minority' myth. Here are two typical quotes from the studies, both by Republican politicians:

> if you look at Asian Americans, for example, in general, they have higher income [sic] than the median of our country, more intact families, more entrepreneurship, higher levels of education.

> There's one distinctive thing about Asian Americans as a constituency, they have not relied on politics to get ahead, as many other disadvantaged groups have done. African Americans have faced terrible disadvantage in this country. Asian Americans certainly faced discrimination. They managed to get ahead in businesses, professions, science, popular culture … they have done it themselves, they haven't had to rely on politics as much as other groups. [224]

While, as we have seen, the 'seemingly positive' 'model minority' myth has racist consequences for both Asian Americans and other people of colour (for example, the notion that 'black people in particular' have pathological cultures provides ideological justification for the reining-in of the RSAs as in the prison-industrial complex and police violence as discussed earlier in this chapter) the myth also impacts negatively on the working class in general, especially under austerity/immiseration capitalism. As Nakagawa puts it:

> That myth is one of the tenets of American racism, used repeatedly for decades to promote the idea that racism and structural racial disadvantage are either non-existent or at least entirely surmountable, while suggesting that some people of color, and Black people in particular, are just whiners unwilling to pull themselves up by their bootstraps. And that belief, that the black poor are just entitlement junkies, has negative consequences for all poor people because the tough 'love' solutions this belief inspires, like cutting back on food stamps and other programs, see no color.[225]

ISLAMOPHOBIA: A BRIEF HISTORY

Although the word 'Islamophobia' was not coined in the English language until 1991, Zaheer Ali documents a major Islamophobic incident in the mainstream US media in 1959, in a television programme entitled *The Hate that Hate Produced*.[226] The programme introduced the Nation of Islam, its leader Elijah Muhammad and spokesperson Malcolm X to the American public, Ali argues, in the most sensationalized way possible, in the hope of scaring whites into supporting more moderate African Americans in the civil rights movement. While at the beginning of the programme the host issued disclaimers distinguishing the Nation of Islam from 'orthodox' Muslims, throughout the broadcast 'Muslim' was loosely used interchangeably or in combination with 'Negro' to emphasize the threat posed by Islam in the African American community. As the host of the programme put it (in sexist language characteristic of the time):

> Negro American Muslims are the most powerful of the black supremacist group. They claim a membership of a quarter of a million Negroes. ... Their doctrine is being taught in 50 cities across the nation. Let no one underestimate *the Muslims* [emphasis added]. They have their own parochial schools like this one in Chicago, where Muslim children are taught to hate the white man. Even the clothes they wear are anti-white man, anti-American, like these two Negro children going to school. Wherever they go, the Muslims withdraw from the life of the community. They have their own stores, supermarkets, barber shops, restaurants.[227]

By the early 1980s, any possible ambiguity between the racialized denigration of Muslims as such and the Nation of Islam had disappeared. The communications ISA, via the mainstream media, made sure that the presence of Muslims in the United States gained the attention of the larger society.[228] One of the first historic studies of Arab American communities commissioned by an Arab American organization (ADC) noted in 1984:

> At a time when the United States is more receptive to cultural pluralism, and ethnicity is no longer socially unacceptable, Arab Americans remain primary targets of defamatory attacks on their cultural and personal character. Thus, much of the activity of the Arab-American community has been directed at correcting the stereotypes that threaten to produce a new wave of anti-Arab racism

in the United States and endanger the civil and human rights of the Arab-American community.[229]

As Hilal Elver argues, the Iran hostage crisis during the Islamic revolution in 1979 and the TWA hijacking in Lebanon in 1985 brought out deep-seated racism in American society. Following the February 1993 World Trade Center bombing in New York City, some newspaper editorials suggested that 'admission of Muslims into the United States ought to be reduced to a minimum or eliminated altogether'.[230] Muslim communities became subject to hate crimes, including the bombing and burning of mosques in several states. In the aftermath of the Cold War, the American public was interpellated to see Islam as the next challenge.[231]

Following the 9/11 attack on the Twin Towers in New York in 2001, the US 'Justice Department detained more than twelve hundred people without charge and without a rational basis'.[232] In 2002, 83,000 young Muslim men living in the United States, from 25 different countries, were forced to register, were fingerprinted, and were questioned by US immigration officials, the strategy soon being abandoned owing to the inability to find evidence of any suspicious activity.[233] As Deepa Kumar puts it:

Since the events of 9/11, the question of political Islam has taken center stage in world politics. The 'war on terror' has transformed the whole discussion on the relationship between Islam and the West. A slew of books and essays have appeared on this topic since then. Predictably, conservative analysts, recycling old Orientalist clichés, have advanced the idea that the West is once again at war with 'Islam'. The underlying logic behind this argument is 'we' are secular and democratic, while 'they' are mired in the backwardness born out of an adherence to Islam. These arguments have become part of the common-sense ideology in the United States and elsewhere.[234]

According to the FBI, anti-Islamic incidents were the second least reported hate crimes prior to 9/11, but following 9/11, they became the second highest reported among religion-bias incidents. From pre-9/11 to post-9/11, a growth of 1,600 per cent took place. In January 2002, the Intergroup Clearinghouse reported that there had been more than 1,700 cases of racism against Arab Americans, Muslim Americans, Sikh Americans and South Asian Americans.[235]

ISLAMOPHOBIA TODAY

Since 9/11, Islamophobia has continued unabated.[236] In April 2009, President Obama addressed the Turkish Parliament and praised Muslim Americans for 'enriching the United States'.[237] Five years after Obama's speech, the Council for American-Islamic Relations (CAIR), America's largest Muslim civil liberties and advocacy organization, whose 'mission is to enhance the understanding of Islam, encourage dialogue, protect civil liberties, empower American Muslims, and build coalitions that promote justice and mutual understanding',[238] reported that in 2013, 36 bills or amendments designed to vilify Islamic religious practices were introduced in the legislatures of 16 states, all of which were originally sponsored solely by Republicans.[239] Thirty-three (92 per cent) of the 2013 anti-Islam bills contained language that was extracted from American Laws for American Courts, template legislation written by David Yerushalmi that forms the core of most of the anti-Islam legislation seen in the United States over the last few years.[240] In 2006, Yerushalmi wrote, 'Our greatest enemy today is Islam. The only Islam appearing in any formal way around the world is one that seeks a world Caliphate through murder, terror and fear.'[241]

Some of the momentum for one of the bills comes from the work of the Islamophobic Act! For America. When asked if Americans should 'resist Muslims who want to seek political office in this nation', founder, president and CEO of Act! For America, Brigitte Gabriel stated:

> Absolutely. If a Muslim who has – who is – a practicing Muslim who believes the word of the Koran to be the word of Allah, who abides by Islam, who goes to mosque and prays every Friday, who prays five times a day – this practicing Muslim, who believes in the teachings of the Koran, cannot be a loyal citizen to the United States of America.[242]

CAIR categorizes US Islamophobia network groups as inner core, whose primary purpose is to promote hatred of Islam and Muslims and whose work regularly demonstrates Islamophobic themes, and outer core groups whose main aim 'does not appear to include promoting ... hatred of Islam and Muslims but whose work regularly demonstrates or supports Islamophobic themes'.[243] The 32 identified groups (about two-thirds of which are inner core) range alphabetically from Abstraction Fund, an inner core group which gave 82 per cent of its total $1,982,930 of contributions and grants to groups known for promoting Islamophobia, to the outer core *Washington Times*, a conservative newspaper whose columnists have continually propagated anti-Muslim sentiments.[244] A search on the newspaper's website for 'Muslim' threw up a story about the proprietor of an Arkansas shooting range who announced on social media that she is banning Muslims from her establishment out of fear for the safety of her patrons. She is quoted as saying:

> This is not a coffee and donut shop. This is a live fire indoor shooting range. People come here to buy, rent, and shoot lethal weapons. In the range, people are shooting guns in close proximity to each other, so my patrons depend on me and my discretion regarding who I allow to shoot beside them. One mistake in judgement on my part could cost innocent people their lives.[245]

Her reasoning is that she is banning Muslims because 'Why would I want to rent or sell a gun and hand ammunition to someone who aligns himself with a religion that commands him to kill me?' The reporter of this piece, Jessica Chasmar, describes herself as follows:

> Registered GOP [Republican]. Libertarian ideologue. MA in political communications …. I enjoy beer, lipstick … and making liberals cry (which isn't difficult.) I'm politically incorrect, and I make no apologies. Let's take America back. La Revolucion![246]

Author of *The Fear of Islam: An Introduction to Islamophobia in the West*, Todd Green points out that the 2016 presidential race already includes a field of candidates with a recent history of Islamophobic rhetoric.[247] For example, Rick Santorum, whose website describes him as a 'conservative committed to restoring the American dream for hardworking Americans'[248] accused Presidents Bush and Obama of giving 'all Muslims a pass for identifying a cancer within their own body'.[249] Rand Paul (according to his website, he and his wife are 'devout Christians and are active in their local church'[250]) compared the Muslims who wanted to build the Park51 Center to the Ku Klux Klan.[251] Meanwhile, Lindsey Graham, 'Ready To Be Commander-in-Chief On Day One',[252] suggested that the decision of the 2015 Charleston killer (the murders are discussed at the end of this chapter) to sit in a bible study group for an hour before opening fire reflects 'Mideast hate' (a euphemism for 'Islamic hate').[253] Finally, Mike Huckabee ('I will fight for the United States military to be the most feared, respected, and capable fighting force the world has ever known'[254]) maintained that Islam 'promotes the most murderous mayhem on the planet'.[255]

CONCLUSION

In this chapter I have provided an analysis of a wide range of histories of and current realities pertaining to racialized groups in the United States. Various groups have been racialized throughout the country's history, and I have tried to include those who continue to be racialized in the first quarter of the twenty-first century. There are a number of differences in these histories and contemporary situations.

Distinctive differences in the experiences of racialized groups do not, of course, detract from the commonalities of racism experienced by racialized communities. Overall, similarities and differences between Native Americans, African Americans, Latina/o Americans, Asian Americans and Muslim Americans underline Adrienne Dixson's analogy with jazz – in unison and out of unison at the same time.[256] As is argued throughout this book, in order for these differences and similarities to be fully understood, they need to be linked to racialization processes and articulated with ongoing changes in the capitalist mode of production and developments in colonialism and imperialism. Racialization processes are themselves intimately connected to migration patterns, which are in turn related to the needs and demands of the capitalist economy.

We cannot but help draw comparisons between the racism inherent in the use of the RSAs and ISAs against US citizens of colour at home, and imperialist adventures overseas. World Socialist Web Site (WSWS) correspondent Patrick Martin writes about the reactionary and vicious character of the Islamic State in Iraq and Syria (ISIS) and the terrible consequences of a half-century of intervention in the Middle East by US imperialism.[257] He notes how US Vice President Joseph Biden condemned the beheading of US journalist Steven Sotloff in a speech at a naval shipyard, declaring that US military forces would pursue ISIS to 'the gates of hell'.[258] As Martin points out, ISIS is not 'an incomprehensible emanation of Satanic evil', as portrayed by the RSAs and the ISAs the world over; rather 'it is a product of the policies of the US government over a protracted period of time'. As he explains, successive US administrations have built up the most reactionary and backward Islamic fundamentalist forces for many decades from the Cold War onwards, including the right-wing Iranian Islamists in support of the 1953 coup that ousted the liberal government that had nationalized the largely British-owned oil industry; and the Muslim Brotherhood in Egypt to undermine the regime of Abdel Nasser who had nationalized the Suez Canal and sought military aid from the then Soviet Union. In addition, in 1977 the CIA backed a coup in Pakistan that established a martial law regime based on Islamist fundamentalism that lasted until 1988. The

United States has played similar roles in Iran and Saudi Arabia. As Martin goes on:

> Islamic fundamentalism became directly linked to terrorist violence through the US campaign of subversion beginning in the late 1970s against the pro-Soviet government in Afghanistan. The CIA, working with Saudi Arabia and Pakistan, recruited Islamic fundamentalists from all over the world, trained them in bomb-making and other terror tactics, and funnelled them to the battlefield in Afghanistan. Prominent among these was the son of a Saudi construction multi-millionaire, Osama bin Laden.[259]

'The veterans of Afghanistan', Martin continues, 'returned to their home countries, from Morocco to Indonesia, spreading the influence of Islamic fundamentalism into countries where it had never before existed'. A key turning point was the 1990–91 Persian Gulf war, when half a million US troops were deployed to Saudi Arabia, prompting bin Laden and other Islamists to declare the United States the main enemy.

Bush's 'war on terror', in the wake of the 9/11 attacks, by no means signified a break with the Islamic fundamentalists, many now operating under the umbrella of Al Qaeda, as later events would show. There remained a murky connection between US foreign policy and the radical Islamists, particularly in Iraq, Libya and Syria, all countries ruled by secular regimes that had largely suppressed the fundamentalist groups. The US invasion and occupation of Iraq killed hundreds of thousands of Iraqis, destroying the social and physical infrastructure, and employing the strategy of divide and rule; the US occupation deliberately fired up Sunni–Shiite sectarian divisions, which led to the growth of the Sunni-based Al Qaeda in Iraq, the forerunner of ISIS.[260]

The US-NATO intervention in Libya in 2011 employed elements that were linked to Al Qaeda as its ground troops, which led to political disintegration and civil war in that country. Finally, in Syria, the CIA and US allies directly armed, financed and trained Islamic extremists to fight the government of President Bashar al-Assad, which was allied to Iran and Russia. Recipients of US aid included both the al-Nusra Front, the Al Qaeda affiliate in Syria, and ISIS, which advocated an even more extreme form of Islamist terrorism than Al Qaeda, including the immediate establishment of a 'caliphate' on conquered territory in eastern Syria and western Iraq.[261]

The United States's first black president has kept the military industrial complex at the top of all agendas, a role, as Paul Carr argues, that is incumbent on the military commander-in-chief.[262] Obama has very willingly been a proponent of drones, much more so than George W. Bush, and drones have been used to kill a range of people in Afghanistan, Pakistan, Yemen and Somalia as well as in other areas. His administration has seen the maintenance of Guantanamo, the extension of militarization in Afghanistan, the continuation of the war in Iraq, the invasion of Libya, the unwavering support of Israel in spite of all the evidence related to transgressions and over-zealous behaviour during the 2014 attacks on Gaza, and so many other incursions.[263] All of this, of course, exacerbates Islamism, which in turn intensifies Islamophobia.

Obama, Carr reminds us, 'has not dismantled the almost unimaginable and unconscionable network of some 900 USA military bases in over one hundred countries'. Moreover, throughout his presidency, Obama has approved more targeted killings than any other modern president, with the administration declining to reveal details of how it places people on 'kill lists', conducts surveillance in the United States and decides whom to detain overseas. As Carr concludes:

> The point here is that if Obama does not willingly wish to have the hard conversations about race when he has the power to do so, who, then, will have them? It is unrealistic to think that a President Bush or others would be interested in doing so. Race, racialization and racism are embedded in the fabric of the American state, and to ignore that reality is to further entrench racial injustice in everything that happens within the state, including incarceration, police behavior, judicial processes and decisions, militarization, economics, politics, education, and day-to-day life. One can understand why he is motivated to not engage in these debates but, given his enormously powerful rhetoric about hope and change, how could he not fight for social justice at the most visceral, fundamental level, knowing that many people of color are facing systemic, institutional and deep-seated racial conflicts? If Obama believes that it's all about 'business as usual', appeasing power-brokers and maintaining a stable capitalist state for investors, then it is almost inconceivable that meaningful change for a large number of racialized peoples could be effectuated.[264]

Pierre Orelus provides a compelling indictment of the Obama years with respect to both domestic and foreign policy. Orelus notes that while Obama, the safest and most pragmatic choice to follow George W. Bush, needs recognition for his progressive achievements on women's and LGBTI rights, and to some extent on healthcare (despite, as Paul Carr notes in the Afterword to the book, the limitations and problems of Obamacare), he has followed and sometimes outstripped his predecessor in the pro-neoliberal capitalist orientation of his domestic policy and the pro-imperialist nature of his foreign policy. Moreover, having stated completely erroneously that 'There's not a Black America and a White America and Latino America and Asian America – there's the United States of America',[265] Obama has not improved 'race relations' domestically or internationally. Obama's professed belief in hope and in change from the bottom up have been proved to be just slogans.

Inevitably, in considering racism in a country with some 320 million inhabitants, there will be some omissions, and I apologize to any groups that are not included in this chapter, and feel that they should be. For example, while Jewish Americans in the contemporary United States are not generally thought of as an oppressed racialized group experiencing racism as documented in this chapter, antisemitism remains a significant blight on US society. As David Grubin has argued while Jewish Americans have flourished in the US, they have also faced racism, being targeted as scapegoats, especially during periods of hardship and war.[266] Moreover, we should not underestimate antisemitic hate crime, which accounts for 60.3 per cent of the total of religious hate crime, compared with 13.7 per cent anti-Islamic and 6.1 per cent anti-Catholic.[267]

I have not in this chapter considered hate groups, of which there are nearly 1,000 operating across the country.[268] These include neo-Nazis, Klansmen, white nationalists, neo-Confederates, racist skinheads, black separatists, border vigilantes and others. Since 2000, the Southern Policy Law Center (SPLC) points out, the number of hate groups has increased by 56 per cent, a surge fuelled by anger and fear over the economy, immigration and the diminishing white majority, symbolized for them by the election of the nation's first African-American president.[269]

In the middle of 2015, white supremacist Dylann Roof shot nine African Americans in a Charleston, South Carolina church – multiple times to make sure they were all dead – in an attempt to start a 'race' war, but he nearly backed out because 'everyone was so nice to him'. He had researched the church and targeted it because it was a 'historic African-American church'. In his confession Roof expressed no remorse or shame.[270] South Carolina is home to 19 known hate groups.[271]

As Frankie Boyle reasons, in a way that is pertinent to the preceding discussion of imperialism, there is 'a genuine question to be asked here: what responsibility does the United States state bear for the Charleston shootings when racist murder seems to be part of its policing strategy and most of its foreign policy?'[272] To exemplify his query, he informs us that presidential candidate Hillary Clinton spoke of the 'racist terrorism' of

Roof, despite being the architect of the US military intervention in Libya. 'The US's record of invasions, assassinations and government overthrows', Boyle goes on, is racist: '[i]magining that you can kill people and seize control of their resources without believing them to be inferior requires a certain amount of intellectual flexibility'. Recalling the ships sinking in the Mediterranean Sea, causing hundreds of migrants to drown, Boyle concludes that this is the 'same sort of intellectual flexibility that allows people to express grief for the migrants who drown in the Mediterranean and hatred for the ones who survive'.

Having now considered the plethora of types of racism historically and contemporaneously in the United Kingdom and the United States, I now turn to Australia, where a similar sad state of affairs has existed for some two and a quarter centuries.

3
Australia

INTRODUCTION

As with the United Kingdom and the United States, and as explicated in general terms in the Introduction to this book, poverty in Australia is related to ethnicity and racism. For example, adults born in countries where English is not the main language face a much higher risk of poverty (18.8 per cent) than those born in Australia (11.6 per cent), or born in an English-speaking country (11.4 per cent).[1] Twenty-nine per cent of adults living in households below the 50 per cent poverty line are from a non-English-speaking country.[2] Aboriginal communities are also far more likely to experience poverty than non-indigenous Australians, with 19.3 per cent living below the poverty line, compared with 12.4 per cent of other Australians.[3] Finally, as far as South Sea Islander Australians are concerned, as we shall see a parliamentary inquiry found very little evidence in the last 20 years of efforts to address their social and economic disadvantage.

Also as in the United Kingdom and the United States, racism in Australia is multifaceted. I begin Chapter 3 with a discussion of older colour-coded racism. This has a number of dimensions. First, I examine racism directed at indigenous peoples. Beginning with invasion, settler colonialism and attempted genocide, I go on to consider the exploitation of Aboriginal land and labour power. Next I look at the 'stolen generations', before addressing indigenous peoples today. Second, I turn my attention to the historical situation of indentured labour and anti-South Sea Islander racism, and then to South Sea Islander peoples today. Third, anti-Asian racism is discussed in the context of the gold rushes and Chinese immigration, which began in the mid-nineteenth century, and anti-Japanese racism in the twentieth. Anti-Asian racism is then addressed in the contemporary context.

Having addressed three dominant forms of colour-coded racism, I then look at older non-colour-coded racism, focusing on anti-Irish racism and antisemitism through history and in Australia today.

The white Australia policy dominated Australian politics for much of the twentieth century, but immigration was mediated by Anglo-Celtic racism. Racism in the latter part of the twentieth century and the beginning of the twenty-first century cannot be understood without an examination of Hansonism and the Howard government, which was formed in the light of the decline of multiculturalism, and which is my next focus.

I then look at newer colour-coded racism, in the form of more recent anti-migrant racism. Next I consider newer hybridist racism in the form of Islamophobia and anti-asylum-seeker racism, followed by a quick look at the proliferation of hate groups.

OLDER COLOUR-CODED RACISM

Invasion, Settler Colonialism and Attempted Genocide

On 26 January 1788, eleven British ships commanded by Captain Arthur Phillip, first governor of the new colony, anchored off the east coast of Australia at Sydney Cove and raised the British flag.[4] Nearly 20 years earlier (29 April 1770), Lt James Cook had marked the beginning of the end for the traditional way of life of Australia's First Nations when he had sailed under instructions, based on the eighteenth-century European law of *terra nullius* (land belonging to nobody), to take possession of the Southern Continent 'if it was uninhabited, or with the consent of the natives if it was occupied'.[5] Upon his arrival, Cook declared the land he called New South Wales (NSW) to be the property of Britain's King George III.[6] The colonization, first of the Eora people in Botany Bay,[7] then of the rest of the country, was fore-shadowed, as we saw in Chapter 2, by centuries of struggle for hegemony amongst European powers in the Americas. As Vilhelm Elklund put it, from 'its experience in America, Europe had developed a legal framework in which colonization was both acceptable and encouraged. Occupation of Australia was practically a foregone conclusion.'[8]

British settlement was a full-scale invasion, with its convicts forming the front line, and adherence to the myth of *terra nullius,* meaning that white 'Australians' were fighting against opponents 'who didn't exist, who didn't have to be pushed off the land that was never theirs to begin with'.[9] Moreover, even when the British discovered evidence of cultivation and land ownership traditions, they refused to acknowledge their mistake.[10]

The reality of what was claimed to be *terra nullius*, then, is very different. Prior to the invasion there were a vast number of different clans speaking some 250 languages.[11] Here is a description of just one small section of a huge nation of different peoples:

For thousands of years prior to the arrival of Europeans, northern Sydney was occupied by different Aboriginal clans. Living primarily along the foreshores of the harbour, they fished and hunted in the waters and hinterlands of the area, and harvested food from the surrounding bush. Self-sufficient and harmonious, they had no need to travel far from their lands, since the resources about them were so abundant, and trade with other tribal groups was well established.[12]

The capitalist way of work was alien to Aboriginal peoples who, moving throughout their country in accordance with the seasons, only needed to spend about 4 to 5 hours per day working to ensure their survival. This large amount of leisure time enabled the development of a rich and complex ritual life – 'language, customs, spirituality and the law – the heart of which was connection to the land'.[13]

From 1790 onwards, ships came out on a regular basis with convict labour and supplies on board. As well as the intra-European struggle for imperial hegemony, another reason for the British to invade Australia, according to Sue Ballyn, was that prisons in Britain had become unbearably overcrowded. Crime rates were rising across Britain as large numbers of people were moving away from rural areas to the increasingly industrialized cities, where unemployment ran high, particularly as machines replaced labour. An estimated 1 million people in Britain were below the bread line in 1788. The congestion in the prisons was worsened by the refusal of America to take any more convicts after the American War of Independence, which ended in 1783.[14]

The Aboriginal Heritage Office describes how disease struck a 'fatal and extensive blow' to Aboriginal people, who had no resistance to smallpox, syphilis and influenza, for example. In less than a year (1788–89), over half the indigenous population living in the Sydney basin had died from smallpox.[15]

In addition to the importation of fatal diseases, the history of settler colonialism is a history of massacre and attempted genocide. To most settlers, the Aboriginal peoples were considered akin to kangaroos, dingoes and emus, 'strange fauna to be eradicated to make way for the development of farming and grazing'.[16] As one senior member of the church put it:

I have myself heard a man, educated, and a large proprietor of sheep and cattle, maintain that there was no more harm in shooting a native, than in shooting a wild dog. I have heard it maintained by others that it is the course of Providence, that blacks should disappear before the white, and the sooner the process was carried out the better, for all parties. I fear such opinions prevail to a great extent. Very recently in the presence of two clergymen, a man of education narrated, as a good thing, that he had been one of a party who had pursued the blacks, in consequence of cattle being rushed by them, and that he was sure that they shot upwards of a hundred. When expostulated with, he maintained that there was nothing wrong in it, that it was preposterous to suppose they had souls. In this opinion he was joined by another educated person present.[17]

The following is part of a chronology of some of the atrocities committed against indigenous Australians, the details of which are vague because of a lack of accurate recording of some of the incidents. The summary should therefore be treated as indicative, rather than definitive:

- between 300 and 1,000 Gunai/Kurnai people killed in East Gippsland, Victoria between 1800 and 1860
- the ambush and massacre of 30 Tasmanian Aboriginal people of the Pennemukeer band at Cape Grim by four shepherds in 1828, whose bodies were thrown into the sea, after which the hill where it occurred was named Victory Hill
- the killing of between 60 and 200 Kilcarer gundidj clan of the Gundit-jmara people over a dispute over the ownership of a beached whale in the Convincing Ground, near Portland, Victoria in 1833 or 1834
- the massacre of between 14 and 25 Aboriginal people in Pinjarra, Western Australia by soldiers and police led by the governor in 1834
- the hacking and slashing to death of 30 to 40 defenceless Aboriginal people by stockmen, which ended with camp drinking and bragging about the killings, at Myall Creek in 1838
- the wiping-out in 1838 at Waterloo Creek by a Sydney mounted police detachment of several hundred people, which amounted to most of the Kamilaroi people
- up to 300 Aboriginal men, women and children shot and burned by settlers, vigilantes and officials in Mowla Bluff, Western Australia, in 1916, after a station manager was beaten up and stabbed for violence and sexual abuse of the local tribespeople
- a massacre of the Kirrae Wuurong people in Noorat, Victoria in 1839, where a mass grave was later discovered
- the 'Black War' in the early years of the nineteenth century in what is now Tasmania, which led to the genocide of the Tasmanian Aboriginal peoples
- the Bathurst massacres in the early 1920s of some 1,000 men, women and children, a third of the entire Wiradjuri population
- the last known massacre carried out at Coniston cattle station,

Northern Territory in 1928, where estimates of the Warlpiri, Anmatyere and Kaytetye people killed vary between 60 and 170.[18]

Adherence to *terra nullius* allowed the white invaders to rationalize their behaviours as 'settlement', and allowed the governments (colonial and later federal) to ignore the people who were not supposed to exist in the first place. It was not until the 1992 Mabo judgment that Australia was finally freed of *terra nullius* as a legal doctrine, but not as an exclusionary practice.

The Exploitation of Aboriginal Land and Labour Power

The exploitation of Aboriginal land and labour has a long history, dating back to the beginnings of colonization, when domestic animals such as sheep, cattle, pigs, goats, donkeys and horses were first introduced. By 1900 there were over 8.5 million cattle and 70.5 million sheep in Australia. At this time sheep were mainly distributed across the semi-arid and sub-humid areas of southern Australia, while cattle were more widely distributed across northern and southern Australia, including many dryland areas where they are not able to flourish.[19] There were two distinct phases in the colonial expansion of pastoral activity in Australia. The first was pastoral settlement from the 1790s, largely confined to the woodlands and grass-lands of south-eastern Australia, and largely focused on sheep. The second was a major expansion of cattle pastoralism into the dry lands and tropical savannas of northern and central Australia in the late nineteenth/early twentieth century.[20]

It was, as Cultural Survival explains (this organization advocates indigenous people's rights, and supports indigenous communities' self-determination, cultures and political resilience), the British Crown's issuing of leases in the Northern Territory during the 1870s that created a trading frenzy, in which 'the lives of Aboriginal people were placed in the hands of gamblers in distant cities'.[21] This was followed by what the organization describes as 'the actual invasion of cattle into the life-sustaining ecosystems'. As they put it, tens of thousands 'of water-guzzling bullocks were driven into the arid N.T. lands. Their monopolization of the grasslands, under the careful supervision of their owners' rifles, was the beginning of a social and ecological disaster'. However the dilemma facing the 'whitefellas' (Anglo Australians) was that if they respected the rights of Aboriginal people as required by the terms of the lease, they would have to greatly modify their social and agricultural practices of cattle rearing. In the event the reaping of profits to repay loans and mortgages won the day, and cattle production was maximized:

The Commonwealth government, formed in 1901, acquired the Northern Territory from a disillusioned South Australia ten years later. The reservation in favor of Aboriginal people continued to be written into the pastoral leases; it also continued to be ignored. Aboriginal people were either pressed into unpaid labor in return for rations, forced to move to government ration stations and reservations or sought refuge on the few cattle stations on which they were permitted to form communities. Aboriginal people were classified not as citizens but as wards of the state. They were expected to die off. They did not.[22]

Thalia Anthony describes the relationship between settlers and Aboriginal peoples as feudal. As she states, where there is a land-dependent workforce, colonial systems can produce feudal relations of production whereby colonists allow indigenous peoples access to conquered land in exchange for their labour power. Feudal land relations, she goes on, were 'a logical framework for colonial expropriation of Australian land' and labour relations in northern Australia. This was in contrast to the industrializing south-eastern Australian colonies, where Aboriginal labour power was largely superfluous and where Aboriginal peoples were forcibly ejected from their land. Aboriginal workers, Anthony explains, with their bush skills and knowledge, became critical to the northern cattle industry, performing station and stock work. Rather than wages, Aboriginal workers – via a modernized form of 'vassalage' – received accommodation, clothing and minimal subsistence for themselves and their families, including tobacco, blankets and simple tools. The availability of a cheap, permanent and large Aboriginal workforce, Anthony goes on, meant that the landowners were able to maintain profits and endure market and climate fluctuations without investing in capital equipment such as pumps, fencing and motorized vehicles.[23]

Perry Anderson has described the dual power sites of the British Crown and private landlords' authority (in this case over the indigenous peoples) as the 'complex unity' of feudal power of the state and lords.[24] Unlike in the south-east where Aboriginal 'bush skills' were not essential, and employers could draw on a much larger settler population for labour power,[25] and where Aboriginal people were incarcerated in government and mission settlements often far removed from home,[26] on the cattle stations it was in the pastoralists' interests to foster Aboriginal family and community life.[27] Aboriginal existence was policed by the pastoralists themselves. As one proclaimed of the 1880s:

Every man was his own policeman; and the letter of the law was often ignored in favour of summary justice .... if no punishment were inflicted it would have been impossible to settle the country.[28]

Anthony describes the climate of fear that permeated pastoral station existence:

The arbitrary powers that pastoralists' exercised brutally on the frontier had consequences for Aborigines in station life. An early stock worker ... claimed that despite infrequent killings, the threat of violence was apparent: 'I was working for some rough men, whitefellas who would pull their gun and kill any Aborigines who stood up to them.' Even when violence was not exercised, the pastoralists' authority was established because of Aborigines' ongoing fear of Europeans.[29]

Anthony concludes that by 'practicing direct control over their Aboriginal workers, pastoralists exuded the status and powers of feudal lords over their land and labour'.

Droving was almost completely performed on foot in the north, until the post-war boom of the 1950s, again in contrast to the south-east, which was dominated by sheep stations and higher levels of mechanization.[30]

It was not until 1967 that Aboriginal and Torres Strait Islander Australians were given full citizenship.[31] Prior to the referendum, each state had different laws for indigenous peoples, while in consistency with the *terra nullius* thesis, the Commonwealth constitution excluded them 'in reckoning the numbers of the people of the Commonwealth'.[32] In 1965 Aboriginal activist Kumantjayi Perkins (known at the time as Charles Perkins) and a group of students from Sydney University led a bus tour through indigenous communities in NSW, followed by the media, which had exposed the segregation and dreadful living conditions in the communities – the first time most non-indigenous Australians had been exposed to the cruel realities of indigenous life.[33]

Citizenship rights were accompanied by a campaign for equal pay for black workers on cattle stations, of which the response of the pastoralists was to move rapidly toward employing white stock workers exclusively, to replace droving with trucking and people on horseback with helicopter mustering.[34] In 1971, the Gibb Committee produced an abysmal report that was silent on the abuse of the reservations protecting Aboriginal interests (just as it was silent on the abuse of reservations concerning environmental degradation).[35] According to Cultural Survival, the Report 'recommended in effect that Aboriginal culture be declared dead and Aboriginal people be fenced in':

in appropriate areas land be obtained by excision, or by sub-lease from the pastoralists for Aboriginal communities for limited village, economic and recreational purposes to enable Aborigines to preserve traditional cultural ties and obligations and to provide the community with a measure of autonomy; such land naturally needs access to adequate water supplies but in addition it should be of such an area and such a quality that some supplementary activities may be encouraged upon it, e.g. pig, poultry and fishing, gardening and artifact making, etc.[36]

In 1976, the Aboriginal Land Rights (NT) Act was passed. This allowed Aboriginal people to lodge traditional land claims to areas of unalienated (vacant) Crown land and to the few cattle stations for which they held the 'whitefella title'.[37] Two years later, the 1978 Commonwealth Act passed by the Fraser government gave self-government to the Northern Territory, thus consolidating white interests. In the same year, the Northern Territory Country-Liberal Party amended the Crown Lands Act with respect to the rights of Aboriginal people resident on cattle stations. This restricted access to educational, medical and other facilities located at the homestead to indigenous people living within 2 km of the homestead.[38]

In 1984, Hugh Morgan, CEO of Western Mining (WMC), one of Australia's largest mining corporations, embarked on a racist campaign denigrating Aboriginal culture, with claims that land rights would promote cannibalism and infanticide.[39] Two years after Morgan's preposterous allegations, at the request of Aboriginal groups, the Anti-Slavery Society visited Australia and reported on the conditions of Aboriginal peoples in the bush and in the town. Among other human rights abuses, it found that the police almost systematically maltreat Aboriginal children both physically and psychologically.[40]

The Stolen Generations

'Stolen generations' is the term used to describe Aboriginal people forcefully taken away (stolen) from their families between the 1890s and the 1970s, many of whom never saw their parents, siblings or relatives again, and many of whom were told they were orphans. The rationale was that by removing children, especially girls, Aboriginal people's cycle of life would be broken, that they would 'die out' as their culture – language, tradition, knowledge, dances and spirituality – was taken away, and their genes were 'bred out' when they eventually had children with white people. In this way, it was hoped that the 'Aboriginal problem' would be solved. 'Adult

Aboriginal people resisted efforts to be driven out of towns by simply coming back. But children taken away were much easier to control.'[41] The reason for taking children away was the claim that Aboriginal parents would neglect them, whereas malnourishment and lack of adequate resources were in reality the effect of white settler-inflicted poverty. The 'stolen generations' were raised on gender-segregated missions, totally estranged from their Aboriginality, with the girls often trained as domestic servants and the boys to be 'stockmen'. Many were physically, emotionally and sexually abused, with babies born to girls raped by white men taken away from them, sometimes as soon as they were born.[42]

In 1997 a landmark report, *Bringing Them Home,* disclosed that as many as 50,000 children and their mothers had endured 'the humiliation, the degradation and sheer brutality of the act of forced separation ... the product of the deliberate, calculated policies of the state'. The report called this genocide. One writer described the voice of an infant screaming as he is wrenched from his mother, who pleads, 'There is nothing wrong with my baby. Why are you doing this to us? I would've been hung years ago, wouldn't I? Because [as an Aboriginal Australian] you're guilty before you're found innocent.'[43]

Indigenous Peoples Today

The quote immediately above is not from the nineteenth or twentieth century. It is 2014, and the writer is campaigning journalist and film maker John Pilger.[44] The grandmother of the little boy demands to know why 'the stealing of our kids is happening all over again', to which the welfare official's response is 'I'm gunna take him, mate.' Pilger argues that this is happening across Australia today in what he describes as 'a scandalous and largely unrecognised abuse of human rights that evokes the infamous stolen generation of the last century'. Assimilation, he goes on, remains Australian government policy in all but name: 'Euphemisms such as "reconciliation" and "Stronger Futures" cover similar social engineering and an enduring, insidious racism in the political elite, the bureaucracy and wider Australian society.' Today, he argues, the theft of Aboriginal children – including babies taken from the birth table – is more widespread than at any time during the last century. As of mid-2013, almost 14,000 Aboriginal children had been 'removed'. According to Pilger, this is five times the number when *Bringing Them Home* was written. Many indigenous mothers, he states, are unaware of their legal rights, while a secretive children's court has become notorious for rubber-stamping removals.[45] Underlining the priorities of the state, in 2012 the co-ordinator general of remote services for the Northern

Territory, Olga Havnen, was removed from her job when she revealed that almost A$80 million was spent on the surveillance and removal of Aboriginal children compared with only A$500,000 spent on supporting the same impoverished families.[46] Havnen pointed out that:

> the primary reasons for removing children are welfare issues directly related to poverty and inequality. The impact is just horrendous because if they are not reunited within six months, it's likely they won't see each other again.[47]

In 1985, when on an academic exchange programme (I taught at Macquarie University in Sydney for a year), I interviewed Aboriginal activist, socialist and educator Helen Boyle. I asked her how racism affects Aboriginal people.[48] In addition to the destruction of Aboriginal traditional society and culture, the forcing on them of the capitalist mode of production, and the norms and mores of capitalism and the cash economy on a pre-industrial society – the building of the whole economy on the backs of black people – and the massacres, some of the key issues she identified were indigenous people's life chances, including incarceration, life expectancy, ill-health, and the importance of land rights. Some 30 years later, like African Americans, Australian indigenous people are massively over-represented in the criminal justice system of Australia. Whereas Aboriginal people make up less than 5 per cent of each state's population, 30 per cent of Australia's prison population are Aboriginal.[49] It is estimated that by 2020, one in two of the prison population will be Aboriginal people. In the Northern Territories, Aboriginal and Torres Strait Islander prisoners make up 84 per cent of the prison population, although they form a little under a third of the NT population.[50] With respect to life expectancy, today indigenous Australians have a life expectancy of around ten years less than non-indigenous Australians.[51]

Ill-health remains a massive blight on the lives of Australia's First Nations. Alyawarre Aboriginal Pat Anderson explained how racism and ill-health are intimately connected. She recalls her first memory of racism when she was 7 or 8 in the early 1950s, when she was told at school that Captain Cook had 'discovered' Australia. At that age, while having any sense about what happened at Botany Bay, she just knew that was not true. As she explains, 'There is no way I can communicate this to the teacher, of course. I don't have the words. All I have is my own experience, as an Aboriginal child, and as part of an Aboriginal family and community'. 'An incident like this,' she went on, 'of having one's own lived experience denied, implicitly or explicitly, is a common one for Aboriginal people.' It is, she argues, 'a profound but subtle form of racism, that has the potential to undermine a person's – particularly a child's – confidence and sense of worth'.[52]

The ways in which racism can be harmful to health are first, that on an individual level it is associated with 'psychological distress, depression, poor quality of life, and substance misuse, all of which contribute significantly to the ill health'. Prolonged 'experience of stress can also have physical health effects such as on the immune, endocrine and cardiovascular systems'. The kind of 'unthinking racism that sees Captain Cook as the person who "discovered" Australia, or the country as "terra nullius" before his arrival can also affect us psychologically'. Anderson points out:

> Subtly but powerfully, such myths tell us that we are unimportant, insignificant, that 'our people' have not achieved anything and by implication we are unlikely to amount to much in the future.[53]

A second way in which racism affects health is because people may be reluctant to seek much-needed services from providers that they perceive to be unwelcoming or that they feel may hold negative stereotypes about them.

Third, health systems do not provide the same level of care to indigenous people as to other Australians. This 'systemic racism', Anderson concludes, 'is not necessarily the result of individual ill-will by practitioners, but a reflection of inappropriate assumptions made about particular racial groups'. The kind of racist incident that she experienced at school, then, is not a one-off episode that affects a single person, but institutional racism – 'a pattern of events and behaviours that contribute to the ill health and disadvantage suffered by First Australians'.[54]

When referring to ill-health, Boyle singled out trachoma, a bacterial infection of the eye, associated with poverty, that can cause complications including blindness. During the twentieth century, separate rooms for sleeping, running water and plumbed sewerage meant that trachoma disappeared from all developed countries – except Australia.[55] This communicable disease is still rife in many outback Aboriginal communities, with disease rates ranging from 2 to 50 per cent.[56] Other indices of ill-health include:

- a lower birth weight for indigenous than for non-indigenous people
- babies born to indigenous women twice as likely to die in their first year as those born to non-indigenous women
- heart and related conditions 1.2 times more common for indigenous people than for non-indigenous people

- the overall incidence rate of cancer slightly higher for indigenous people than for non-indigenous people, and indigenous peoples more likely to die from it than non-indigenous people
- the overall death rate for diabetes seven times higher for indigenous people than that for non-indigenous people
- indigenous adults almost three times more likely to feel high or very high levels of psychological distress than non-indigenous adults
- indigenous peoples more than twice as likely to be hospitalized for 'mental and behavioural disorders' as other Australians
- indigenous peoples twice as likely to die from 'intentional self-harm' as non-indigenous people
- end-stage kidney disease seven times more common for indigenous people than for non-indigenous people
- indigenous people twice as likely as other Australians to be admitted to hospital for injuries
- indigenous people almost three times more likely than other Australians to be admitted into hospital for a respiratory condition, and twice as likely to die from respiratory disease
- a hospitalization rate for indigenous people 1.3 times higher than that for non-indigenous people for diseases of the ear and mastoid process
- more indigenous adults than non-indigenous adults suffering from edentulism (losing all of their teeth), especially at younger ages
- communicable diseases almost all much higher for indigenous than non-indigenous Australians.[57]

Susan Allan documents an escalating wave of Aboriginal youth suicides which stem from the endemic unemployment, poverty and social problems afflicting indigenous communities. She quotes George Georgatos, a senior national consultant to the Aboriginal and Torres Strait Islander Suicide Prevention Evaluation Project, who states that there is a rapid increase in suicide numbers, with the median age of suicides getting younger, and the 'majority of the suicides … found within concentrations of acute poverty'.[58] According to the Australian Bureau of Statistics, between 2007 and 2011, 53 children under the age of 15 committed suicide in Australia, 17 of whom were Aboriginal. The rate of suicide for indigenous children was 1.2 per 100,000 – six times the rate for non-indigenous children. For Aboriginal youth aged between 15 to 24, the suicide rate is 42 per 100,000, compared with 8 per 100,000 for non-Aboriginal youth.[59]

In 2014 the Productivity Commission delivered a report, *Overcoming Indigenous Disadvantage*, which noted that, despite a slight improvement in life expectancy for the Aboriginal people, suicide rates, self-harm, mental health and incarceration had got worse, as had access to basic services. For example, admissions to hospital for intentional self-harm increased by 48 per cent between 2004–05 and 2012–13, and the proportion of adults reporting high or very high psychological distress rose from 27 to 30 per cent.[60]

Allan recounts the tragic story of Peter Little, an 11-year-old Aboriginal boy in the Western Australian city of Geraldton in 2014. Little was playing with other children outside his grandparents' house at around 5 pm, when he told one of the other children that he was going to kill himself and walked across the road into the bush. He was later found by a child hanging from a tree. He was rushed to the local hospital but pronounced dead. Peter Little was buried just metres from Julieka Dhu, a 22-year-old Aboriginal woman who died in police custody in the same year Little died, having been found dead in a police lockup, after being imprisoned for the non-payment of approximately $1,000 in various fines. Her boyfriend was imprisoned in the cell next to her. Warren Mundine, the government's chief indigenous adviser, argued that Peter Little's death was part of 'an epidemic ... quite frankly you are looking at a society in collapse. I am a father and I cannot get it through my head that at the age of eight or nine a child can't see a future for themselves.'[61]

At the end of 2013, the Tony Abbott government announced cuts of $13.4 million over four years to indigenous legal aid. In the 2014 May budget, cuts of $534 million over five years were announced to indigenous social programmes, including a $160 million cut to the indigenous health budget. The only increase was $54 million for seven new police stations in remote communities.[62]

Anderson refers to the debate centred on Abbott's stated intention to repeal Section 18C of the Racial Discrimination Act, which she argues, should be seen in the light of the evidence such as that I have outlined above. Section 18C 'makes it unlawful to 'offend, insult, humiliate or intimidate' a person or group because of their 'race, colour or national or ethnic origin'. Much of the debate over its repeal, she points out, has focused on issues of free speech versus morality (multiculturalism and good 'race relations' is a moral requirement). Opposing the amendment, Anderson argued that Aboriginal people need to educate all Australians that racism, however casual, however apparently light-hearted, however off the cuff, has implications for other people's health. It is worth quoting Anderson at length, as she makes links between health and general well-being and how these are crucially related to the retention of indigenous culture, but also to not being cut off from mainstream society:

> people – any people – cannot thrive if they are not connected. We have long known that as Aboriginal and Torres Strait Islander people,

we need to ... feel connected with our families, communities and cultures to have genuine health and wellbeing. But we are also part of this nation – an important part, I would argue – and must also therefore be connected to the rest of society, Racism cuts that connection. At the same time, racism cuts off non-Indigenous Australians from all the unique insights and experiences that we, Australia's First Peoples, have to offer. As a nation, we have to get over this idea that Aboriginal experience and ideas don't count. We need to get past the myth that everything significant on this continent began in 1788.[63]

Indentured Labour and Anti South Sea Islander Racism

Between 1863 and 1904, over 62,000 people from the Melanesian archipelagos provided the colony of Queensland with cheap labour power in the form of indentured workers for its emerging agricultural industries.[64] From 1863 to 1878, islanders were employed in cotton growing, sheep and cattle rearing, pearl shelling, fisheries and domestic service industries.[65] However, from 1880, when Melanesians were restricted to employment in 'tropical and semi-tropical agriculture', island labour was effectively concentrated in the cane fields.[66] Given the abolition of slavery, in the latter part of the nineteenth century indentured labour provided the intensive labour power that was required for the pre-mechanization sugar plantations. The islanders worked under limited-term contracts and for wages, but with similar working conditions to slaves. According to Reid Mortensen, the abuses that made indentured labour akin to slavery were first, 'the engagement of islanders who did not appreciate the nature or conditions of indentured service', combined with 'blatant misrepresentation', and second, physical abduction, euphemized as 'blackbird-hunting' or 'blackbirding'. Blackbirding entailed the 'enticing of islanders onto ships on the pretence that the crew wanted to barter or to offer them a short pleasure cruise, or ambushing villages and seizing the inhabitants'.[67]

At the time, it was believed that Europeans were unfit to work in the tropics. As one plantation owner put it:

> It has been conclusively proved ... that white men cannot and will not do the work done by niggers in the field, and ... that if white labour were available, it would only be at wages which the planters could never afford to pay. The sugar industry is entirely dependent upon coloured labour.[68]

Emma Roberts described the journey to Queensland, which was so treacherous that many islanders died en route, with little sympathy from the ships' masters. If heavy weather set in, islanders were confined below deck, which encouraged the spread of diseases, often with fatal results.[69] As Kay Saunders points out, the Queensland governor had openly declared that the life of a white man was more sacred than that of a black man.[70] Roberts also referred to the appalling working conditions and the failure to account for islanders' health or cultural requirements,[71] while Lyndon Megarrity noted that first-time recruits were paid less than one-tenth the wages of 'white ploughmen'.[72] Moreover, Saunders pointed to a study of plantation workers by two doctors in 1880 that reported that the kind of work performed was too strenuous for young recruits, with a high potential for mortality.[73]

Accommodation consisted of huts (which Melanesians often constructed themselves from grass) which were overcrowded and poorly ventilated, so they were breeding grounds for disease.[74] Food given to the labourers was mostly unpalatable meat with carbohydrates such as white bread or rice, unsuitable for the islanders who were commonly vegetarians in their home communities.[75] A high risk of infection, primarily because of poor living and working conditions, was very prevalent on plantation, with the mortality rate of South Sea Islanders (mainly young males) five to six times higher than the rate amongst the whole European population.[76]

The problem of disease was exacerbated by inadequate medical care for the islanders. The few hospitals that treated labourers had strict segregation policies, with islanders kept outside in 'rotten tents', even in seasons of severe rain, and forced to lie on the often flooded ground in saturated clothes and blankets. Islanders were all grouped together, irrespective of their medical problem, thus encouraging the rampant spread of disease.[77]

There is also documentation of abuse by employers such as beatings, withdrawal of food, deprival of leisure time and separation of couples.[78]

Debates over the importation of South Sea Islanders as cheap 'coloured' labour to engage in work that was thought unsuitable for European workers, and concerns over whether they were kidnapped slaves or indentured labourers, went right to the heart of arguments over the nature of the British-type society being established in northern Australia. At the same time, there were also serious worries about long-staying islanders who failed to return home after completing their initial contracts, as well as general concerns about the kidnapping of labour and an unacceptably high death rate among new recruits.[79] After the 1884 Pacific Island Labourers Amendment Act, the islanders were to be limited to field work in tropical agriculture, removing them from working in sugar mills, the pastoral and maritime industries, and effectively limiting them to the coast. There was a full exemption from this clause for all islanders who had arrived in

Queensland before 1 September 1879. This created restrictions on employment opportunities, the harbinger of the racist legislation introduced in the first years of the Commonwealth, discussed in the next section of this chapter.

The 1884 Act was the model for the Commonwealth legislation from 1901 to 1904, including the Pacific Islanders Labourers Act 1901 and the Immigration Restriction Act 1901. The former ordered the recruitment of the South Sea Islanders to cease after 1903, and gave the federal authorities the power to deport any islander found in Australia after December 1906. The only islanders allowed to stay were those who had arrived in Queensland prior to 1 September 1879, those working as crew on ships, and those granted certificates of exemption under the Immigration Restriction Act, which granted compensation to the sugar industry and ordered the introduction of white labour on a just wage.[80]

These two Acts provided the legislative basis for the white Australia policy (also discussed in the next section of this chapter). The 1884 Act had the effect of stratifying islanders on social class lines, with indentured labourers limited to tropical agriculture; time-expired labourers, some likewise limited to tropical agriculture and others who could work anywhere in the colony; and lastly 'ticket-holders', the pre-September 1879 immigrants who were bound only by the normal laws of Queensland.[81] The impact of deportation was dramatic: in 1902, 85.5 per cent of Queensland sugar was produced by 'coloured' labour, whereas by 1908, 87.9 per cent was produced by white labour.[82] However, about 2,500 South Sea Islanders managed to stay behind (both legally and illegally), often by marrying into Aboriginal communities.[83]

Remaining islanders were forced to assume subjugated positions in society through segregation; trains had carriages specifically for non-Europeans, and islanders had to purchase goods from 'Kanaka stores'.[84] From 1909 until 1942 South Sea Islanders living in Australia experienced considerable hardship: legislation prohibited their employment in the sugar industry, unions resisted their employment elsewhere, and they could not obtain financial assistance from banks. Moreover, without extended family in Australia to assist and support them, the ageing original South Sea Islanders faced a great deal of hardship in the lead-up to the Second World War.[85]

The Australian Human Rights Commission argues that islanders were usually treated with racism similar to that faced by Aboriginal people.[86] For example, in Central Queensland:

Islander women were relegated to the 'black ward' at Rockhampton Base Hospital, which was separated from the main maternity section and overlooked the morgue. Islander and Aboriginal women gave birth in their beds, while the labour ward was the preserve of white women. Isolated and out of earshot, at the end of the veranda, they found the experience frightening.[87]

There were at least 40 pieces of racist Queensland legislation between 1900 and 1940, directed at South Sea Islanders who had stayed on in Australia.[88] Most of these laws restricted employment and income-earning opportunities, while the Liquor Act 1912 prohibited the supply of alcohol to islanders. At the same time, trade unions refused membership to islanders and industrial awards restricted employment to union members.[89] Full citizenship was not granted until 1967, three years after the ban on 'coloured labour' in the sugar industry ended. Many Australians at the time did not differentiate between South Sea Islanders and Aboriginal people, discriminating against both groups equally. Thus research by the Royal Commission into Human Relationships in 1977 reported that South Sea Islanders were not eligible for benefits provided for Aboriginal people unless they identified as being Aboriginal, thereby giving up their South Sea Islander origins.[90]

In 1992, the Human Rights and Equal Opportunity Commission (HREOC) documented detailed findings of the ongoing disadvantage faced by Australian South Sea Islanders as a result of racist practices by governments and the general community over the previous century. For example, the report noted that, although more than two-thirds of Australians at the time were home owners, this was the case for less than one-third of islanders. In response to the report, in 1994 the Commonwealth government officially recognized the Australian South Sea Islander community as 'a distinct ethnic group in Australia with its own history and culture.'[91] Two years later, consultations between the government and Australian South Sea Islander communities in Queensland and northern NSW made public that, as a result of the recognition, many South Sea Islanders were unable to access the indigenous services they had used prior to recognition. In 2000 the Queensland government formally recognized Australian South Sea Islanders as a distinct ethnic and cultural group, and acknowledged their contribution to Queensland's development. The government also recognized the discrimination, injustice, disadvantage and prejudice experienced by Australian South Sea Islanders throughout history, and the significant disadvantage the community still faces.[92]

South Sea Islander Peoples Today

In 2013, South Sea Islander people called on the Commonwealth government to make a formal apology for the hardships endured by their ancestors,[93] and in 2014, they pushed to be included as a separate ethnic group in Australia's 2016 national census.[94] The Queensland Australian South Sea Islander Survey of 2014 found a large degree of dissatisfaction. For example, 'less [than] half of respondents (43.7 per cent) felt the Queensland Government did a good job of acknowledging the unique history and culture of Australian South Sea Islanders', while less than a quarter (23.0 per cent) felt 'Queenslanders in general acknowledged Australian South Sea Islanders' cultural uniqueness'.[95] The following issues were identified by the South Sea Islanders:

- Australian South Sea Islander history and culture should be taught as a part of Queensland's school curriculum.
- The economic contribution of Australian South Sea Islanders and their ancestors should be properly recognized.
- There should be better acknowledgement of the harsh and often discriminatory history of Australian South Sea Islanders.
- There should be greater acknowledgement of Australian South Sea Islanders' distinct ethnicity (in relation to Aboriginal and Torres Strait Islanders and other culturally diverse peoples).
- There should be a greater understanding of Australian South Sea Islander associations with their ancestors' original home islands, extended family connections and the problems caused by past removals.
- Specific identification, assistance, consultation and action be granted to Australian South Sea Islanders.[96]

In 2015, over 20 years later, the Commonwealth government officially recognized the islanders as a distinct ethnic group. South Sea Islander Greg Sutherland, chair of the National South Sea Islander Working Group, whose mother is a direct descendant of labourers were brought from Vanuatu to Queensland and northern NSW to work on cane farms, told ABC News that not much has changed, and that 'big problems remain around unemployment, housing, health and education'. Sutherland went on to suggest that the reason for lack of change is that people don't like to recognize that South Sea Islanders are the equivalent of the enslaved peoples of the United States (see Chapter 2 for a discussion of the latter).[97]

In the same programme, Liberal National Party of Queensland (LNP) backbencher George Christensen, who represents a seat which includes one of the highest populations of Australian South Sea Islanders in the country, reported that a parliamentary inquiry revisiting recognition, which had looked at what had been achieved in the previous 20 years, found very little evidence of efforts to address the social and economic disadvantage – despite the recommendations from HREOC, and a commitment that each and every one of the recommendations be implemented. Reporter Melissa Maddison pointed out that the inquiry was shocked to hear that when some Australian South Sea Islanders visit hospitals, they are told to just tick the Aboriginal or Torres Strait Islander (ATSI) box, so that they can access services. To clarify, Sutherland stated that 'South Sea Islanders fully appreciate, fully understand and fully acknowledge that Aboriginal people and Torres Strait Islander people are the Indigenous peoples of Australia. We were the original boat people.'[98]

Anti-Asian Racism

Anti-Chinese Racism

In 1851 a 'grain of gold' was discovered in a waterhole near Bathurst, NSW. The ensuing gold rush was followed by neighbouring Victoria, which yielded even more gold. As a result the total population of Australia trebled from 430,000 in 1851 to 1.7 million in 1871. After NSW and Victoria, deposits were uncovered throughout most of Australia. Gold's discovery accelerated the abolition of convict transportation to Australia, which was in effect giving free passage to potential gold diggers who would not want to work for a living when a fortune awaited them on the goldfields.[99]

Of the new immigrants to Australia, 40,000 were Chinese, and in 1861 Chinese immigrants made up 3.3 per cent of the Australian population.[100] Phil Griffiths has noted that central to the 'Chinese experience in Australia has been racism and political exclusion'.[101] From 1854 onwards, according to Ian Welch, media artists started presenting a variety of racist images, at first highlighting 'humorous' perceived 'ethnic differences', but in later years becoming increasingly malicious.[102] Anti-Chinese laws were passed in 1855 in Victoria, 1857 in South Australia (SA) and 1861 in NSW. While these were soon repealed because the 'danger' represented by large-scale Chinese immigration was thought to have passed, the second round of anti-Chinese laws, starting in Queensland in 1877, and then SA, NSW and Victoria in 1881, were never repealed. In all cases these were strengthened in the late 1880s as a result of the sense of impending disaster created in 1887–88, when the fear of a potential Chinese invasion of the north of Australia, which was seen as providing an 'open door', reached crisis point.[103]

The years 1877–88 saw a rise in trade union militancy, culminating in great strikes in 1890 and 1891. With the formation of Labor parties in

NSW, Queensland, SA and Victoria, Griffiths argues that 'a more radical, quasi-socialist outlook took root amongst many working class people', and there is good reason to believe that anti-Chinese racism was used to limit this challenge from below.[104] James Supple suggests that the main reason for moving towards the exclusion of Chinese workers, and what eventually became the white Australia policy, was strategic fears that large-scale Asian immigration would create a 'fifth column' that would side with China in the event of a war. Asians, particularly Chinese immigrants, Supple points out, were seen as competitors with Europeans in a race to colonize Australia.[105]

According to the Gold! website, working-class anti-Chinese racism had its beginnings in 1854, when an angry group of European and American miners met in Bendigo, Victoria, and declared that a 'general and unanimous rising should take place … for the purpose of driving the Chinese off the goldfield'. However, local constables acted quickly to prevent the uprising. The event was only the beginning of greater anti-Chinese tensions. Gold! has provided details of some of the anti-Chinese racist violence on the gold fields:

- At Buckland River gold field, Victoria in 1857, following a meeting of white miners, a small group began to charge through the Chinese camp, tearing down tents and demanding that the Chinese leave. After a tense but orderly few minutes, acts of violence increased as the European crowd gained momentum. With the mob shouting, 'Come on and let us drive the long tailed devils off at once', Chinese miners were trampled, robbed and beaten. A European wife of a Chinese miner was beaten and nearly killed, another Chinese miner had his finger severed for a gold ring, as tents, a joss house and other property were looted and burned around them. There were 2,500 Chinese miners expelled from their camps, three died from exposure and another was said to have drowned. All but four of the arrested white rioters were acquitted, as local juries believed their anger was understandable.
- In Ararat, Victoria, after a violent incident in a Chinese store, a small group charged a Chinese camp. Eyewitnesses stated that European and American diggers attacked the Chinese with timber and axe handles, felling Chinese 'senseless to the earth' as 'Chinamen were to be seen flying thick and numerous, like scattered sheep before dogs'. The Chinese were finally forced from the field in 1858.
- At Lambing Flat, NSW, a Miner's Protective League formed, petitioning for the removal of the Chinese 'for the protection of native industry'. In 1861, a brawl resulted from a 'roll-up' and 1,500 Chinese fled. With the guidance of police, the Chinese returned to the field. A full brass

band trumpeting 'Rule Britannia' fuelled 2,000 to 3,000 white diggers marching on the Chinese camp. The ringleaders had made anti-Chinese banners, and marched on the unprepared Chinese shouting and chanting themselves into a frenzy. They hunted and whipped the Chinese men, knocking them down with the butt ends of their whips, in many cases pulling their pigtails out by the roots, and planting them on their banners. They then set fire to the camp. Miners who stayed to hide their gold in mine shafts were buried alive. Over 1,000 Chinese miners fled, and almost 500 were injured. Once peace was restored, police arrested three white miners involved in the riot. This brought 3,000 angry miners to the police camp, and the police released the prisoners.[106]

As Griffiths explains, three great issues came together in 1887, when the Chinese government sent a special mission to Australia to report on the conditions faced by its people living in the country: 'the renaissance of Chinese military might; the belief that China was now Britain's key ally in the East; and loss of confidence in British loyalty towards Australian interests'.[107] The agenda for their visit was spelled out in a journal article which attacked countries that hunger 'for land they do not and cannot make use of', expressed outrage at the abuses suffered by Chinese people in various colonies, pointed to China's revitalized military, and promised that one of the immediate aims of Chinese foreign policy would be 'the amelioration of the condition of her subjects residing in foreign parts'.[108]

After the visit, the *Sydney Morning Herald* interpellated its readers that public concern over Chinese immigration had been significantly increased by their visit, and that there was 'the belief that [their] report ... is likely to be followed by a Chinese invasion of Australia'.[109] It was at this moment, Griffiths points out, in the weeks following the visit of the Commissioners, that the Premier of Victoria initiated a discussion in 1887 among colonial premiers about joint legislation to further restrict Chinese immigration.[110] As the premier put it at the time:

Members of the European family of nations joining our community become amalgamated with the general population ... their habits of life, their style of civilization, their religion and morals, and their physique, are so much on an equality with our own that they blend readily with the population and are heartily welcome. The Chinese stand out in marked contrast ... and occupy an isolated position in every community where they are found .... The Chinese, from all points of view, are so entirely dissimilar as to render a blending of the peoples out of the question.[111]

As Griffiths argues, key figures in the colonial ruling class feared the development of a racially divided population, and drew on 'the mainstream liberal theory of anti-slavery, and John Stuart Mill's theory that representative government required social homogeneity to construct and legitimise their position'. Comments, articles and speeches, Griffiths points out, by influential colonial figures often combined elements of both. The supposed 'servility' of Chinese people, for example, could support the notion that their presence in numbers might lead to some form of quasi-slavery and be an expression of the belief that cultural differences between Chinese and Europeans made assimilation impossible. As Griffiths puts it:

> These two influences were brought together by Australian perceptions of the experience of the United States. Slavery had created corrupt, backward and immoral societies in the South and those two incompatible systems, slavery and free labour, had led to an appalling civil war that had cost a million lives. After the civil war, African-Americans remained unassimilated and racial conflict was seen as endemic. The majority ruling-class opinion in Australia was to avoid both aspects of American racial division.[112]

Australia became a country in its own right, rather than six colonies as it was previously, in 1901,[113] and white Australia was made law in the same year by the Immigration Restriction Act. This Act set in motion a dictation test for would-be immigrants, which could be in any European language. In 1905, the Act was changed so it could be given in any language at all. The Test was given 805 times in 1902–03, with 46 people passing, and 554 times in 1904–09, with only six people successful. After 1909 no person passed the dictation test, and people who failed were refused entry or deported. The Act, frequently amended, remained in force until 1958.[114]

The white Australia policy was also, Griffiths argues, a means to secure their physical control over a vast portion of the earth's land mass in the face of the supposed threat from China, and the need to incorporate the middle and working classes into a new Australian nationalism, loyal to the British Empire. As Griffiths points out, 'the anti-Chinese movement served to limit and contain the development of class consciousness in Australia'. Key ruling-class leaders were able to 'construct a new hegemonic ideology of Australian nationalism that was white rather than English'. A major factor in this incorporation was the anti-Chinese laws which, with the willingness of the labour movement to mobilize against Chinese immigration, helped drive through white Australia. Griffiths concludes that this was the final act in the long struggle by capital to get the kind of economy and labour force they wanted: 'free' and white wage labour, although as we have seen, for reasons outlined above, rural Aboriginal labour remained unfree for many decades.[115]

Supple notes a major need of the ruling class to move to federation:

> The colonial ruling class had possession of an entire continent, large parts of which had no permanent European inhabitants, in particular the tropical north closest to Asia. Defence was one of the key motivating factors for the ruling classes of the British colonies spread across Australia to adopt Federation.[116]

Debates over immigration policy at the time of Federation, Chad Cooper points out, 'reveal how federal parliamentarians managed the complex and arguably contradictory task of fostering a national ideology based on racial exclusivity whilst remaining a civilised member of a diverse British Empire'. The new Parliament, he goes on, had to manage the sometimes competing interests of the fledgling 'independent' Australia, with those of the British Empire which was its imperial overlord, and whose 'size and reach' meant that the majority of British subjects were Indian or African.[117] Moreover, the United Kingdom had important trade and strategic interests in China and Japan. For these reasons, its government was opposed to overt racism on the part of Australia.[118] As Cooper puts it, how 'to build and maintain a white Australia without upsetting the Empire was clearly a matter of concern to the new Parliament'.[119] While some contributors to the debate hedged their bets, Australia's first prime minister, Sir Edmund Barton, was unequivocal:

> I do not think either that the doctrine of the equality of man was really ever intended to include racial equality. There is no racial equality. There is that basic inequality. These races are, in comparison with white races – I think no one wants convincing of this fact – unequal and inferior. The doctrine of the equality of man was never intended to apply to the equality of the Englishman and the Chinaman. There is a deep-set difference, and we see no prospect and no promise of its ever being effaced. Nothing in this world can put these two races upon an equality [sic]. Nothing we can do by cultivation, by refinement, or by anything else will make some races equal to others.[120]

So the meaning of equality is that which exists between white men. As Griffiths has argued, by 'making White Australia fundamental to national identity, the ruling class created the illusion of a common interest between workers and employers, and between ordinary Australians and the blood-soaked British Empire'.[121] The 'white Australia' policy dominated Australian politics for much of the twentieth century, but immigration was mediated by Anglo-Celtic racism, resulting in a hierarchical racialized and gender-segmented labour market, with four main groups: white English-speaking immigrant males, non-English-speaking immigrant males, English-speaking immigrant women and non-English-speaking immigrant women.[122] Beneath these four segments were and are, as we have seen, indigenous men and women, marginalized to permanently unemployed, fringe-dweller status.[123]

Anti-Japanese Racism

If China was viewed as a threat to Anglo-Australian hegemony over the continent in the nineteenth century, Japan played that role in the twentieth.[124] During my year of teaching at Macquarie University in 1985, living in a small community on the North Shore of Sydney, the only place you could go for a beer was the local RSL (Returned and Services League). The RSL badge has a crown at the top, signifying allegiance to the Queen. Below the crown are the national flowers of Australia, Wales, England, Scotland and Ireland. I do not remember the exact wording on the copy of the constitution that the RSL club gave me, but I do remember it made a reference to loyalty to the British Empire written in the present tense. During a three-way conversation with my Anglo-Australian co-sponsors, very soon after joining, the one of them mentioned casually that 'the only good Jap is a dead one'. When I challenged this, he asked me why. I told him that it was racist. He then asked me what my politics were, and I told him I was antiracist and a socialist, whereupon he said that had he known that, he wouldn't have co-sponsored me.[125]

When the Immigration Restriction Act was introduced into parliament, attorney-general and future prime minister Alfred Deakin declared it was 'primarily aimed against the Japanese' and to 'uphold the purity of the British race and exclude alien Asiatics as well as the people of Japan'.[126] A few years later, Japan's victory over Russia in their 1904–05 war, according to Griffiths, 'saw militarism grip Australian politics'. The Deakin government, he went on, supported by Labor, flouted Britain and started building an independent Australian navy, at huge expense, with money that he claimed had been earmarked for unemployment benefits and pensions.[127] The UK government soon used fear of Japan to get the Australian Labor government of 1910–13 to prepare for war against Germany, a war in which 60,000 young Australians would die.[128] After the First World War, at the Versailles Peace Conference of 1919, Japan tried to get a resolution passed against racism, while the Japanese delegation proposed a 'racial equality clause' in the Covenant of the League of Nations:

The equality of nations being a basic principle of the League of Nations, the High Contracting Parties agree to accord, as soon as possible, to all alien nationals of States members of the League, equal and just treatment in every respect, making no distinction, either in law or in fact, on account of their race or nationality.[129]

Australian Prime Minister Billy Hughes opposed the motion, announcing at a meeting that 'ninety-five out of one hundred Australians rejected the very idea of equality'.[130]

By the time of Pearl Harbor in December 1941 (when Japan made a surprise attack on American soil during the Second World War at a naval base near Honolulu, Hawaii), Griffiths argues that 'Australians had been conditioned to expect a "race war" for more than forty years'.[131] Mary Nakashiba described how her life was completely changed at that time. She and her family were arrested at their Darwin home, then transported south by ship. Disembarking after two weeks in Sydney, the 15-year-old was accosted by an angry mob as she stepped off the gangplank. As she put it:

They were screaming, 'Kill them! Shoot the bastards!' .... I couldn't believe it – these were Australians, people of my own country. I'll never forget it. I was in total, utter shock. That was the point that I realised my life would never be the same. [132]

As Christine Piper explains, despite being born in Australia, Mary and her siblings were considered 'enemy aliens', along with their Japanese-born father who had migrated to Australia 50 years earlier. Mary's brother was also separated from the family and sent to the men's camp. Her mother objected because he was only 17 years old. 'But the soldier said, "No, he's got to go." We didn't hear from him until we were all released.' Even though Mary's mother was free to go, she decided to stay with her family and they spent three years behind barbed wire in rural Victoria. Although there was scant evidence that civilians were acting as spies, Piper points out, people of Japanese origin were interned as 'a preventative measure' and most were repatriated to Japan when the war was over, thus diminishing their ability to speak out about their experience. Despite being grouped together under the banner of 'enemy alien', the 4,301 Japanese civilians internees in Australia were extremely heterogeneous and many did not even share the same language, some having come from Allied-controlled countries such as the Dutch East Indies, New Caledonia, Vanuatu and the Solomon Islands. As Piper notes, the authorities took a 'collar the lot' approach, interning 98 per cent of all male Japanese 'aliens' registered in Australia, compared with 32 per cent of Italian and German males. Internees suffered from loss of assets: businesses were looted, properties destroyed, belongings stolen and vehicles misappropriated. After Japan surrendered, following the dropping of atomic bombs on the cities of Hiroshima and Nagasaki, nearly all Japanese internees were forcibly repatriated to Japan unless they were born in Australia or had an Australian-born spouse. Some had lived in Australia for more than 50 years.

The official white Australia policy ended only when it became a liability, as Asian countries gained independence after the war, and as the policy damaged trade with the developing countries. So, as Griffiths concludes, there were strong incentives to get rid of it. He also singles out the role of the Communist Party of Australia in building working-class sympathy for Asian people. Finally, the mass movements against the Vietnam War in which Australia was involved for over a decade 'had to confront the racism of pro-war arguments which were rooted in the myth of the "yellow peril"', as millions of ordinary Australians came to see the white Australia policy as reactionary. In 1975, the policy was completely dismantled by the Gough Whitlam Labor government with the passing of the Racial Discrimination Act. However, the Act did not do away with anti-Japanese racism. In 1980 the Iwasaki tourist development in Queensland was bombed, and in the late 1980s there was a racist campaign against Japanese investment in Australia and a proposed hi-tech city in the country.[133]

Anti-Asian Racism Today

On an Australian talk show in late 2014, mining multi-millionaire and founder of the right-wing Palmer United Party Clive Palmer referred to officials in Beijing as 'Chinese mongrels' who were trying to 'take over this country'. (He later apologized after Prime Minister Abbott and China's Ministry of Foreign Affairs condemned his remarks.) The following day, a then member of Palmer United, Senator Jacqui Lambie, stated that successive governments had failed to build an Australian military capable of stopping 'our grandchildren from becoming slaves' to the Chinese.[134]

It is not just small right-wing populist parties that continue the anti-Asian rhetoric of the nineteenth and twentieth centuries. In 1970, Humphrey McQueen said of the Australian Labor Party, which had its genesis in the early 1890s, that it 'was racist before it was socialist'.[135] Nearly half a century later, writing in Australia's most popular newspaper, the right-wing *The Australian*, commentator Tony Bramston described a speech by Labor Party leader Bill Shorten in 2014 as 'inexcusable'. As Bramston put it, in 'opposing the mooted purchase of Japanese submarines, Shorten roused his flag-waving union audience with references to race, fear and protectionism'. 'Under Labor', he promised, 'we will build ships and submarines in Australia because we love this country!' His overtly nationalist audience responded with wild cheers. He moved on to the historical fear of invasion, which as Bramston said is 'deeply ingrained in the psyche of old Australia': 'For goodness sake, Tony Abbott, buy a map of the world', he said. 'We are an island, Tony Abbott, and our navy matters'. Australian Manufacturing Workers Union national secretary Paul Bastian responded: 'Japanese subs on the way. Do you feel betrayed?' to which the union workers responded 'Yes!'

Referring to events during the Second World War, one of them added, 'Last time we had Jap subs, they were in bloody Sydney Harbour'. As Bramston said, this gave Shorten the chance to reject this view and make it clear that Labor opposed importing submarines because it undermined the local shipbuilding industry and risked jobs, however retrograde such a view is. Instead Shorten used the moment to amplify the racist rhetoric: 'This is a government with a short memory. In the Second World War, 366 merchant ships were sunk off Australia'. Bramston concluded that 'the figure was wrong but the message was clear'.[136] Some 70 years after the war ended, Japan was still Australia's enemy.

Earlier in the same year (2014) a man posted on YouTube a video of the interaction between a white Australian woman and an Asian Australian woman on a train. These included the white woman pulling her eyes back into slants and yelling out a string of 'gook' abuses, mocking the man holding the camera, and repeatedly calling him a 'bogan' (a derogatory term for the white working class that has been compared to the United Kingdom word 'chav' and the US 'white trash'). She claimed that he 'can't get a regular girlfriend, he's got to get an Asian' (the man pointed out that he was unrelated to the Asian Australian, and was married to someone else). The white racist also stated that 'he's too lazy to jerk-off, he can only get a gook!' She also repeatedly imitated the Asian Australian's accent in a very racist way, before asking her 'What's wrong with Hong Kong? Why did you come to this country? This is our country'. The white Australian woman concluded that the Asian Australian woman was with the 'bogan' (although they had said she wasn't) because 'she probably thinks he's rich'. The white woman later apologized, excusing her racist behaviour on the grounds that she was having a bad day, couldn't get a job and had been swindled out of a large sum of money by a man she had met on a dating site.[137]

This incident was followed at a later date by further racist abuse of an Asian Australian on a train by an Aboriginal woman. It was part of a series of abuses on public transport against people of Asian descent in Australia starting in 2013, including one by a group of teenage girls against a female Asian passenger, and a man criticizing some Asian tourists on a Sydney bus.[138]

OLDER NON-COLOUR-CODED RACISM

Anti-Irish Racism

On 12 March 1868, during the first ever visit to Australia by a member of the British Royal family, Prince Alfred, one of Queen Victoria's sons, was the victim of an unsuccessful assassination attempt in Sydney by an Irish man, Henry James O'Farrell.[139] Colonial writer Elizabeth Rickets Hall described O'Farrell as a 'miscreant' who at one stage was said to be involved with the Fenians (fighters for Irish independence). However, she noted, it was 'most unlikely that he was', with some saying he was insane 'as his defence maintained'. O'Farrell's 'obsession with Fenianism and the wrongs of Ireland', she suggested, caused his erratic behavior.[140]

After the shooting, there were public 'indignation meetings' around the country. Australians were aware of Fenian 'terrorism' in England from reports in newspapers, but it was the attempted assassination that spawned an anti-Irish Catholic and non-loyalist movement which lasted for many years. By the end of 1868, the Orange movement in Australia had become ultra-British and ultra-Protestant, with racism directed at all people of Irish descent, irrespective of religion.

At the time of the attempted assassination Henry Parkes was the colonial secretary and the 'principal ministerial contact with the head of the Prince's entourage'.[141] According to historian Charles Manning, Parkes had by that time 'degenerated into a political demigod with Czar-like propensities, who had no other object in life than to crush his political foes and hold political power'. In pursuit of this, he drummed up anti-Irish and anti-Catholic sentiment into a wave of hysteria.[142] Parkes had previously referred to the Irish as 'jabbering baboons and disruptive trouble makers'.[143] The Irish, he now claimed, multiplied too fast, the Church had become a political movement, the priests a coven of spies, and he had it on good authority that the Fenians had planned the murder of the Prince.[144] According to Jeff Shaw:

> The uproar in Parliament that followed these repeated utterances was erased from Hansard, fist fights broke out on the floor of the Assembly, and Protestant women outside in Macquarie Street kissed Parkes, the new anti-papist hero. Parkes modestly admitted in

meetings he was an instrument and vessel of Almighty God, chosen specially by Jehovah to administer New South Wales.[145]

In private, Shaw claims, 'fearing their votes, he reassured the Irish Catholics that he had their best interests at heart'. Courting the Irish vote was also an integral part of the white Australia policy. Indeed, the most significant example of colonial ruling-class determination to build a homogeneous society, Griffiths suggests, was its handling of Irish Catholic immigration and assimilation. As he explains, 'colonial governments wanted as much labour as possible and poor Irish Catholics were easier to get as potential immigrants, but their politics and religion were unwelcome'. Despite NSW premier Henry Parkes's militant Protestantism, for example, the campaigns against Chinese immigration actually succeeded in uniting Catholics and Protestants, creating the impression of a common interest amongst 'white' people. Griffiths summarizes the meaning of white Australia:

> This … is the real significance of the concept of a 'white' Australia. Any attempt to develop a nationalism that described itself as 'English' or 'British' would alienate a substantial proportion of Irish Catholics. 'White Australia' meant that immigrants of Irish, and especially Catholic origin, could identify with Australia and Australian nationalism, even if some found it difficult to identify with the empire to which the Australian state was committed. This also applied to the substantial numbers of northern European immigrants, whom most politicians believed could assimilate easily into their 'British' society.[146]

Anti-Irish Racism Today

In May 2014 Padraig Gaffney, originally from Lanesborough in Co. Longford and who had lived in Australia for ten years, was fined A$10,000 after getting drunk, and causing damage to his hotel by setting off the fire hydrant. He had travelled from Queensland to Melbourne for a romantic break to celebrate his birthday with his girlfriend, to whom he intended to propose. When police had knocked on the door of Gaffney's room, he told them he had no memory of activating the fire hydrant. He reportedly told the police that he was 'Sorry, so sorry.' Asked why he had flooded the hotel, Gaffney said to the court, 'Why would anyone have a reason for that? I'd just like to say I'm very, very sorry. I can't remember a goddamn thing.' Gaffney was quoted as saying, 'This entire thing has ruined my life completely.'[147]

The headline in *The Age* newspaper was 'Drunk Paddy's $500k flood of tears', referring to the amount of damage it was claimed he had caused. This was followed by incessant Australian national media 'jokes': 'Isn't that what all ye Irish do down here?' 'Ah, ye Paddys always drinking or fighting.' Gaffney was so affected by this racist abuse that he committed suicide. Campaigner Eoin Hahessy commented that the destruction of some floors of a hotel was 'undeserving of a national punch line'. Racism 'towards the Irish, cloaked in a smile, is extremely common Down Under. It starts with your accent and progresses to your pronunciation. The Irish inability to express "th" is a constant source of merriment.' Hahessy goes on to refer to a Dubliner who, when applying for a job in 'a respected organisation', was greeted by the laughing HR manager: 'I must tell you why I am laughing, my colleague said to me "don't mention potatoes"'. As Hahessy notes, this is not 'something to cause you to flock to the barricades', but it nevertheless shows how acceptable it is to be racist against the Irish in Australia. Hahessy also describes how Alan Joyce, CEO of Qantas, was mocked in *The Australian* when making a statement in relation to an engine explosion investigation: 'Tiz too arly ter judge waaat dat issue is an' 'oy long it 'ill take ter be fixed … It cud be ahn issue wi' de casin' or it cud be an issue wi' de turbo-ines.' A few years earlier, Joyce received a typed letter sent to his home, which read, 'It's coming soon Paddy. You can't even see it! The Unions will fight you …. Qantas is our airline, started & staffed by Australians, not foreign filth like you. All your evil plans … will come back to you very swiftly, & kick you (sic) Irish FOREIGN ARSE out of the country.'[148]

Some four months after Gaffney killed himself, the *West Australian* published a cartoon portraying four Irish nurses all called Colleen dancing an Irish jig with a leprechaun at the bedside of two patients. This was in response to a row over the recruitment of 150 Irish nurses in Western Australia, which the Australian Nursing Federation had said unfairly prioritized the employment of foreign nurses over Australians.[149]

Antisemitism

Antisemitism as a form of non-colour-coded racism has a long history in Australia, particularly in ruling-class circles. As Andrew Markus notes:

> open expression of anti-Semitism and a degree of discrimination was a feature of Australian life. The Jewish immigrants who arrived in the inter-war period, particularly the larger numbers of the late 1930s, faced open hostility. This was manifested in newspapers, particularly *Smith's Weekly* and *The Bulletin*, and expressed by some

members of federal and state parliaments. In the immediate pre- and post-war periods, openly racist comments could still be made and limitations were placed on economic and social interaction with Jews. Discrimination was entrenched in some of the professions, including the law; Jews were denied admittance to the Melbourne Stock Exchange and membership of the Melbourne Club, tennis and golf clubs.[150]

As Tess Lee Ack explains, antisemitism flourished in the 1930s as the Nazis came to power in Germany, and with the rise of Australian fascist movements, the best-known being the New Guard, founded in February 1931.[151] It came as a result of a period of intense class struggle and working-class radicalization that led to the election of a reformist state Labor government amidst the worst economic crisis in the history of world capitalism. Sections of business and the ruling class began to encourage fascism.[152] At one point the New Guard made plans to kidnap the NSW premier and stage a coup d'état to place NSW under martial law. There was open admiration for Benito Mussolini and Italian fascism, and the way he had banned all opposition political parties and newspapers. For example, according to Tom Orsag, when he returned from Italy in 1923, the Nationalist Premier of Victoria, Harry S. W. Lawson, proclaimed Mussolini as the one 'whom Providence wanted to lead Italy', while the manager of the Melbourne branch of the Australian Bank of Commerce described him as 'certainly one of the most wonderful men I have ever seen'.[153] During the 1925 seafarers' strike, the *Sydney Morning Herald* interpellated its readers that 'Italy … was only saved from Red Dominance by the heroic remedy of Fascism – a dreadful medicine for sure, and yet less bitter than the plague it stopped.'[154] During Anzac Day parades from 1930 to 1937, Italian fascists marched as a distinct group, with their trademark salutes drawing no adverse comments in the newspapers. As Orsag points out, anti-democratic ideas became respectable, and the press argued openly that militias might be necessary if Labor was re-elected or things got 'out of hand'.[155]

New Guard's leader, Eric Campbell, was a Sydney solicitor who took pride in his descent from Australia's 'elite, pioneering stock'.[156] In 1933, he went to Europe to make contact with leading fascists in Germany and Italy, as well as Sir Oswald Mosley in Britain.[157] As Lee Ack points out, typical 'of a fascist organisation, the membership of the New Guard "largely comprised members of the petty bourgeoisie, insurance clerks, motor garage proprietors and small businessmen."'[158] However, Moore (quoted here) goes on, fascism was admired and supported by many among Australia's ruling class, including future Liberal Prime Minister Robert Menzies, as well as senior figures in the police, government, the church, academia and business. While Lee Ack concludes that it could be argued such support in some cases owed more to fear and hatred of the working class, there was no repudiation or criticism of antisemitism.[159]

Between 1939 and 1953 immigrants to Australia had to declare in writing whether they were 'Jewish', and from 1946 a numerical quota limited Jewish passengers on ships and planes travelling to Australia. In addition, Jews were excluded from participation in the first stage of the Displaced Persons (DP) programme. On the other hand, there was lax screening of non-Jewish DPs, resulting in the admission of a number of war criminals.[160]

Mark Aarons has estimated that hundreds of fascists and Nazi collaborators were accepted as immigrants between 1947 and 1951, a number of whom found an amiable political home in the Liberal Party. One example was Lyenko Urbanchich, dubbed 'little Goebbels' by the Yugoslav War Crimes Commission, who became a powerful force in the NSW Liberal Party.[161]

Antisemitism Today

Late in 2013, eight or so young men shouting antisemitic abuse, including 'F•••ing Jews', violently attacked four men and a woman as they returned from a Shabbat (the Jewish day of rest) evening meal in Bondi Beach.[162] The Jewish group sustained injuries including a fractured skull, facial fractures, a broken nose, cuts and bruising, with television footage showing victims bleeding profusely from their heads and faces. Jeremy Jones of the Australia/Israel and Jewish Affairs Council, who has been tracking antisemitic incidents for 25 years, described the incident as the most extreme that he had heard of in the country.[163]

The number of antisemitic physical assaults trebled to 15 between 1 October 2013 and 30 September 2014, according to the Executive Council of Australian Jewry's (ECAJ's) annual antisemitism report. The majority of these attacks (eleven) took place in NSW, while two took place in Victoria and one in each of Western Australia and Queensland. The most serious incident apart from the assault in Bondi was an attack on a 28-year-old man wearing a T-shirt with Hebrew writing on it in Melbourne.

The author of the report, Julie Nathan, put much blame on the media which, she argues, helped antisemitism move from the margins of society to the mainstream. Nathan highlights three instances: an article in the *Sunday Mail* of Adelaide, in which it was claimed that Jews were 'oppressive' while Palestinians were 'the best, kindest, most stoic and eloquent people'; antisemitic comments that were left unmoderated on the ABC's

Four Corners Facebook page for up to five weeks; and a cartoon in the *Sydney Morning Herald*, which showed a classic negative stereotype of a Jew with a hook nose, kippah and a Magen David (Star of David) on the back of his chair looking over Gaza while holding a remote.[164] As Nathan puts it in the report:

> When major media outlets, including the national broadcaster, are prepared to publish or host unsubstantiated claims and irrational bias, that is combined with outright demonising of Jews, then a signal is sent that anti-Semitism is acceptable and even respectable, and Jew-haters feel emboldened to promote their views and to act on them.[165]

Nathan singles out another incident of antisemitic terror in the Executive Summary of the ECAJ report: the invasion of a school bus in Sydney in August by a group of drunks, and the threats and intimidation they directed at young Jewish children on board, after which Jewish parents were quoted in the media as being afraid to send their children to school. Nathan concluded:

> The year in review began with a vicious physical assault in Bondi against five Jews walking home on the Sabbath, and ended with the fallout from the Israel–Gaza war and neo-Nazi leaflets being letterboxed on the Jewish New Year in Sydney suburbs with a high percentage of Jewish residents. These events bookended a year of heightened antisemitic activity in Australia in comparison to the previous year.[166]

Overall between 1 October 2013 and 30 September 2014, the total number of antisemitic incidents, which includes physical assaults; abuse; harassment or intimidation; property damage and vandalism; graffiti; and threats via email, Facebook, mail, telephone and posters, logged by the Jewish community roof bodies in each state and the ACT, the community security groups and the ECAJ, increased from 231 in 2013 to 312 in 2014, an annual increase of 35.06 per cent.[167] However, it is known that other organizations and individuals also received reports of incidents that may or may not have been passed on to the Jewish State roof bodies, the community security groups or ECAJ, and it is also 'known anecdotally that many other incidents, especially of casual anti-Jewish racism, are not formally reported at all'.[168]

Nathan told the *Australian Jewish News* that in the anti-Israel protests in

2014 there 'was a clear undertone of anti-Semitism', and in the report stated that at 'any given protest in Sydney, the majority of placards had either overt or subtle antisemitic themes'. Nathan also notes in the report that there were 'very few public condemnations of the antisemitism of the protesters' and that 'the media and political focus was on the Islamist nature of the protests, especially in Sydney'.[169] As an academic writing from the other side of the world, who was not present at any of these protests, I am not in a position to comment on this specifics of the Sydney demonstrations, but given a lifetime of involvement with Left politics, I find her charge that a *majority* of placards were antisemitic unlikely. I agree, of course, that any Islamist presence should be condemned, and that equally antisemitism should be condemned, but I do not accept that the majority of anti-Zionist protestors are antisemitic, which could be read from Nathan's comments.

While I cannot comment of the specific composition of the Sydney protests, I do feel able to comment on the relationship between anti-semitism and anti-Zionism. As I wrote in Chapter 1, contemporary antisemitism needs to be seen in the context of hegemonic global US capitalism and imperialism, in which Israel is a key player. I went on to argue that it is vital to make a distinction between antisemitism, and anti-Zionism and the State of Israel's close relationship with the United States. This is particularly important for Marxists and other Left factions whose brief must be total and unremitting opposition to all forms of racism, including antisemitism and that emanating from Islamists. Like all forms of racism, I concluded in Chapter 1, antisemitism is not directed at people because of their political viewpoints, but because of their perceived 'race', ethnicity, nationality, culture or religion. Of course, political viewpoints can be falsely equated with ethnicity, as when all Jewish people are (obviously wrongly) equated with Zionism and the policies of the state of Israel. The same arguments apply to Islamophobia (discussed below), when all Muslims (again obviously wrongly) are equated with Islamism.

Daniel Randall describes an incident that occurred in London during a 2014 demonstration against Israel's assault on Gaza. It is equally relevant to our discussion of Australia, or indeed anywhere else where anti-Zionist or pro-Palestinian demonstrations take place. Given that I find myself broadly in agreement with Randall's analysis, I shall briefly recount it here.

On the demonstration, Randall encountered a man carrying a placard that read 'Research: The Protocols of the Learned Elders of Zion', with an image of a star of David, dripping blood, and '666' in the centre. As he explains, the *Protocols* are an antisemitic forgery, dating back to Tsarist Russia, purporting to expose a Jewish conspiracy to dominate the world: 'They were used in their time, and have been used since, to whip up racist hatred, often violent, against Jews.' Randall told the man with the placard that racism had no place on the demonstration, that his presence harmed the Palestinian cause, and that his placard was promoting a racist hoax. During his self-acknowledged tirade, Randall mentioned that he was Jewish. The response from the placard-carrier was overtly antisemitic: 'Well, you're blinded by your bias because you're a Jew. Only Jews make the arguments you're making.' Some onlookers backed Randall, but others continued the antisemitic abuse and one threatened physical violence.

As Randall comments, explicit 'anti-Jewish racism of the kind displayed on the man's placard has been rare on Palestine solidarity demonstrations in Britain'. I am sure the same can be said of Australia. But as Randall states:

> the fact that it was present at all, and that it could find even a handful of defenders in a crowd of other demonstrators, is deeply worrying. Pointing to its rarity, and dismissing the problem as restricted solely to fringe elements, would be to bury one's head in the sand …. it is an undeniable fact that there are anti-Semites in the global Palestine solidarity movement, and ones prepared to violently express their anti-Semitism. That must not be allowed to infect the movement.[170]

I agree with Randall's contention that if people with such politics want to attend solidarity demonstrations to peddle them, 'they should find themselves isolated, and face constant harangue. They shouldn't be entitled to a moment's peace.' While outward displays of 'classical' antisemitism are rare, Randall concludes, subtler themes are more common. Placards and banners comparing the Israeli state to Nazism, and its occupation of Palestine to the Holocaust, and images melding or replacing the Star of David with swastikas, are 'while far from universal, relatively commonplace'. Randall makes a direct comparison between antisemitism and anti-black racism, and the governments of Israel and the United States:

> 'Zionism = Nazism', 'Star of David = Swastika', and 'The Occupation = The Holocaust' all use collective cultural trauma as a weapon to attack Jews. The fact that those who take such placards on demonstrations intend only to target the Israeli government, and not Jews in general, is no defence or excuse. The barbarism of Israeli state policy does not make the Jewishness of its government fair game, any more than Barack Obama's imperialism excuses racist attacks on him.[171]

An equally important point for the Left is that right-wingers in the Jewish community use instances of antisemitism to discredit the Palestinian cause, and to dissuade Jews from acting to support it. On this, instrumental, level, antisemitism harms the Palestinians, but any form of racism should have no place in any solidarity movement, not because it is bad PR, but because the politics of solidarity should be anathema to any form of racism.[172]

HANSONISM

The rise and fall of multiculturalism

In order to understand the phenomenon of Hansonism, it is first necessary to dwell briefly on assimilation, followed by the rise and fall of multiculturalism at the level of the state. Because of the 'white Australia policy' which, as we have seen was in effect from the late nineteenth century until it was dismantled in 1975, the vast bulk of (non-British and Irish) post-Second World War labour immigrants to Australia, as Scott Poynting notes, were 'white', including displaced persons from continental Europe, with immigrants encouraged from northern Europe in the first instance. When these were insufficient to meet labour market demands, as it was always known they would be, immigrants were sought from elsewhere.[173]

As Chris Cunneen, David Fraser and Stephen Tomsen explain, increasing automation into ever new sectors of production, the accelerated use of electronic apparatus, the economic profitability of the rearmament process and the 'arms race' and the ability of capital to tap vast markets through mass production were at the heart of economic growth in the advanced capitalist countries.[174] In Australia, capital was forced to turn to pools of labour from southern Europe. Increasing numbers of workers were recruited from Italy, Greece, Yugoslavia and Malta in the 1950s, followed by Turkish migrants in the 1960s, and migrants from Latin America in the 1970s. Racist treatment of Italian, Greek and Yugoslavian workers was widespread, and unfair practices in the workplace were common.[175] As Poynting puts it, 'these groups were discriminated against and popular and institutional racism towards them was endemic, with assimilation (and its later more tempered variant, "integration") official policy and culturally expected until the 1970s advent of multiculturalism'.[176] The racist term 'wog' was used, and is still used, to describe southern European Australians.

The social democratic Labor government of 1972–75 cut back on immigration, finally removed most of the 'racial' barriers to immigration, and focused on the millions of post-war migrants who had become permanent settlers. By 1975 citizenship had become easier to obtain, and a series of programmes had been drafted, including the expansion of government grants to minority ethnic groups to employ welfare workers, state-funded radio broadcasting in minority languages, and a multicultural education programme.[177]

Multiculturalism continued under the incoming Liberal/Country (National) Party, in power from 1975 to 1983 and led by Malcolm Fraser, and became, according to Lee Ack, 'primarily an attempt to rebadge Australian nationalism as more "inclusive" and thus avoid social fracture'.[178] The 1978 Galbally Inquiry into Migrant Services and Programs signalled an important turning point. The report 'urged the adoption of cultural diversity as a means of developing the sense of nationalist loyalty amongst migrants', and contributed to the 'development of a multiculturalism that was conceptualised primarily as [a] mechanism for consolidating national unity'.[179] As such, Lee Ack argues, multiculturalism entailed co-opting a layer of middle-class migrants to help discipline militant workers within their own communities, thus diverting their anger and discontent into safe channels. Developed within a nationalist framework, although it created space for anti-racist arguments, multiculturalism under Fraser was limited in its capacity to challenge racism, and racism continued unabated during this period.[180]

In 1984, conservative historian Geoffrey Blainey, in typically inter-pellative style, wrote of the 'realistic concern felt by so many' about the overwhelming increase in the number of Asian faces. The solution, he argued, in order to resist the drive towards an Asian 'invasion' or takeover, was to reject the concept of multiculturalism and reassert the core values of the Anglo-Saxon founding fathers of Australia.[181] As Michael Grewcock argues, as well as generating a revival of anti-Asian racist activity, this:

> succeeded in returning to the mainstream assumptions that multi-culturalism was potentially divisive because it accorded special privileges to minorities and undermined cultural homogeneity. In particular, Blainey was influential in labelling multiculturalism as the product of a powerful minority lobby and an 'industry' that had captured the ear of government.[182]

Despite Blainey's intervention, multiculturalism continued under the Labor government of Bob Hawke which succeeded Fraser in 1983. In 1986, multi-culturalism was expanded to include principles of equitable access by all to government resources; rights to political participation; rights to practice one's own culture, language and religion; and early in 1987 the Office of Multicultural Affairs (OMA) in the Department of Prime Minister and Cabinet was established.[183] As under Fraser, multiculturalism was linked to 'Australian national identity'.[184] In 1988, however, it was argued in the FitzGerald Report that the philosophy of multiculturalism was not widely understood, and the 'ensuing uninformed debate' was 'damaging the cause it seeks to serve'.[185]

The report found an increasing resentment of what some members of the public thought multiculturalism meant – 'special preference to migrants in gaining services, and an emphasis on the continuation of separateness and divisions between groups'. As Andrew Jakubowicz puts it, 'the old assimilationist sentiments were still out there, and the Committee identified those concerns in its report'. Hawke defended multiculturalism, on the grounds that it was an important and central part of the social contract, a view that prevailed at the time.[186] Soon after the election of the John Howard government in 1996, Howard dropped the multicultural portfolio by closing down the OMA, restricting access to the Adult Migrant Education Program to new migrants, and reducing funding and consultation for minority ethnic organizations.[187] Poynting and Mason summarize the disastrous effects of multiculturalism's demise:

> The multiculturalism which had been developed in Australia in the early 1970s was designed to meet particular social and historical circumstances, amounting to practically unprecedented and elsewhere unmatched levels of cultural diversity, and the failure of assimilationist policies to cope with these. The set of policies which evolved served well for a quarter of a century, in guaranteeing a measure of social inclusion, ameliorating ethnically structured inequalities, and inhibiting racist extremism and violence. The retreat from multiculturalism and the assimilationist discourse of the New Integrationism ... present dangerous implications for both domestic protection of religious freedom and Australia's wider adherence to international human rights obligations.[188]

Hansonism and the John Howard Government

Racism in the latter part of the twentieth century and the beginning of the twenty-first cannot be understood without an examination of Hansonism. Pauline Hanson was disendorsed as the Liberal candidate for Oxley in Queensland after she wrote a letter to a local newspaper complaining about Aboriginal 'privileges'. She then stood as an independent and won the seat in 1996. Foregrounding 'commonsense' and her experience as a mother, sole parent and small businesswoman, in her initial speech she invoked 'reverse racism' and complained of 'political correctness and those who control the various taxpayer funded "industries" that flourish in our society servicing Aboriginals, multiculturalists and a host of other minority groups'. Hanson went to state that 'Aboriginals' enjoy privileges over other Australians. Implicitly denying thousands of years of a huge nation of flourishing cultures, with peoples speaking some 250 languages, encompassing a rich and complex ritual life, as outlined at the beginning of this chapter, she said:

> This nation is being divided into black and white, and the present system encourages this. I am fed up with being told, 'This is our land.' Well, where the hell do I go? I was born here, and so were my parents and children. I will work beside anyone and they will be my equal but I draw the line when told I must pay and continue paying for something that happened over 200 years ago. Like most Australians, I worked for my land; no-one gave it to me.[189]

She followed this with a tirade against the 'Aboriginal industry' that ended with a call to get rid of the Aboriginal flag: 'To survive in peace and harmony, united and strong, we must have one people, one nation, one flag.'[190] 'One Nation' subsequently became the name of Pauline Hanson's party. Later in the speech, Hanson moved on to immigration and multiculturalism, claiming that most Australians want immigration 'radically reviewed' and 'multiculturalism abolished'. Echoing Margaret Thatcher's famous 'swamping' remarks, she proclaimed:

> I believe we are in danger of being swamped by Asians. Between 1984 and 1995, 40 per cent of all migrants coming into this country were of Asian origin. They have their own culture and religion, form ghettos and do not assimilate. Of course, I will be called racist but, if I can invite whom I want into my home, then I should have the right to have a say in who comes into my country. A truly multicultural country can never be strong or united. The world is full of failed and tragic examples, ranging from Ireland to Bosnia to Africa and, closer to home, Papua New Guinea. America and Great Britain are currently paying the price.[191]

To underline the fact that she was promoting the return of the white Australia policy, she then quoted the immigration minister in the Labor government from 1945 to 1949 and leader of the Australian Labor Party from 1960 to 1967. Arthur Calwell wrote the pamphlet 'I stand by White Australia'. The pamphlet ends with a reference to 'the evils of miscegenation' and, like Hanson's speech begins, ends with an appeal to 'common sense'.[192] Hanson said:

Arthur Calwell was a great Australian and Labor leader, and it is a pity that there are not men of his stature sitting on the opposition benches today. Arthur Calwell said:

> Japan, India, Burma, Ceylon and every new African nation are fiercely anti-white and anti one another. Do we want or need any of these people here? I am one red-blooded Australian who says no and who speaks for 90 per cent of Australians.

I have no hesitation in echoing the words of Arthur Calwell.[193]

Moving on to the abolition of multiculturalism and immigration, she claimed that this would save 'billions of dollars and allow those from ethnic backgrounds to join mainstream Australia'. 'Immigration', she affirmed, 'must be halted in the short term.' Hanson then called for the introduction of compulsory national service as a safeguard against a future war.

Prime Minister John Howard welcomed her speech as a blow to 'political correctness' and a triumph for 'free speech',[194] noting that people should be able to 'talk about certain things without living in fear of being branded as a bigot or as a racist'.[195] As Lee Ack argues, Hanson got more that her fair share of 'free speech', in that her initial speech was published in full in the daily newspapers. The media, Lee Ack points out, 'even when they editorialised against her views ... reported her every utterance, followed her every move and made her a celebrity'.[196] Lee Ack quotes Robert Manne, who wrote that 'For many ordinary people she became a heroine .... When she appeared on television her views seemed to command overwhelming approval. When she arrived in country towns or walked through shopping malls her progress was cheered.'[197]

Howard went on to feed the climate of racism by his response to the Wik judgement, his refusal to apologize for the stolen generations, and implementation of policies on refugees.[198] I shall deal with each in turn.

In The Wik Peoples v The State of Queensland & Ors; The Thayorre People v The State of Queensland & Ors [1996] HCA 40 ('Wik'), the High Court held that native title rights could coexist on land held by pastoral leaseholders, but that if there is any inconsistency between the rights of the native title holders and the rights of the pastoralist, the rights of the native title holders must yield. This means that if there is a conflict of rights, the native title holders come off second best. If there is no conflict, the rights of each coexist.[199] Howard's response was to give a specific set of guarantees that no pastoral leaseholder would lose '*anything at all*'.[200]

The government's reaction to Wik was the so-called Ten Point Plan, which formed the basis of the Native Title Amendment Act of 1998. This effectively extinguished native title not only on pastoral leases, but also on a range of other land tenures, vacant Crown land in towns and cities, and over waterways and airspace. It delivered, in the words of National Party leader and Deputy Prime Minister Tim Fischer, 'bucket loads of extinguishment'.[201]

As Lee Ack points out, the Northern Territory Emergency Response, known as the Intervention, opened up what she describes as a 'new and terrible phase in attacks on Indigenous rights'. Using the pretext of what it turned out were false claims of endemic child sex abuse, Howard sent troops into indigenous communities, installed white 'business managers' to run them, and signalled plans to force communities off their land and into 'hub towns'.[202] The Western Australian Pastoralists and Graziers Association acclaimed the Intervention:

> We've been advocating what Howard's suggesting should happen now for the last 40 years. We've been suspicious of the way that Aboriginal affairs have been going ever since there was the equal opportunity and wage decisions made back in the sixties.[203]

With respect to the stolen generations, following the *Bringing Them Home* report, which looked into the separation of Aboriginal and Torres Strait Islander children from their families (discussed earlier in this chapter), Howard refused to apologize to indigenous peoples during his terms as prime minister from 1996 to 2007. Moreover, in 2008 he defended his decision not to say sorry to Australia's Aboriginal Peoples during his eleven years in power, and criticized the Kevin Rudd government's apology in 2008. He went on to say:

> I do not believe as a matter of principle that one generation can accept responsibility for the acts of earlier generations. In some cases, children were wrongly removed, in other cases they were removed for good reason, in other cases they were given up and in other cases, the judgement on the removal is obscure or difficult to make.[204]

As far as the issue of refugees is concerned, as Supple points out, Howard implemented many of Hanson's policies such as temporary protection visas for refugees, intended to discourage 'boat people' by restricting the rights they would be entitled to once they had arrived, including not being able to bring family members over.[205]

Howard also ordered the turning around of refugees on the MV *Tampa* in 2001 to win over Hanson's supporters. This Norwegian cargo ship rescued 433 boat people from the distressed Indonesian fishing vessel

Palapa, off the coast of Christmas Island, Australia. The Australian government summarily denied admission to the passengers, mostly refugees fleeing from war-torn Afghanistan. As Peter D. Fox argues, the government's hard-line stance 'marked the dawn of a prolonged state policy aimed at deterring future asylum seekers that held sway until a change in political leadership in 2007'. Fox goes on:

> Though the Howard government's tough posture drew world-wide condemnation, it galvanized the governing Liberal Party of Australia to harden its stance on immigration in the midst of a re-election campaign With this went all the rhetoric about refugees being 'illegals', 'queue jumpers' and possibly even 'terrorists'. This language, and boasts like that by Howard that, 'we will decide who comes to this country', served to conflate refugee and immigration policy – even though the numbers arriving on boats have never been more than 2 or 3 per cent of total annual immigration.[206]

Supple claims Howard successfully used racism to remain in power, and ride out opposition to his continuation of the neoliberal agenda, allowing him to get away with introducing the GST (goods and services tax) benefiting the rich at the expense of the working class, 'running a union busting agenda, targeting unions like the Maritime Union of Australia and construction unions, passing anti-union laws and pushing through budget cuts'. Supple concludes that 'Howard's was a government that consistently ruled for the rich, and needed to sow division in order to get away with it.'[207]

Underlining the fact that the interests of politicians do not always coincide with those of capitalists, as I argued in the Introduction, Lee Ack points out that many capitalists were worried about the level of support for Hanson's anti-Asian policies – not because they opposed racism, but because it was 'bad for business'. This became clear, she goes on, when the Business Council of Australia, together with the Council of Social Services, religious leaders and – disgracefully – the Australian Council of Trade Unions (ACTU), issued a joint statement condemning One Nation's Asian immigration policy but ignoring its racism towards indigenous people. As Lee Ack points out, this was no oversight: 'anti-Aboriginal racism is good for business and featured prominently in the business community's campaign against native title.'[208]

There were a number of reasons for the decline of Pauline Hanson and One Nation from 1999 onwards (internal war, amid a welter of accusations and counter-accusations; resignations, suspensions and expulsions; a growing revolt of party branches against the organization's undemocratic structure; and the aftermath of the Queensland election result, where One Nation attracted nearly one quarter of the vote, potentially jeopardizing parliamentary stability at the national level and generating a mainstream backlash),[209] but this did not lead to any decline in the Howard government's racism. As Lee Ack explains, while in deference to business interests there was less talk about Asian immigration, attacks on Aboriginal people continued unabated. However, the Howard government's commitment to pastoral leaders was not enough to satisfy Australian capitalism, and in particular the mining industry, which wanted even more mineral-rich Aboriginal land. To facilitate this, the Howard government started talking about 'economically unviable' Aboriginal communities in remote areas, complaining about the cost of delivering basic services to them and insisting that the 'experiment' of Aboriginal self-determination had failed. In 2004 the Aboriginal and Torres Strait Islander Commission (ATSIC), the Australian government body through which indigenous Australians were formally involved in the processes of government affecting their lives, was abolished 'amid hyped claims of corruption and dysfunction and vilification of Aboriginal leaders'.[210]

NEWER COLOUR-CODED RACISM

Anti-Migrant Racism

People of Chinese and Japanese origin are not the only Asian groups to be at the receiving end of Australian racism. In 2008, for example, Indian taxi drivers in Melbourne and Adelaide demonstrated against racist assaults, including the killing of some of them.[211] In the same year, assaults on Indian students, the second largest group of foreign students in Australia after those from China, started to surface, peaking with a number of vicious attacks in May and June 2009, which resulted in one student being left in a coma.[212] Students claimed the attacks were racist, but police and government authorities maintained that they were mainly opportunistic. The assaults spread to West Sydney. There were a number of protests by the students, with those in Sydney and Melbourne complaining not just about the earlier attacks, but also about substandard private colleges, poor courses aimed at South Asian students, low-quality housing, exploitative work conditions, and the need for local benefits like travel concession cards to improve safety.[213] Lee Ack argues that the protests were as much about the response of the authorities as the attacks themselves, with victims complaining that police were both reluctant and slow to respond and were often racist towards them, or blamed the victims themselves for the assaults.[214]

Gautam Gupta of the Federation of Indian Students in Australia stated that 'institutional racism in the police force and the media and political elites means Australia is ill-equipped to deal with the problem in an open, honest manner'.[215] This assertion was substantiated when a number of Victorian police officers, including three superintendents and several inspectors, circulated emails with a video of an Indian train passenger being electrocuted, suggesting that this could be a way to 'fix Melbourne's Indian student problem'.[216]

African migrants have also been on the receiving end of racism. In 2007, 19-year-old Sudanese refugee Liep Gony was beaten to death with a metal pole, his murderer having painted 'F--- da niggas' on his living room wall, and having been heard to say, 'these blacks are turning this town into the Bronx. I'm going to take my town back. I'm looking to kill the blacks' before randomly attacking Gony.[217] The response of Kevin Andrews, the then immigration minister in the Howard government, was to blame the victim:

> I have been concerned that some groups don't seem to be settling and adjusting into the Australian way of life as quickly as we would hope and therefore it makes sense ... to slow down the rate of intake from countries such as Sudan.[218]

The barrage of racist stereotyping, following media interpellation about Sudanese gangs, led to an investigation and a published report.[219] Interviews with young people with African backgrounds and community workers revealed the problem was not Sudanese gangs, but the Victorian police, who systematically target and often verbally or physically abuse young African men. A year later, following payouts by the police, Tamar Hopkins of the Flemington and Kensington Community Legal Centre, which represented the men, stated:

> Many police are using excessive and unlawful force against ordinary Victorians and in particular minorities. These civil claims represent a tiny fraction of the complaints that are made. Excessive, unnecessary force, and indeed racism, is very much a part of everyday policing.[220]

NEWER HYBRIDIST RACISM[221]

Islamophobia: A Brief History

David Marr and Marian Wilkinson describe how in the run-up to the 2001 federal election the Howard government, very unpopular at the time and with Labor's prospects good, appealed to and encouraged fears of an 'invasion' by 'Muslim boat people', using the *Tampa* incident (see pages 174–5) and the 'children overboard' episode (see page 187) to block Labor and thereby win the election.[222] However, as Lee Ack argues, Islamophobia runs much deeper, and is more than an election ploy:

> Fostering hostility towards Muslims was a deliberate strategy which served a number of purposes. It was used to justify the crimes conducted under the umbrella of the War on Terror: principally the invasions of Afghanistan and Iraq, the trashing of civil liberties with new anti-terror laws that extended and strengthened the repressive apparatus available to the state, and the inhuman treatment of desperate asylum seekers and refugees.[223]

Jack Holland has argued that John Howard's language from 11 September 2001 to mid-2003 helped to enable the 'War on Terror' in an Australian context in three principal ways. The first was via contingent and contestable constructions of Australia, the world and their interrelationship; the second, by emphasizing shared values, 'mateship' and mutual sacrifice in war in a way that appealed to 'battlers' and disillusioned Hansonites; and the third was by positioning any alternatives as 'un-Australian'.[224]

Following the London (England) bombings, on 7 July 2005 (7/7), a series of coordinated Islamist suicide attacks on London Transport in which 52 people died and over 700 were injured, Howard met with Muslim leaders and told them that the 30 Muslim schools in Australia must teach 'Australian values'. He also informed them that his government was ready to 'get inside' the schools and mosques to ensure that they were not promoting terrorism.[225] Federal education minister Brendan Nelson issued a provocative media message the following day, that 'if people don't want to be Australians and they don't want to live by Australian values and understand them, well then they can basically clear off'.[226]

In September of the same year, also in the aftermath of the London bombings, the government set up a 'Muslim Community Reference Group', said to have been 'hand-picked' by Howard. Poynting and Mason suggest that this was not about community consultation at all, but 'to obtain intelligence for security services in their "war on terror" and to co-opt the communities into collaboration with security officers and police through informing on an ongoing basis'.[227]

Anti-Lebanese Racism: The Cronulla Riots

On Sunday 11 December 2005, more than 5,000 people gathered at North Cronulla, a beach resort 30 km south of Sydney. Men of Arabic appearance were assaulted, large groups of Lebanese Australians from south-west Sydney mounted big reprisal attacks, police and rioters clashed, dozens of people were seriously injured, and 104 were charged with offences.[228] As Paul Daley explains, the tensions that led to the 'Cronulla riots' began with the alleged harassment of local women by Lebanese Australian men and boys, and the subsequent assault of two white volunteer life savers. The NSW police report describes the beginning of the confrontation as follows:

> three Caucasian members of the North Cronulla Surf Life Saving Club … passed … [a] group of Middle Eastern men, the members of each group were staring at each other. A verbal exchange took place in which a member from each group accused the other of staring at him. At this time one of the Middle Eastern men said to [name deleted] in response to the staring accusation, 'I'm allowed to, now f••k off and leave our beach.' [name deleted] said during this verbal exchange, 'I come down here out of my own spare time to save you dumb c••ts from drowning, now piss off you scum.' As this verbal confrontation took place the Middle Eastern group formed a half-circle around the Caucasian males. There was an attempt by one of the Middle Eastern men to calm the situation and it appeared that he had been successful and the confrontation was over. However, at this time the Middle Eastern male who was involved in the initial verbal altercation swung a punch at [name deleted] which missed. Some pushing then occurred between both groups which escalated to a fight.[229]

After the incident, an SMS message urged the following: 'This Sunday every Fucking Aussie in the Shire, get down to North Cronulla to help support Leb and wog bashing day … let's show them this is our beach and they're never welcome back.'[230] During the ensuing attack on the Lebanese Australians, the Australian flag was appropriated and worn as the 'Cronulla cape', becoming a symbol of aggressive territorial claim and exclusion, what Paul Daley describes as 'a hideous distillation of Anglo-Australian racism'.[231]

Alan Jones, a radio shock-jock and fervent Howard supporter, played a central role in inciting the riots, calling for 'a community show of force' against 'Middle Eastern grubs'.[232] Jones also referred to Lebanese men as 'vermin' and 'mongrels' who 'simply rape, pillage and plunder a nation that's taken them in'.[233] Despite all the evidence to the contrary, both Howard and his deputy and the then Labor leader denied that the riot was racist, with Howard describing it as primarily an issue of law and order, and Labor leader Kim Beazley declaring it 'simply criminal behaviour, that's all there is to it'.[234]

I have classified anti-Lebanese racism as 'newer' because Lebanese Muslim settlement in Australia is a relatively new phenomenon. This was the third of three periods of migration, the first two of which occurred in the 1880s and after the Second World War, and were mainly of Christians. The third mainly Muslim settlement occurred after the Lebanese Civil War which began in 1975.[235] Islamophobia is an important component of anti-Lebanese racism. I have categorized it as 'hybridist' because the build-up to the Cronulla riots, and the riots themselves, very much reflect a racism of Anglo-Celtic origin directed at people of Lebanese or Arab 'appearance'. The right-wing media used Cronulla to intensify Islamophobia. In a detailed analysis of coverage in *The Australian*, Nahid Kabir found a consistent pattern of conflating the Lebanese community with 'Muslim extremists'. She concluded that 'the message reverberating in *The Australian* during this period was clear: Muslim extremists pose a threat to Australian national security', and that the event 'was generally an occasion to cast aspersions on "Muslim Australians."'[236] Lee Ack exemplifies the interpellative power of the Murdoch press with respect to both the working and middle classes when she writes:

> Unlike its News Ltd stablemates such as the *Herald Sun* and the *Daily Telegraph*, *The Australian* is not a paper with a large working class readership. Its target audience is the middle class and the business community – though of course all these newspapers reflect the political views of their owner, Rupert Murdoch. The Murdoch press does not simply pander to the prejudices of its working class readers – it seeks to reinforce them and to actively stir up racism when it is politically expedient to do so, not just among workers, but among the middle class.[237]

Cronulla: The Aftermath

In 2006, the attorney-general used his invitation at the start of Eid-al-Adha to the largest mosque in NSW, the Lakemba Mosque, to warn his audience that they must obey Australian law, and be tolerant towards others. As Poynting and Mason point out, the congregation, mainly Arab immigrants, had been on the receiving end of horrific racism for nearly two decades.[238] Also in 2006, the deputy leader of the Liberal Party attacked what he called 'mushy misguided multiculturalism', and cautioned that Australian values were 'not optional'.[239] Those who did not share these values, he went on, should have their citizenship revoked. The citizenship pledge should be a 'big warning sign' to Muslims wishing to live under sharia law: 'Before becoming an Australian you will be asked to subscribe to certain values. If you have strong objection to those values don't come to Australia.'[240] Later in 2006, Howard wrote in the Murdoch-owned mass-circulation *Daily Telegraph*:

> it is an undeniable fact that some who have come here are resisting integration. There are pockets of this resistance in different migrant groups but it is perhaps most visible at this time in a small section of the Islamic community.[241]

A few weeks after Howard's *Telegraph* article the first ever conference of Australian imams took place in Sydney (in mid-September 2006) and participants endorsed the federal government's proposed tests for citizenship and permanent residency. They also made recommendations that 'Muslim clerics preach in English and that they be accredited by a national board of Islamic leaders.'[242] Dr Ameer Ali, president of the Federation of Islamic Councils, who had also been chair of the Muslim Community Reference Group, enjoined Australian Muslims to cease complaining about being victimized, which was exactly what the federal and state governments, security forces and police *were* engaged in.[243]

As Tabar and colleagues argue, this incorporation of key Muslim community leaders needs to be seen in the context of the jockeying for public respectability, political influence and government largesse, while at the same time maintaining intracommunity standing though representing and advocating the real needs of their constituencies, which has characterized 'ethnic leader' multiculturalism in Australia since about 1978.[244] Following Gramsci, Poynting and Mason recognize that establishing hegemony is always backed up by 'the armour of coercion', by the state apparatuses, in the form of police harassment, arrest, and raids on mosques and households.[245]

Such intrusions also demonstrate 'a disregard for basic rights of religious freedom' and 'threaten to undermine Australia's observance of its obligations under a number of international treaties that it has ratified'.[246] The Howard government claimed unsurprisingly that events since 9/11 called for greater state intervention in Muslim cultural and religious matters. Poynting and Mason's retort to this is twofold. First, while the International Covenant on Civil and Political Rights (CCPR) states that in times of public emergency, the state may take necessary action, the proviso is that 'such measures are not inconsistent with their other obligations under international law and do not involve discrimination solely on the ground of race, colour, sex, language, religion or social origin.'[247] The interventions of the Howard government, they argue, are clearly directed at Muslim communities on the basis of their religion. This is exacerbated by that government's rejection of multiculturalism, in favour of 'Australian values'.

Poynting and Mason's second response is that in the 'light of the existing demonisation of, and discrimination against, Muslim communities by the state apparatus, increasingly coercive measures can only be counter-productive'. As they put it, the 'fear-mongering and the normalising of Hanson style racism undertaken by the Howard government ... [did] much to create a "permission to hate" Muslims, with its attendant discrimination and vilification.'[248] Poynting and Mason conclude by citing Paul Hoffman, who argues that:

> a state's failure to adhere to fundamental human rights norms makes it more likely that terrorist organizations will find it easier to recruit adherents among the discontented and disenfranchised and among the family and friends of those whose human rights have been violated.[249]

When a Labor government was returned in 2007 with Kevin Rudd as prime minister, there was no return to active support for multiculturalism. However, after the 2010 election of Julia Gillard, the Australian minister for immigration and citizenship announced the restoration of the portfolio and full-on multiculturalism, including antiracism strategies, expressing the view that if 'Australia is to be free and equal, then it will be multicultural. But, if it is to be multicultural, Australia must remain free and equal.'[250] The Australian Multicultural Council was officially launched by Gillard the following year. However, Gillard's 'multiculturalism' was greatly influenced by the 'new integrationism' that had been fostered under Howard. As Gillard put it, multiculturalism:

> is the meeting place of rights and responsibilities where the right to maintain one's customs, language and religion is balanced by an equal responsibility to learn English, find work, respect our culture and heritage, and accept women as full equals .... Where there is non-negotiable respect for our foundational values of democracy and the rule of law, and any differences we hold are expressed peacefully .... Where old hatreds are left behind, and we find shared identity on the common ground of mateship and the Aussie spirit of a fair go.[251]

'True multiculturalism', she went on, was the face of 'a new migrant studying hard in an English language class, working two jobs to put their kids through school or lining up to vote for the very first time'. It is 'an expression of progressive patriotism in which all Australians, old and new, can find meaning'.

Islamophobia Today

Liberal Party leader Tony Abbott became the 28th prime minister of Australia in 2013. A year later, in October 2014, the Australian parliamentary authorities ruled that Muslim women wearing burqas, niqabs or other face-covering veils would be banned from the public galleries and restricted to sound-proof glass enclosures usually reserved for children, allegedly on the grounds that the garments could be used to hide weapons.[252] Senator Jacqui Lambie, of the right-wing populist Palmer United Party, plans to present a private members bill for a total ban on face-covering veils in public places. As Richard Phillips points out, the parliamentary ruling has nothing to do with security, since anyone entering the public gallery has to pass through screening devices; moreover, there have been no reported cases of a Muslim woman wearing a niqab or burqa even attempting to enter the building. The ban is better seen as upping the climate of Islamophobia to justify Abbott's involvement in the US-led war in Iraq and Syria, and to further instigate 'divide and rule' between Muslim and non-Muslim Australians amid rising social tensions at home. As Phillips goes on, Abbott told the media he was against governments 'telling people what to wear' but felt 'confronted' by Muslim women wearing full veils, and wished that they 'weren't worn'.[253]

Following widespread condemnation, Abbott backed down and the rule was changed to temporarily removal of facial covering for security checking. The Department of Parliamentary Services said, 'Once this process has taken place, visitors are free to move about the public spaces of the building, including all chamber galleries, with facial coverings in place'.[254] Lambie labelled the backdown on the burqa ban a morale booster for Islamic extremists:

> The decision today to allow burqas and other forms of identity concealing items of dress to be worn in Australia's Parliament will put a smile on the face of the overseas Islamic extremists and their supporters in Australia.[255]

In the current toxic political climate, racists, interpellated by the political and communications ISAs, have defaced mosques, while Muslim women have been abused and had their veils pulled off. A cursory glance at Islamophobia Watch Australia revealed the following instances of Islamophobia for the month to December 2014:

- Alan Jones, the shock-jock who played a central role in inciting the Cronulla riots discussed earlier, was ordered to pay $10,000 to a Muslim community leader after a nine-year legal battle. The tribunal found Mr Trad's complaint of racial vilification over the comments was substantiated.

- The 'Boycott Halal' movement in Australia is set to escalate with a petition to federal parliament in the New Year demanding the Corporations Act 2001 be changed to mean only Muslims bear the cost of halal certification on everyday products. The movement is supported by extremist groups including the 'Islam-critical' Q-Society, Restore Australia, the Australian Defence League and the Patriots' Defence League.

- Between October and December, one Muslim woman has been abused three times by strangers who have taken offence against her Islamic dress. Referring to politicians who were advocating banning the burqa in Australia, she stated, the 'government isn't doing anything to address these issues and I'm an innocent victim of their ignorant bigoted comments by the parliament members. We need to hold people accountable from the top.'

- There has recently been a surge in reports of violence and harassment against Australian Muslims, mainly women, and often in the presence of children.

- The head of the Australian Defence League was one of three people charged over a brawl near a mosque in west Sydney. Police were told the fight followed derogatory remarks allegedly made by two men towards people attending the mosque.

- A Queensland bar and grill put up a sign, '2000 years ago Jesus Christ made headlines turning water into wine. The tradition continues .... We turn money into beer. (Sorry no Muslims).'

- A Muslim woman was forced to attend a Christian church service during a 60-day jail stint. She alleged that she was threatened with solitary confinement if she did not attend, and that another correction officer and a Baptist mocked her when she refused to actively participate.

- Sydneysiders paying their respects to siege victims at Martin Place following the Sydney siege in December 2014 were shouted down by a group of anti-Islamic protesters. Four men waving Australian and Southern Cross flags shouted slogans including 'Islam is evil' and 'not all cultures are evil – Islam is inferior'. The men also accused Muslims of being 'murderers' and supporting female genital mutilation, according to a witness. The group bore signs proclaiming 'Muslim terrorists not wanted here – neither are their leftist supporters', 'Tony Abbott – Will you protect us from multiculturalism?' and 'We didn't start the fire!' One of the men was Nick Folkes, who has previously been associated with the fringe Australian Protectionist Party and is now the 'chairman' of the 'Party for Freedom', which calls for an end to Muslim immigration and 'state-sanctioned multiculturalism'.

- The local head of ACT branch of the Patriots Defence League which claims to defend the Australian 'way of life' allegedly spat on a Canberra driver with whose car he crashed in the car park while monitoring the activities of a local Islamic centre, according to police. The man is accused of spitting on the man's cheek and saying, 'Look what you have done you f—ing idiot, you stupid idiot, you Muslim c—.' He then allegedly spat through the man's open window. He called police after the crash, allegedly telling them: 'If he says one more word, I will knock him out, useless f—ing Arab c—.'
- Assistant commissioner of Sydney police Michael Fuller said police dealt with a number of 'hate and bias' crimes following the Sydney siege, including one man who allegedly made threatening phone calls to a mosque in western Sydney.[256]

Anti-Asylum-Seeker Racism

Settlement patterns for refugees in Australia were as follows in the year 2013–14: Afghanistan 2,531, Myanmar 1,145, Iraq 829, Bhutan 312, Syria 297, Iran 269, Congo (DRC) 241, Eritrea 187, Somalia 185, Ethiopia 129, Others 376.[257] As discussed earlier in this chapter, the term 'boat people' entered the Australian lexicon from the mid-1970s, when boats arrived carrying people seeking asylum in the aftermath of the Vietnam War. The first boat arrived in Darwin in 1976. Over the next five years, there were over 2,000 Vietnamese boat arrivals, with the last in 1981.[258] At the time of the 1977 federal election, there were references in the press to an 'invasion', a 'flood' and to the 'yellow peril'. At the same time, the Darwin branch of the Waterside Workers' Federation in 1977 called for strikes to protest at the 'preferential treatment' refugees were receiving.[259] The Fraser government, however, set up a programme that became the most generous in the world, and by 1979 Australia had accepted 48,000 Vietnamese refugees, more on a per capita basis than the United States.[260] The vast majority of the 90,000 Vietnamese immigrants and refugees who settled in Australia in the 1970s and 1980s arrived by aircraft, after being processed in camps in South-East Asia.[261]

Fraser explained the rationale for this some years later:

> I strongly felt that we had been fighting alongside a lot of these people, that the Americans in particular had given them assurances and we had an obligation to them, rather than just leaving them behind, which had been the original decision of the Whitlam government. But when we made the contrary decision, Gough did not oppose it.[262]

As Mike Steketee explains, while Whitlam's government was responsible for formally ending the white Australia policy, the Labor prime minister was strongly against accepting refugees from Vietnam: 'Even as Saigon fell to communist forces in April 1975, bureaucratic delays by the Whitlam government prevented about 55 Vietnamese staffers at Australia's embassy in Saigon from gaining sanctuary in Australia.'[263]

Referring to his decision to accept the asylum seekers, Fraser said, 'I was so convinced it was the correct decision, I thought it would demonstrate ultimately that the white Australia policy really had been buried.' Fraser also revealed John Howard had approached him in a corridor following a cabinet meeting in May 1977 and said, 'We don't want too many of these people. We're doing this just for show, aren't we?'[264]

The second period of boat arrivals (1989–98) spanned the prime ministerships of Bob Hawke, Paul Keating and John Howard. Those arriving were routinely held in detention, a measure introduced by the Keating government, often for long periods, which according to Katharine Betts was at first a major news topic, but became largely forgotten as time went on, as periods spent in detention were reduced and most arrivals were sent back.[265] A 1998 report from the HREOC on the policy of mandatory detention argued that the policy breached international human rights standards, and that when detention was prolonged many of the conditions in which people were detained became unacceptable and breached Australia's human rights obligations. The report also called for children and other vulnerable people to be detained only in exceptional circumstances.[266]

The third major period of boat arrivals began in 1999, and numbers started to increase significantly. As a result of the *Tampa* incident discussed earlier (see page 174), the Howard government introduced in 2001 the policy of transporting asylum seekers to detention centres on islands in the Pacific rather than allowing them to land on the Australian mainland. The so-called 'Pacific solution' meant that the asylum seekers on board the *Tampa* were subsequently transferred to the island of Nauru.[267]

In 2001, a warship fired warning shots at a fishing boat overloaded with asylum seekers to prevent it from entering Australian waters. The following sequence of events then ensued, as chronicled by Alison Delitt. Asylum seekers held children in the air to alert the Australian navy that there were children on board, with one parent holding a child over the side of the boat so that it could defecate. A confused navy communication sent to immigration minister Philip Ruddock told of threats to throw a child overboard, and based on this, Ruddock stated that children had been thrown overboard. A navy report was subsequently sent to Prime Minister Howard, Ruddock and other ministers which did not mention children being thrown overboard. Later the same day, Howard condemned the 'sickening behaviour' of asylum seekers in throwing children overboard. When the boat sank, Ruddock accused the asylum seekers of destroying it deliberately, but no evidence was given. Photographs of the sinking ship with frightened asylum seekers in the sea were emailed to Defence Minister Peter Reith's senior staff. Meanwhile the Department of the Prime Minister was informed that there was no evidence that children had been thrown overboard, while the ship's commander made the same declaration. Reith then released two close-up pictures of children in the water, and told the media that they were of children that had been thrown overboard. Howard and Reith conferred on the phone, and both claimed later that Reith did not tell Howard that the allegations about the children were false. Howard then addressed the National Press Club and yet again claimed the children had been thrown into the sea, despite the fact that his key advisors, Reith and his office staff all knew that this was false information. During the 2001 election campaign, Howard was depicted with clenched fists, accompanied by the slogan, 'We decide who comes to this country', which was sent to all voters in marginal seats, and published in full-page newspaper advertisements. Howard won the election with an increased majority.[268]

In 2004 HREOC published a report that was highly critical of the mandatory detention of children, viewing its implementation as fundamentally inconsistent with the Convention on the Rights of the Child (CRC). The inquiry further found that children in long-term immigration detention were at risk of serious mental harm, and that failure to remove children from detention together with their parents constituted cruel, inhumane and degrading punishment.[269] The Howard government rejected the findings and recommendations of the report, and reaffirmed its commitment to the policy of mandatory detention, including children, but in the following year, after pressure from his backbench, Howard announced a softening of immigration detention policy, which included the release of families with children into community detention arrangements. However, the principle of mandatory detention remained, along with the excision of territory for migration purposes, offshore processing and if necessary turning boats around at sea.[270]

The 'Pacific solution' was formally ended in 2008, when the Rudd government announced that the centres on Manus and Nauru would no longer be used, and that future unauthorized boat arrivals would be processed on Christmas Island, a territory of Australia in the Indian Ocean.[271] The policy has been widely criticized. For example, Bem and colleagues write about the poor mental health and general condition of the detainees, in both the immediate and the longer term. Medical figures, they point out, paint a shocking picture of psychological damage, including '45 people engaged in a serious hunger strike, multiple incidents of actual self-harm and dozens of detainees suffering from depression and other psychological conditions each year and being treated with anti-depressants or anti-psychotic medication.'[272] Moreover, the Pacific solution failed to uphold Australia's commitment under international law to provide for non-refoulement of refugees – the principle that forbids sending a refugee back to a place where they might face persecution. It also violated the principle of burden-sharing – all nation states contributing towards the solution, Australia being the first 'developed country' to engage in making other countries do the work – by offloading asylum seekers on poorer Pacific countries, and expecting other resettlement countries or transit countries such as Malaysia or Indonesia to host them.[273]

The cessation of offshore processing was temporary, however, and the Julia Gillard Labor government reintroduced it in 2012, after arrangements with the governments of Nauru and Papua New Guinea, the latter to use Manus Island again.[274] The Gillard government had also the previous year signed a memorandum of understanding (MOU) with the government of Afghanistan and the UN High Commissioner for Refugees (UNHCR) allowing for failed Afghan asylum seekers to be involuntarily returned to Afghanistan.[275] As Lee Ack argues, during her time as prime minister, Gillard engaged under in a 'race to the bottom' with Liberal leader Tony Abbott as they canvassed ever more brutal strategies to 'stop the boats'.[276]

Anna Pha has described Gillard's reintroduction of offshore processing as 'one of the darkest in Australia's history since colonial invasion'. As Pha explains, the legislation goes further than arbitrary detention: detention is mandatory and indefinite, whereas release is arbitrary. Referring to the causes of people seeking asylum, she states:

> Whether it be Vietnam, Yugoslavia, Iraq, Afghanistan, Somalia, Sudan, Libya, Syria, Iran, each new imperialist intervention or war adds to the millions of desperate people fleeing for a safe haven.[277]

As Green Senator Sarah Hanson-Young argued, it would not save lives. It was a callous, hard-hearted political manoeuvre to try to neutralize Opposition leader Tony Abbott's populist 'stop the boats' line in the 2013 federal elections, even removing some of the protections legislated by Howard in 2001. The government rushed the legislation through both Houses, and the Communications ISA 'faithfully repeated all the government's lies about "fairness", protection of people and saving lives'.[278] Green Senator Penny Wright summed up the intention of the bill:

we are being asked to compromise so that we can treat some people so harshly that it will send a message of punishment and deterrence to others contemplating making the journey. We will have to treat them so harshly that it compares with the situations they are fleeing from.[279]

The government admitted that 'the asylum seekers will initially be housed in tents, behind barbed wire fencing, drop pits (toilets) and bucket showers, and limited power on Nauru', with the risk of malaria on Manus Island.[280]

Two years after the Gillard legislation, Doherty and Evershed, writing in *Guardian Australia*, described conditions on Manus Island at the end of 2014. Almost a quarter of the 1,028 asylum seekers on the island had 'needed medical isolation, hospitalisation or other treatment in the past eight months', while 18 had underwent emergency evacuation to Australia with life-threatening illnesses. Manus Island detainees, they went on, were being placed in medical isolation at a rate of nearly one a month. Asylum seekers argue that their care is getting worse. Detainees who were beaten during unrest on the island in February, 2014 said they were still suffering with their injuries at the end of the year, while others said they had had medication taken from them, and had been given drugs past their expiry date. Still others said they had waited months for treatment. Two detainees died in 2014, one beaten with a wooden pole and having had a rock dropped on his head in the February riots, the other having died in hospital when a skin infection turned septic, and his transport to a Brisbane hospital was delayed by a visa hold-up.[281]

The Queensland representative for the Australian Medical Association, Dr Richard Kidd, said there were 'huge question marks' over the standard of healthcare being provided to detainees on Manus. As Kidd pointed out, many of the detainees were survivors of torture and trauma in their home countries, and they were arriving in Australian detention weakened, often dehydrated and malnourished, from the boat journey:

On a place like Manus Island, I would expect high rates of typhoid and hepatitis. Gastroenteritis is going to be rife, particularly if there is limited access to clean latrines, and certainly if you have trouble removing sewage cleanly and safely.[282]

'It's really an evil policy', he concluded, 'they are saying publicly they want to crush these people so others don't come. To deliberately harm another human being, that is completely unacceptable, it is morally wrong and just indefensible.' *Guardian Australia* received no response to questions directed at the authorities. Australian government staff had told the UN Committee Against Torture in November 2014 that healthcare in the detention centres was comparable to that available in Australia.[283]

The remarks of Nicole Judge, a former Salvation Army worker at the camp, sum up the inhuman conditions on Nauru and Manus:

> When I arrived on Manus Island during September 2013, I had previously worked on Nauru for one year. I thought I had seen it all: suicide attempts, people jumping off buildings, people stabbing themselves, people screaming for freedom whilst beating their heads on concrete. Unfortunately I was wrong; I had not seen it all. Manus Island shocked me to my core. I saw sick and defeated men crammed behind fences and being denied their basic human rights, padlocked inside small areas in rooms often with no windows and being mistreated by those who were employed to care for their safety.[284]

In an Australian TV programme in 2014, naval personnel pointed out that successive Australian governments, both Labor and Liberal-National, had illegally ordered Navy crews not to rescue asylum seekers on sinking boats, deliberately allowing refugees to drown in an effort to frighten people away from seeking asylum in Australia. They also described the sickening task of retrieving the bodies of dead asylum seekers or coping with ill and distressed people, including children.[285]

After the Abbott government took office in September 2013, one Navy officer said, refugees were further put in danger by offloading them into lifeboats and pushing them away from Australian waters. The Abbott government also reintroduced temporary protection visas, first initiated by the Howard government in 1999, providing visas for three to five years, but not permanent residency.[286] Abbott stated:

> We always said that three things were necessary to stop the boats – offshore processing, turning boats around and temporary protection visas. Last night the final piece of policy was put in place.[287]

Paul Power, chief executive of the Refugee Council of Australia, criticized the legislation as a 'shattering blow for asylum seekers who face the grave risk of being returned to danger'.[288]

At the end of 2014, the Australian government flatly rejected, and directly defied, a report by the Geneva-based UN Committee Against Torture (CAT) stating that the country's refugee policies could be in breach of the UN Convention Against Torture.[289]

A year earlier, the UK broadsheet the *Guardian* built up over the course of a week, through interviews and inspections, a picture of daily life in detention on Manus. There were at the time about 1,100 male asylum seekers detained in the facility, from countries such as Afghanistan, Burma, Lebanon, Iran, Iraq, Pakistan, Somalia, Sudan and Syria.

In the piece, Graeme McGregor describes the living conditions, which are hot, extremely cramped and with poor ventilation and no privacy. In one dormitory, conditions are so bad that Amnesty International put them on a par with torture. The building has a low, curved metal roof and sleeps over 100 men on bunk beds with no space between them, no windows and two floor fans. The stench is thus overwhelming and the heat stifling. 'P Dorm' flooded when it rained and the asylum seekers reported snakes in the room. McGregor writes of a series of 'unnecessary humiliations', with the men spending several hours each day queuing for food, showers and toilets in the intense heat and pouring rain. There is no shade or shelter. The men are referred to by their 'boat ID', rather than their names. Nearly all are not allowed shoes, and most have had their belongings confiscated by people smugglers or staff on the island.

The 500 men in the 'Oscar' compound get only half a litre of water a day, as opposed to the 5 litres recommended. There is one toilet for every 30 people, and the toilets are often dirty or broken. The men are not given enough toiletries, mosquito repellent or washing powder. Contact with loved ones is limited to two 15-minute telephone conversations a week, 'strictly regulated, often in the middle of the night' and with no privacy.

The men have no activities to keep them busy, and McGregor describes one dormitory where a man had drawn a large television, DVD player, complete with electrical cords, and games controllers made of cardboard with buttons on them. One of the men explained, 'We use this to pass the time. It is no laughing matter. We pretend to play and it brings back memories of home.'

The facility cannot treat serious illnesses, and receives no response from the Australian authorities for basic requests to improve health and sanitation. All this combined with no processing and no information means that the pressure to return home is huge. One asylum seeker told McGregor:

We just need to have some certainty. I have lived in war zones, with bombs and explosions. I have never experienced what I am experiencing here with the uncertainty we face. If we had died in the ocean, that would have been better. I just need to know my destiny so that I can sleep at night. Just to know, so I can be prepared for what will happen.[290]

As Will Borrow, writing in 2015 for the World Socialist Website, puts it, the situation on Manus Island 'is an indictment of the criminal anti-refugee policies of the Australian state'. He quotes Immigration Minister Peter Dutton as stating: 'My message today is very clear to the transferees on Manus and in other facilities… the absolute resolve of me … is to make sure that… they will never arrive in Australia.'[291] In the same year, the Australian High Court, in a flagrant violation of international law, upheld the Australian government's imprisonment of asylum seekers on the high seas and their forced removal to other countries, 'regardless of whether they face persecution'.[292]

CONCLUSION

In this chapter I have provided an analysis of a wide range of histories of and current realities pertaining to racialized groups in Australia. Various groups were racialized throughout the country's history, and I have tried to include those who continue to be racialized in the first quarter of the twenty-first century. Inevitably, there will be some omissions, and as in Chapters 1 and 2, I apologize to any groups who are not included here, and feel that they should be. As in Chapter 2, I have not included in this chapter a full consideration of hate groups. As Alex White has argued, Australia has a long history of white supremacist groups, and many are now cashing in on Islamophobia, with more forum activity and recruitment efforts. White lists the following:

- Australian Defence League, an offshoot of the English Defence League: one of Australia's largest anti-Muslim groups, which uses stalking tactics and the posting of Muslims' photos online, accompanied by abuse.
- Southern Cross Hammerskins: anti-Asian, Islamophobic and antise-mitic, one of the biggest skinhead groups in Australia. The group targets young men at heavy metal music festivals and gigs.
- Blood and Honour Australia: white supremacist, spawned from chapters in the United Kingdom and the United States. Several members have

been linked to death threats against supporters of immigration. It has been linked to the Southern Cross Hammerskins.

- Crazy Whiteboys; neo-Nazi, antisemitic, anti-Asian and anti-African.
- Combat 18: neo-Nazi, its name a code for Adolf Hitler's initials: antisemitic, Islamophobic, and anti-all 'non-white' peoples.
- Patriotic Youth League, more recently known as Eureka Youth League: radical nationalists who play sport, which is a requirement for membership, as is being anti-immigration. Played a key role in the run-up to the Cronulla riots (discussed in this chapter) by handing out white power pamphlets.
- Creativity Movement: committed to the survival of the white 'races', and expansion through non-violence, promotes hatred under the guise of religion.[293]

As suggested in Chapter 2, distinctive differences in the experiences of racialized groups do not detract from the commonalities of racism experienced by racialized communities. As is argued throughout this book, in order for these differences and similarities to be fully understood, they need to be linked to racialization processes and articulated with ongoing changes in the capitalist mode of production and developments in colonialism and imperialism. Racialization processes are themselves intimately connected to migration patterns, which are in turn related to the needs and demands of the capitalist economy.

Conclusion

There are a number of important similarities and differences between the three Anglophone countries that are the focus of this book. While all three have been settled for thousands and thousands of years, the United Kingdom has no identifiable indigenous population whereas the United States and Australia still have sizeable, and on the whole highly visible, racialized indigenous minorities. The last US census listed over 5 million 'American Indian and Alaska Native' Americans, or 1.7 per cent of the total population, and in Australia there are over half a million 'Aboriginal and Torres Strait Islander peoples', or 2.5 per cent of the total.[1]

While some forms of racism in the United Kingdom are very much related to the days of the British Empire and the United Kingdom's vast array of colonies, both the modern-day United States and contemporary Australia are, of course, the products of European colonialism, which had its origins on the first continent in 1492, and on the second nearly 300 years later, in 1770. In addition, in both countries, invasion was followed by settlement, originally in 1565 by the Spanish in what is now the United States, and in 1788 by the British in what is now Australia (see Chapters 2 and 3).

As we have seen throughout the book, peoples at the receiving end of racism encompass a vast plethora of different constituencies including, of course, indigenous peoples in the United States and Australia, who have both been subject to the excesses of the RSAs and ISAs from the start of the colonizations. In the United Kingdom, people in the colonies were racialized both in their home countries and when they arrived in the United Kingdom in the post-Second World War period. In the United Kingdom, we also see older non-colour-coded racialized communities, created by the racism directed at the Irish, also racialized in Australia, and at the Gypsy Roma and Traveller communities. There are also newer groups of racialized people such as Eastern Europeans. The United States has a long history of racialization and racism, exploitation and oppression directed at African American and Latina/o American communities. In both the United States and Australia, Chinese and Japanese peoples have been racialized, exploited and oppressed over the centuries, and in the United Kingdom, the Chinese too have been on the receiving end of racism. The racialization of asylum-seekers is common to both the United Kingdom and Australia, and exists in a number of appalling dimensions. As we shall see in this Conclusion, disparities in wealth are increasing, and it is racialized groups that bear the brunt of poverty and unemployment, as detailed throughout this book.

Antisemitism is a serious problem in the United Kingdom and Australia, and Islamophobia is rampant in all three countries. Both antisemitism and Islamophobia are set to escalate, as the 'war on terror' at home and abroad spawns further reaction from dispossessed Islamists, who utterly mistakenly view Jewish people worldwide rather than Zionism as a major threat to Muslim people in the Israeli occupied territories.

As we saw in Chapters 1 and 3, multiculturalism has a long history in Australia and the United Kingdom, but at the level of the state it diminished in Australia in the late 1990s under Howard, only to be revived by Gillard, albeit in a very nationalist guise, influenced by Howard's 'new integrationism', in the second decade of the twenty-first century.[2] By contrast, in the United Kingdom that decade saw multiculturalism's decline, at least with respect to state policy. Multiculturalism in the Australia context was, by sleight of hand, designed to provide Australians with a triumphalist nationalism, in an attempt to shrug off a racist past. This repressive characteristic ultimately meant that multiculturalism was incapable of providing a convincing narrative of national identity – which explains the Hanson phenomenon (see Chapter 3 for a discussion).

Multiculturalism, as Stratton and Ang point out, is however unimaginable in the United States. To assert multiculturalism there 'would be challenging fundamental aspects of American self-perception'. While the United States is of course a pluralist society, the official rhetoric is that 'America is America: it has a unified national identity'. As Stratton and Ang put it, 'while everyday US social reality is so clearly multicultural, multiculturalism is alien to the way American national identity is imagined'.[3] Thus as we saw in Chapter 2, despite all the evidence to the contrary, Obama was able to deny the very existence of multiculturalism, and indeed racism, in the interpellation, 'There's not a Black America and White America and Latino America and Asian America – there's the United States of America.'

Whereas in the United Kingdom, the Right has always forged the myth of an imagined community[4] of long-existing '(white) Britons' with 'British values', both the United States and Australia, as colonialist settler societies, were faced with the problem of how to create a distinctive national identity without recourse to a pre-existing distinctive common culture as raw material.[5] But while the United Kingdom and the United States designed their national identity through ideological means, Australia did it traditionally through cultural means. As Stratton and Ang put it:

> While culture – and therefore ethnicity – were elided from the discourse of American national identity, race was not. Race, not

ethnicity, has been understood by Americans as the fundamental site of difference within the US nation-state.[6]

The 'Anglo-Australian race' was believed to be a new product of the multiplying British stock, the 'race' which, in the heyday of British imperialism saw itself as superior to all other 'races' and therefore possessing the duty and destiny to populate and 'civilize' the rest of the world. (See Chapter 1.) It is this distinctly Australian racism that undergirded the White Australia policy, which, as discussed in Chapter 3, was sanctioned by the adoption of the Immigration Restriction Act in 1901. In the United States, on the other hand, the one-ness of the American people was sought in a shared ideology (that of the messianic principles enshrined in the Declaration of Independence).[7]

Throughout the book, I have made connections between capitalism and imperialism and colonialism, both older UK imperialism and newer and neo-imperialism, of which the United States is the major player. As World Socialist Web Site (WSWS) writer Chris Marsden argues, for almost a quarter of a century since the dissolution of the Soviet Union and the reintroduction of capitalism in Russia and China, world imperialism has been seeking to bring about what President George Bush senior proclaimed in 1991 to be the 'new world order'.[8] As Bush put it, the end of the 1990–91 Gulf War against Iraq (when coalition forces from 34 countries led by the United States attacked Iraq in response to its invasion and annexation of Kuwait) would herald a world 'where diverse nations are drawn together in common cause to achieve the universal aspirations of mankind [sic] – peace and security, freedom, and the rule of law'.[9]

Since Bush senior's pledge, the major imperialist powers have visited destruction and death on millions of people – overwhelmingly Muslims and people of colour – in wars in the Balkans, the Middle East, Central Asia and Africa. Over and over again, they have proven their indifference to human suffering.[10] Shortly after 9/11 (11 September 2001) George W. Bush junior declared the 'war on terror'. The purpose of this 'war', as Marsden argues, both in its international and domestic manifestations, is 'to provide a political rationale for the re-division of the world between the major imperialist powers'. Military interventions in Afghanistan, Iraq, Libya, Syria and elsewhere, he goes on, have taken place to install puppet regimes in order to secure control of oil, gas and other geostrategic resources, as part of an attempt at global hegemony. In the course of these bloody conflicts, the 'imperialist powers have rained down bombs on defenceless civilians, carried out torture and assassination, and committed war crimes. Entire countries have been ravaged'.[11]

In the Iraq War alone (from the US-led invasion in 2003 to 2011), according to a 2013 report by university researchers in the United States, Canada and Baghdad in cooperation with the Iraqi Ministry of Health, in stark contrast to Bush senior's promise of peace, security, freedom and the rule of law, nearly half a million people are estimated to have died from war-related causes. As the lead author of the report, Amy Hagopian, points out, violence caused most of the deaths, but about a third were indirectly linked to the war, and these deaths have been left out of previous counts.[12]

Underlining what we have seen in Chapters 1, 2 and 3 with respect to racism and the racialization of minority and immigrant communities, Marsden states:

> No one can seriously believe that such actions do not have a profound impact on domestic political life. In a globalised world economy, where populations have become more ethnically and nationally diverse, the indignation created by imperialism's crimes knows no borders. This is especially the case within the minority and immigrant communities that have borne the brunt of attacks on workers' living conditions, leaving millions without work and faced with conditions of desperate poverty.[13]

While modern imperialism is unquestionably implicated in global Islamophobia, its reach is boundless. All the imperialist powers, including the United States, the United Kingdom and Australia, are taking a full role in the 'struggle for spheres of influence'. 'Every area of the globe is a source of bitter conflict: not only the former colonies and semi-colonies in the Middle East, Africa and Asia but also the Arctic, Antarctic and even outer space and cyberspace.'[14]

The orchestrated removal of socialism from the political agenda, Marsden concludes, 'has created conditions in which the most disoriented and desperate elements can be steered toward terrorism as a way of protesting the social, political and cultural oppression they face'. However, while the 'war on terror' goes on and on overseas and at home, austerity/immiseration capitalism means that it 'would be a fundamental political error to believe that the vast repressive apparatus being assembled is to be used against only one section of the population', since everywhere, 'the working class is being reduced to penury as jobs are destroyed, wages slashed, exploitation ramped up and vital social services destroyed'.[15]

Five years before Bush senior's promise of a 'new world order', Margaret Thatcher stated in 1986, with respect to UK capitalism, but by implication generalizable, '[p]opular capitalism is nothing less than a crusade to enfranchise the many in the economic life of the nation. We Conservatives are returning power to the people.'[16] Some 30 years later, the International Labour Organization (ILO) compiled a *Global Wage Report, 2014/15*. As Patrick Martin argues, perhaps the most devastating revelation in it is the following statement: 'Overall, in the group of developed economies, real wage growth lagged behind labour productivity growth over the period 1999 to 2013.' This means, Martin points out, that throughout this 14-year period the share of national income going to the working class declined, while the share of national income going to the tiny minority of capitalists steadily increased.[17]

At the beginning of 2015, Oxfam estimated that on current trends, within a year 1 per cent of the world's population will own more wealth than the other 99 per cent, with the share of the best-off increasing from 44 per cent in 2009 to 48 per cent in 2014, and the least well-off 80 per cent owning just 5.5 per cent. At the same time, the wealth of the richest 80 people doubled in cash terms between those years.[18] Such is the result of the financial crisis of 2007/08 and the onset of austerity/immiseration capitalism, and such is the reality of the interpellation, 'we're all in it together'. When a mere 80 people own the same amount of wealth as more than 3.5 billion people, it gives credence, as Larry Elliott and Ed Pilkington remind us, to Thomas Piketty's warning of a drift back to the levels of wealth concentration in the nineteenth century.[19]

This current growth of inequality is, of course, directly related to the ruling class's strategic response to 2007/08 and the insolvency of major banks, which was to pump some $12 trillion dollars into the financial markets via bank bailouts, near-zero interest rates, and central bank money-printing (known as quantitative easing). As Andre Damon puts it:

> This virtually free cash was used to drive up the world's stock markets and corporate profits to record highs. The same governments and central banks pursued brutal austerity policies against the working class, driving tens of millions into poverty.[20]

As Damon goes on, emblematic of the parasitism of global capital, 'the financial and insurance sector minted more billionaires than any other industry'.

Moreover, as Sandra Polaski, ILO's deputy director-general for policy, explains, '[w]age growth has slowed to almost zero for the developed economies as a group in the last two years, with actual declines in wages in some'.[21] To take the United Kingdom as a prime example, as Gerry Gold argues, predicting a mass revolt, 'the austerity we've seen so far [is] only the warm-up for the main event':

The scale of future cuts proposed by the Tories is so vast and almost unimaginable that it's impossible to envisage any government carrying them through without provoking massive social and civil unrest. In effect, the ConDems ... [in December, 2014] declared all-out war on the people. Left unstated by chancellor George Osborne, the political choices are as stark as a further 60% reduction in the state's budget the chancellor set out in his autumn statement. Osborne was short on detail. No wonder. The Tories are talking about taking government spending back to the levels last seen in the 1930s, when a global slump prefigured a second world war.[22]

As Gold continues, austerity is patently self-destructive – 'of people's lives and livelihoods, jobs and services. But it's all capitalism can come up with.' With respect to the concerns of this book, it has been clearly demonstrated in the first three chapters that while the target of austerity is the working class as a whole, statistically it is overwhelmingly the racialized fractions of that class in the United Kingdom, the United States and Australia whose resulting poverty is greatest.

Martin notes that currently nearly 200 million workers are unemployed worldwide, and that another 400 million will enter the job market looking for work in the next decade. How, he asks, 'will capitalism provide 600 million new jobs under conditions of worldwide economic stagnation? What wages will be offered? What will be the working conditions? What will be the level of exploitation?'[23]

Without doubt, unless capitalism and imperialism are successfully challenged, the racialized workers and communities who bear the greatest brunt in the present will also bear the maximum burden in the future. Fearful of the response from workers worldwide, the 'ruling classes of the world are preparing accordingly, heaping up weapons, building armies of police, intensifying their attacks on democratic rights and spying on the entire population of the world'.[24] The 'war on terror' provides part of the justification for this.

All the world conflicts breed the tensions that lead to 'ethnic divisions' and communal fighting. There are fundamental contradictions in the capitalist system between the development of a global capitalist economy and the division of the world into antagonistic nation states, in which the private ownership of the means of production is rooted.[25] Capitalism is not capable of organizing the world economy rationally, and it contains the seeds of its own destruction, because:

[t]he collision of imperialist and national state interests expresses the

impossibility, under capitalism, of organising a globally-integrated economy on a rational foundation and thus ensuring the harmonious development of the productive forces. However, the same contradictions driving imperialism to the brink provide the objective impulse for social revolution. The globalisation of production has led to a massive growth of the working class. Only this social force, which owes no allegiance to any nation, is capable of putting an end to the profit system, which is the root cause of war.[26]

Commenting on calls from sections of the ruling class, such as the aptly and ideologically named Coalition for Inclusive Capitalism, to be wary of escalating inequalities, Damon concludes: 'warnings about the growth of inequality are rooted in fears within the financial aristocracy that the ever more obvious and repulsive gap between the super-rich and everyone else will have revolutionary consequences'.[27]

Some 25 years after George Bush senior promised a 'new world order' of peace, security and freedom, and 30 years after Margaret Thatcher's pledge of 'power to the people' and her insistence that popular capitalism is a crusade of enfranchisement of the many, the United States, with the United Kingdom, Australia and others as partners, is engaged in a permanent 'war on terror', while neoliberal capitalist governments throughout most of the world are increasingly encroaching on human rights, and preparing to crank up measures to prolong austerity. At the same time, the political and communications ISAs interpellate the populace that the 'war on terror' is the only way to deal with the 'terrorist threat', and that 'we are all in it together' as far as austerity is concerned, to which 'there is no alternative'.

Over 40 years ago, American Marxist Harry Magdoff summed up the way in which we are interpellated with the false consciousness that imperialism and racialized capitalism are 'common sense', something that permeates and saturates the capitalist world, thus undermining a revolutionary response:

> The major obstacle to such enlightenment is the pervasiveness of the ideological rationalization for imperialism. The extent of this pervasiveness is not easy to perceive because such rationalization is deep-seated. Its roots are intertwined with the accepted, conventional modes of thought and the consciousness of a people. Thus, they are located in the false patriotism and racism that sink deeply and imperceptibly into the individual's sub-conscious; in the traditions, values, and even aesthetics of the cultural environment – an environment evolved over centuries during which self-designated 'superior'

cultures assumed the right to penetrate and dominate 'inferior' cultures. These roots are also buried in the sophisticated theorems of both liberal and conservative economics, sociology, political science, anthropology, and history. For these reasons, citizens of an imperialist country who wish to understand imperialism must first emancipate themselves from the seemingly endless web of threads that bind them emotionally and intellectually to the imperialist condition.[28]

As feminist revolutionary historian Roxanne Dunbar-Ortiz argues, the most important task for the antiwar and social justice movements in the United States today is to assume the responsibility of being citizens of an empire that must be dismantled.[29]

As I noted in the Introduction, space has prevented a consideration of the myriad forms of antiracist struggle on three continents, hence I am proposing to write another volume, provisionally entitled *Antiracism: a Critical Analysis*. Lack of space has also meant no proper discussion of an alternative to the nightmares of imperialism and permanent war, to the horrors of austerity/ immiseration capitalism, and no analyses of solutions to a dystopian world of institutional racism and ongoing racialization, to processes by which the rich get richer and richer and the poor get poorer and poorer, and the racialized poor even more so. From the perspective of human survival, let alone morality, a replacement for imperialism, neoliberalism, capitalism, racialization and racism is, for me, self-evidently imperative.

There are other directions for humankind. In the course of my discussion of Marxism and neo-Marxism in the Introduction, I made some brief comments about socialism. Elsewhere with political scientist and Latin American scholar, Sara Motta and other writers, I have discussed at length the many different attempts to for a socialism of the twenty-first century in Latin America.[30] Such struggles are to be distinguished from the Stalinist distortions of 'socialism', known universally and erroneously as 'communism',[31] and involve a fundamental reassertion of 'good sense'. This requires nothing less than the redistribution of wealth, participatory democracy in the workplace and the polity, as well as the growth of communal councils and communes. All this needs to be in the context of the movement towards equality for all, including of course racialized indigenous peoples and peoples of African descent. Crucially, women play a major role in socialist developments in Latin America.

In the context of the bleak and depressing scenario depicted in this book, and in the spirit of Gramsci's dictum, 'pessimism of the intellect, optimism of the will', there is much that the United Kingdom, the United States and Australia can learn from ongoing developments on that continent.

Notes

Introduction

1   S. Rose and H. Rose (2005) 'Why we should give up on race: as geneticists and biol-ogists know, the term no longer has meaning,' *Guardian*, 9 April, www.theguardian.com/world/2005/apr/09/race.science; see also A. Darder and R. D. Torres (2004) *After Race: Racism After Multiculturalism*, New York: New York University Press, pp. 1–12, 25–34.

2   Rose and Rose (2005).

3   Rose and Rose (2005).

4   S. D. Ashe and B. F. McGeever (2011) 'Marxism, racism and the construction of "race" as a social and political relation: an interview with Professor Robert Miles,' *Ethnic and Racial Studies*, 34(12), p. 2,018.

5   I would like to thank Alpesh Maisuria for suggesting this to me.

6   J. Kovel (1988) *White Racism: A Psychohistory*, London: Free Association Books.

7   A good example is when in early 2015, a group of Chelsea FC (a UK football club) supporters physically prevented a black man entering a Paris metro train, with chants of 'We're racist, we're racist and that's the way we like it, we like it, we like it,' emanating from the carriage. Football matches are good examples of cultural events that stimulate racism.

8   Socialism is a greatly misunderstood concept. Its general features are workers' ownership and democratic control of the means of production, distribution and exchange; and public services under state ownership and democratic workers' control. There would be universal free health care for all, incorporating the latest medical advances. There would be no need for private health. There would universal free comprehensive education for all and no need for private schooling. There would be free comprehensive leisure facilities for all, with no fee for health clubs, concerts and so on. There would be free housing, and employment for all. There would be no racism, and full rights for women, for the lesbian, gay, bisexual, transgender and intersex (LGBTI) communities, all members of minority ethnic groups, and disabled people. There would be full freedom of religion. There would be no ageism. There would be no war, no hunger and no poverty. I return to the notion of twenty-first as opposed to twentieth-century socialism in the Conclusion to this book.

9   People of colour ('color' in US spelling) is a common nomenclature in the United States, and is becoming increasingly popular elsewhere. It needs to be differentiated from the now defunct and offensive nomenclature, 'coloured [colored in US spell-ing] people'. As indicated earlier, we see in Chapter 1 of this book that racism is not only directed at people of colour, but can be non-colour-coded.

10 D. Gillborn (2006) 'Critical race theory and education: racism and anti-racism in educational theory and praxis,' *Discourse*, 27(1), p. 20. CRT has a long history in the United States, dating back to the 1980s. For a thorough analysis of the strengths of CRT, see D. Gillborn (2008) *Racism and Education: Coincidence or Conspiracy?* London: Routledge; for a Marxist critique of CRT, see M. Cole (2016a) *Critical Race Theory and Education: A Marxist Response*, 2nd edn, New York and London:

Palgrave Macmillan; and M. Cole (2016b) *New Developments in Critical Race Theory and Education: Revisiting Marxism in Austerity*, New York and London: Palgrave Macmillan.

11   Gillborn (2006), p. 21.

12   Gillborn (2006), p. 22.

13   W. F. Tate (1997) 'Critical race theory and education: history, theory, and implications,' in M. W. Apple (ed.), *Review of Research in Education*, 22, Washington DC: American Educational Research Association, p. 234, cited in Gillborn (2006), p. 9.

14   Tate (1997), p. 235, cited in Gillborn (2006), p. 9. I personally prefer not to use the disablist term 'colour blindness'. We could use a non-disablist term, perhaps 'colour-discounting,' for the belief that people should treat everyone equally regardless of 'race'. If there are any doubts in your mind about the use of 'blind' in this way being offensive, it is probable that you have not worked with a blind colleague or taught a blind student. The same applies with the term 'deaf'. The common expressions 'Are you blind?' and 'Are you deaf?' take on new (offensive) meanings when they are used by those working with or teaching blind, sight-impaired, deaf or hearing-impaired students.

15   Gillborn (2006), p. 22.

16   Gillborn (2006), p. 23.

17   For instance, N. Gotanda (1995) 'A critique of "Our Constitution Is Color-Blind"', in K. Crenshaw, N. Gotanda, G. Peller and K. Thomas (eds), *Critical Race Theory: The Key Writings that Formed the Movement*, New York: New Press; R. Delgado and J. Stefancic (2001) *Critical Race Theory: An Introduction*, New York: New York University Press, pp. 21–3.

18   Delgado and Stefancic (2001), p. 22.

19   Cole (2016a), ch. 1.

20   R. Delgado and J. Stefancic (2000) 'Introduction' in R. Delgado and J. Stefancic (eds), *Critical Race Theory: The Cutting Edge*, 2nd edn, Philadelphia, Pa.: Temple University Press, cited in Gillborn (2006), p. 10.

21   Gillborn (2006), p. 24.

22   Delgado and Stefancic (2000), p. xvii, cited in Gillborn (2006), p. 13.

23   Gillborn (2006), p. 25. Gillborn is referring to the work of M. E. L. Bush, especially (2004) 'Race, ethnicity, and whiteness,' *Sage Race Relations Abstracts*, 29 (3–4); R. Delgado and J. Stefancic (eds) (1997) *Critical White Studies: Looking Behind the Mirror*, Philadelphia, Pa.: Temple University Press; and M. Fine, L. Weis, L. C. Powell and L. Mun Wong (eds) (1997) *Off White: Readings on Race, Power, and Society*, New York: Routledge.

24   Gillborn (2006), p. 25.

25   Marx and Marxism, including the works of founders of Marxism Karl Marx (1818–1883) and Friedrich Engels (1820–1895), are widely misunderstood and extensively misinterpreted. For a comprehensive overview of Marx, his life and to read the works of Marx and Engels, go to the Marx and Engels Internet Archive (n.d.): www.marxists.org/archive/marx/

26   For an explanation of the LTV, see K. Marx (1887) *Capital, Vol. 1*, www.marxists.org/archive/marx/works/1867-c1/, especially ch. 1; for a brief summary, see M. Cole (2011) *Racism and Education in the U.K. and the U.S.: Towards a Socialist Alternative*, New York and London: Palgrave Macmillan, pp. 42–4.

27   T. Hickey (2000) 'Class and class analysis for the twenty-first century,' in M. Cole (ed.), *Education, Equality and Human Rights: Issues of Gender, 'Race,' Sexuality, Special Needs and Social Class,* London: Routledge, p. 168.

28   F. Engels (1892) [1977] 'Socialism: utopian and scientific,' in K. Marx and F. Engels, *Selected Works in One Volume,* London: Lawrence & Wishart, p. 411.

29   Male-centred and sexist language was the norm before the advent of the twentieth-century feminist movement. I shall thus resist the temptation to comment each time it occurs in citations in this book. Today male-centred and sexist language tends to be absent from the printed word. When it occurs, we must presume it is there out of ignorance, or because the writer is deliberately being male-centred and sexist.

30   K. Marx (1859) 'Preface to *A Contribution to the Critique of Political Economy,'* www.marxists.org/archive/marx/works/1859/critique-pol-economy/preface.htm

31   K. Marx and F. Engels (1845–6) *The German Ideology Part I: Feuerbach. Opposition of the Materialist and Idealist Outlook: The Illusion of the Epoch,* www.marxists.org/ archive/marx/works/1845/german-ideology/ch01b.htm

32   See Cole (2011), pp. 23–4.

33   Marx (1887), p. 751.

34   K. Taylor (2011) 'Race, class and Marxism,' SocialistWorker.org, 4 January, http:// socialistworker.org/2011/01/04/race-class-and-marxism, pp. 4, 8.

35   Taylor (2011), p. 8.

36   L. Kolakowski (1978) *Main Currents of Marxism,* trans. P. S. Falla, 3 vols, Oxford: Oxford University Press.

37   Antonio Gramsci (1891–1937), once leader of the Communist Party of Italy, was imprisoned under the fascist regime of Benito Mussolini during the Second World War. His major work, written in prison, was published as *Selections from Prison Notebooks* (London: Lawrence & Wishart, 1978).

     The words 'communist' and 'communism' are greatly misunderstood. 'Communism' was used by Marx to refer to the stage after socialism when the state would have withered away and when we would live communally. In the period after the Russian Revolution up to the demise of the Soviet Union, the Soviet Union and other Eastern European countries were routinely referred to as 'communist' in the West. The Soviet Union, founded in 1922, actually referred to itself, following Marx, as 'socialist'. Some Marxists (e.g. T. Cliff (1974) *State Capitalism in Russia,* www. marxists.org/archive/cliff/works/1955/statecap/index.htm) have described what became of the Soviet Union and other Eastern European countries as 'state capitalist'. It is ironic that the West falsely designated these states 'communist'. In reality (despite the fact that many had a number of positive features: full employment, housing for all, free public and social services, safety for women to walk the streets at night and so on), they were undemocratic dictatorships with special privileges for an elite and drudgery for the many. These Eastern European societies were not real socialist states, and were also far removed from Marx's vision of communism. Marx and Engels also made reference to early pre-capitalist social formations – stages of communal living – for example, 'the ancient communal and State ownership which proceeds especially from the union of several tribes into a city by agreement or by conquest, and which is still accompanied by slavery' (Marx and Engels, 1845/6).

38   Louis Althusser (1918–1990) was a professor of philosophy at the École Normale Supérieure in Paris, and a long-time member of the French Communist Party.

39   K. Marx 1852) *The Eighteenth Brumaire of Louis Bonaparte*, www.marxists.org/archive/marx/works/1852/18th-brumaire/

40   Taylor (2011), p. 7.

41   Marx–Engels correspondence 1893: Engels to Franz Mehring. Source: *Marx and Engels Correspondence*, International Publishers (1968) www.marxists.org/archive/marx/works/1893/letters/93_07_14.htm

42   This is actually part of a real campaign by the Tea Party, a very right-wing faction in the US Republican Party (Common Sense Campaign (n.d.) http://commonsensecampaign.org/site/index.php/home-page/about-us.html), leading lights of which adopt a 'deport them all' stance on immigration (C. Vargas (2015) 'On immigration, will the Tea Party dominate the new Congress?' *The Hill*, 7 January, http://thehill.com/blogs/pundits-blog/immigration/228723-on-immigration-will-the-tea-party-dominate-the-new-congress).

43   It should be pointed out that in Australia in popular usage 'Asian' usually refers generically to Chinese, Korean, Japanese and South-East Asian people. People of Indian, Pakistani and other origins from South Asia are more usually referred to specifically by nationality. In the United Kingdom 'Asian' generally refers to South Asia: India, Pakistan and Bangladesh; and in the United States, people whose origins are in the whole Asian continent.

44   Taylor (2011), p. 7.

45   D. Coben (1999) 'Common sense or good sense: ethnomathematics and the prospects for a Gramscian politics of adults' mathematics education,' in M. van Groenestijn and D. Coben (eds), *Mathematics as Part of Lifelong Learning. The Fifth International Conference of Adults Learning Maths – A Research Forum, ALM-5.* London: Goldsmiths College, University of London, in Association with ALM, www.nottingham.ac.uk/csme/meas/papers/coben.html, p. 206.

46   L. Althusser (1971) 'Ideology and ideological state apparatuses,' in *Lenin and Philosophy and Other Essays*, London: New Left Books, www.marx2mao.com/Other/LPOE70NB.html, p. 175.

47   Althusser explains:

> [c]aught in this quadruple system of interpellation as subjects, of subjection to the Subject, of universal recognition and of absolute guarantee, the subjects 'work,' they 'work by themselves' in the vast majority of cases, with the exception of the 'bad subjects' who on occasion provoke the intervention of one of the detachments of the (repressive) State apparatus. But the vast majority of (good) subjects work all right 'all by themselves,' that is, by ideology (whose concrete forms are realized in the Ideological State Apparatuses). They are inserted into practices governed by the rituals of the ISAs. They 'recognize' the existing state of affairs … that 'it really is true that it is so and not otherwise,' and that they must be obedient. Subjects recognize that 'the hail' was really addressed to them, and not someone else and respond accordingly: 'Yes, that's how it is, that's really true!' Their subjection is thus freely accepted. Thus when confronted with the 'inevitability' of global capitalism, the response is 'That's obvious! That's right! That's true!' (Althusser, 1971, pp. 144–5)

48   Althusser (1971), p. 181.

49   E. Laclau (1977) *Politics and Ideology in Marxist Theory*, London: New Left Books, p. 100.

50   'Social democracy' is a form of government that aims to provide security and equal opportunities for all its people and actively reorders society so that it is conducive to such developments. Such changes should be brought about gradually, legitimated by a democratically elected majority, and the capitalist system is retained.

51   LTV, as developed by Marx, explains that it is workers not capitalists who in reality create wealth (see note 25 to the Introduction).

52   Althusser (1971), pp. 142–4. The ISAs operate primarily, though not totally, through ideology, and the RSAs similarly via force (Althusser (1971), pp. 144–5).

53   Althusser (1971), p. 181.

54   S. Hall (2010) 'Interpreting the crisis: Doreen Massey and Stuart Hall discuss ways of understanding the current crisis,' in R. S. Grayson and J. Rutherford (eds), *After the Crash: Re-inventing the Left in Britain*, London: Lawrence & Wishart (a Soundings ebook).

55   E. J. Hobsbawm (1977) 'Gramsci and political theory,' *Marxism Today*, www. amielandmelburn.org.uk/collections/mt/pdf/07_77_205.pdf, p.209.

56   S. Hall (1978) 'Racism and reaction,' in BBC/CRE, *Five Views of Multi-Racial Britain*, London: BBC/CRE.

57   Gillborn (2008), p. 1.

58   See e.g. Cole (2016a, 2016b).

59   See e.g. C. Mills (1997) *The Racial Contract*, New York: Cornell University Press.

60   See e.g. J. Preston (2007) *Whiteness and Class in Education*, Dordrecht, Netherlands: Springer; J. Preston (2010) 'Concrete and abstract racial domination,' *Power and Education*, 2(2).

61   Gillborn (2008), pp. 34–6.

62   R. Miles (1993) *Racism after 'Race Relations,'* London: Routledge, pp. 50–2.

63   R. Miles (1989) *Racism*, London: Routledge, p. 79.

64   Miles (1989), p. 75.

65   Miles (1989), p. 7.

66   Maria Papapolydorou (Review of *Critical Race Theory and Education: A Marxist Response* by Mike Cole,' *Race and Class*, 51(4) (2010)) has reminded us that for Miles (1989) racism is associated with modes of production but not limited to capitalist modes of production, and that, according to Miles, racialization and racism predate capitalist societies. As Miles puts it, neither are 'exclusive "products" of capitalism but have origins in European societies prior to the development of the capitalist mode of production' (1989, p. 99). While I acknowledge this, and the Crusades are but one obvious example, my focus in this book is specifically on the way in which racialization connects to capitalist modes of production (and to patterns of migration). This is not to say, of course, that all instances of racism in capitalist societies are directly or even indirectly linked to capitalism, economics and politics. In racialized societies, racism is experienced with massive and constant frequency in countless situations, an insistence for which I have credited CRT. The point I am making is that without the neo-Marxist concept of racialization, it is impossible to have a full understanding of racism under capitalism, both historically and contemporaneously. For a discussion of different uses of the

concept of racialization, both (neo-)Marxist and non-Marxist, see K. Murji and J. Solomos (eds) (2005) *Racialization: Studies in Theory and Practice,* Oxford: Oxford University Press.

67 R. Miles (1982) *Racism and Migrant Labour: A Critical Text,* London: Routledge & Kegan Paul; Miles (1989, 1993); Ashe and McGeever (2011).

68 W. Macpherson (1999) *The Stephen Lawrence Enquiry, Report of an Enquiry by Sir William Macpherson,* London: HMSO, www.gov.uk/government/uploads/system/uploads/attachment_data/file/277111/4262.pdf

69 Macpherson (1999), 6.34.

70 G. Dale (1999) 'Capitalism and migrant labour,' in G. Dale and M. Cole (eds), *The European Union and Migrant Labour*, Oxford: Berg, p. 308.

71 Mills (1997), p. 37.

72 'We are the 99 per cent' is a widely used political slogan, first coined by the Occupy movement (www.occupytogether.org/aboutoccupy/).

73 Mills (1997), p. 1.

74 Mills's 'racial contract' refers to his belief that racism is at the core of the 'social contract,' rather than being an unintended result, because of human failing. Social contract theory, which is nearly as old as philosophy itself, is the view that people's moral and/or political obligations are dependent on a contract or agreement among them to form the society in which they live (Internet Encyclopedia of Philosophy (IEP), www.iep.utm.edu/soc-cont/).

75 Mills (1997), p. 33.

76 Mills (1997), p. 20.

77 Mills (1997), p. 3.

78 See e.g. C. Chadderton (2015) 'UK secondary schools under surveillance: what are the implications for race? A critical race and Butlerian analysis,' in A. Kupfer (ed.), *Power and Education: Contexts of Oppression and Opportunity*, London: Palgrave Macmillan, p. 130.

79 M. Cole (2009) *Critical Race Theory and Education: A Marxist Response*, 1st edn, London: Palgrave Macmillan.

80 Mills (1997), pp. 78–9.

81 Mills (1997), p. 79.

82 Mills (1997), p. 79.

83 Mills (1997), p. 81.

84 Mills (1997), p. 80.

85 Mills (1997), p. 78.

86 In Ashe and McGeever (2011), p. 2,019.

87 In Ashe and McGeever (2011), p. 2,019.

88 C. W. Mills (2009) 'Critical race theory: a reply to Mike Cole,' *Ethnicities*, 9(2), p. 275.

89 A. Bhattacharyya (2009) 'The Daily Mail vs. the Nazis?' *Socialist Worker*, www.socialistworker.co.uk/art.php?id=19454

90 Althusser (1971).

91 Bhattacharyya (2009).

92 Bhattacharyya (2009). This was also the case with the xeno-racist political party UKIP in the run-up to the 2015 UK general election (see Chapter 1 for a discussion).

93 M. Smith (2010) 'Nazis in the election, racists on the streets... the BNP and EDL,' *Socialist Review*, March, p. 13.

94 Bhattacharyya (2009).

95 Bhattacharyya (2009).

96 The following analysis draws on Cole (2016a).

97 C. W. Mills (2003) *From Class to Race: Essays in White Marxism and Black Radicalism*, Lanham, Md.: Rowman & Littlefield, p. 156.

98 K. Crenshaw, N. Gotanda, G. Peller and K. Thomas (1995) 'Introduction,' in K. Crenshaw, N. Gotanda, G. Peller and K. Thomas (eds), *Critical Race Theory: The Key Writings that Formed the Movement*, New York: New Press, p. xxvi.

99 Mills (2003), p. 157.

100 Mills (2003), p. 157.

101 Crenshaw et al. (1995), p. xxvi.

102 Mills (2003), p. 157.

103 Mills (2003), p. 158.

104 Mills (2003), p. 158.

105 Mills (2003), p. 158.

106 Social class is of course also gendered, and there is a substantial and substantive literature on Marxism and feminism, the latest of which is S. Mojab (2015) *Marxism and Feminism*, London: Zed. Many feminists have rejected Marxist feminism in favour of intersectionality (discussed later in this Introduction).

107 K. Marx (1870) [1978] *Ireland and the Irish Question*, Moscow: Progress, p. 254.

108 Taylor (2011), p. 1.

109 E. Mitchell (2013) 'I am a woman and a human: a Marxist feminist critique of intersectionality theory,' libcom.org, https://libcom.org/library/i-am-woman-human-marxist-feminist-critique-intersectionality-theory-eve-mitchell, p. 1.

110 Gillborn (2008), p. 37.

111 Cole (2016a).

112 Gillborn (2008), p. 36.

113 K. Crenshaw (1989) 'Demarginalizing the intersection of race and sex: a black feminist critique of antidiscrimination doctrine, feminist theory, and antiracist politics,' University of Chicago Legal Forum, p. 140.

114 Crenshaw (1989), p. 140.

115 S. Smith (2013/14) 'Black feminism and intersectionality,' *International Socialist Review*, 91, http://isreview.org/issue/91/black-feminism-and-intersectionality, p. 3.

116 N. Yuval-Davis (2011) 'Power, intersectionality and the politics of belonging,' Aalborg: Institut for Kultur og Globale Studier, Aalborg Universitet, Denmark, http://vbn.aau.dk/files/58024503/FREIA_wp_75.pdf, p. 4.

117 The Socialist Equality Party that publishes on the World Socialist Web Site (WSWS) is an example of such an organization. While I find their analyses of neoliberal and austerity/immiseration capitalism enlightening and most insightful, and make use of them throughout this book, I take issue with their frequent marginalization of issues other than social class.

118 Mitchell (2013), p. 7.

119 M. Rectenwald (2013) 'What's wrong with identity politics (and intersectionality theory)? A response to Mark Fisher's "Exiting the Vampire Castle" (and its critics),' *North Star*, www.thenorthstar.info/?p=11411, p. 2.

120   Patricia Hill Collins, cited in B. Guy-Sheftall (1995) *Words of Fire: An Anthology of African-American Feminist Thought*, New York: New Press, p. 345.
121   Smith (2013/14), p. 13 (emphasis added).
122   Ashe and McGeever (2011), p. 2,017.
123   K. Raja (2013) 'Poverty and racism inextricably linked, says UN expert,' *Third World Resurgence*, 278, October, www.twnside.org.sg/title2/resurgence/2013/278/human1.htm
124   Cited in Raja (2013).
125   Cited in Raja (2013).
126   M. Cole (2016c) *Antiracism: A Critical Analysis* (forthcoming).

1 The United Kingdom

1   Policy Exchange (2014) A Portrait of Modern Britain, 6 May, www.policyexchange.org.uk/publications/category/item/a-portrait-of-modern-britain
2   H. Barnard (2014) 'New report fails to highlight most important fact about poverty and ethnicity,' Joseph Rowntree Foundation, www.jrf.org.uk/blog/2014/05/most-important-fact-ethnicity
3   I. Grosvenor (1987) 'A different reality: education and the racialisation of the black child,' *History of Education*, 16(4); I. Grosvenor (1989) 'Teacher racism and the construction of black underachievement,' in R. Lowe (ed.), *The Changing Secondary School*, Lewes: Falmer.
4   M. Greenfields (2006) 'Stopping places,' in C. Clark and M. Greenfields, *Here to Stay: The Gypsies and Travellers of Britain*, Hatfield: University of Hertfordshire Press.
5   S. Poynting and V. Mason (2007) 'The resistible rise of Islamophobia: anti-Muslim racism in the UK and Australia before 11 September 2001,' *Journal of Sociology*, 43(1).
6   M. Cole (2012a) 'Racism in the UK: change and continuity,' in M. Cole (ed.), *Education, Equality and Human Rights: Issues of Gender, 'Race,' Sexuality, Disability and Social Class*, 3nd edn, London: Routledge.
7   A. Sivanandan (2009) 'Foreword' to L. Fekete, *A Suitable Enemy: Racism, Migration and Islamophobia in Europe*, London: Pluto. While Islamophobia fuels Islamism and vice versa, it is imperative for antiracists to be vigilant against attempts to legitimize Islamophobia as a response to Islamism. In addition, while such groups as Islamic State (IS), itself a product of decades of western imperialism (see P. Martin (2014) 'ISIS atrocities and US imperialism,' WSWS, 4 September, www.wsws.org/en/articles/2014/09/04/pers-s04.html), pose a very real threat to non-Muslims and Muslims alike, it is also necessary to be aware that such threats, whether real (as with IS) or fabricated (as with Sadam Hussein's 'weapons of mass destruction'), are used as an excuse for the expansion of imperialist conquest.
8   A. Sivanandan (2001) 'Poverty is the new black,' *Race and Class*, 43(2).
9   L. Fekete (2009) *A Suitable Enemy: Racism, Migration and Islamophobia in Europe*, London: Pluto.
10   I deal with each form of racism separately for analytical clarity. Of course, there may be overlap between them. For example, some at the receiving end of older colour-coded racism will be Muslim and subject to Islamophobia; some Eastern European

workers are Muslim or of Roma origin, and subject to Islamophobia and anti-GRT racism; many asylum seekers are Muslim, some are Eastern European and so on. I have not included a discussion of people who are 'mixed race,' since, while the 2011 census revealed a million people who identify as 'mixed race,' and while there is evidence of a growing consciousness and interest in being mixed, it is difficult to speak of a coherent mixed group or experience in the United Kingdom (see M. Song (2010) 'Is there "a" mixed race group in Britain? The diversity of multiracial identification and experience,' *Critical Social Policy*, 30 (3)).

11 J. Hunt (1864) 'On the Negro's Place in Nature,' *Journal of the Anthropological Society of London, 2, p. xvi* http://www.jstor.org/stable/3025197?loginSuccess=true&seq=2#page_scan_tab_contents

12 V. G. Kiernan (1969) *The Lords of Human Kind*, London: Weidenfeld & Nicolson, p. 316. Kiernan draws a convincing parallel between the European male ruling class's simple notion of the right to rule 'natives' or to fight them, and its perceptions of the place of women in society.

13 B. Semmel (1960) *Imperialism and social reform*, London: George Allen & Unwin, p. 24.

14 Semmel (1960), p. 24

15 J. M. MacKenzie (1984) *Propaganda and Empire: The Manipulation of British Public Opinion 1880–1960*, Manchester: Manchester University, p. 150.

16 MacKenzie (1984), pp. 150–1.

17 D. A. Lorimer (1978) *Colour, Class and the Victorians: English Attitudes to the Negro in the Mid-Nineteenth Century*, Leicester: Leicester University Press, p. 107.

18 J. A. Mangan (1986) 'The grit of our forefathers: invented traditions, propaganda and imperialism,' in J. M. MacKenzie (ed.), *Propaganda and Empire: The Manipulation of British Public Opinion, 1880–1960*, Manchester: Manchester University Press.

19 R. Williams (1961) *The Long Revolution*, London: Chatto & Windus, pp. 168–72.

20 R. Miles (1982) *Racism and Migrant Labour*, London: Routledge & Kegan Paul, pp. 110 and 119.

21 P. Summerfield (1986), 'Patriotism and Empire: Music-Hall entertainment, 1870–1914,' in J. MacKenzie (ed.) *Imperialism and Popular Culture*, Manchester: Manchester University Press, p. 42.

22 J. S. Bratton (1986) 'Of England, home, and duty: the image of England in Victorian and Edwardian juvenile fiction,' in McKenzie (1986).

23 J. Springhall (1986) '"Up Guards and at them!"; British imperialism and popular art, 1880–1914,' in MacKenzie (1986).

24 Pitman's *King Edward History Readers* (for Juniors) 1901, pp. 5–6, cited in V. Chancellor (1970) *History for Their Masters*, Bath: Adams & Dart, pp. 127–8.

25 R. Miles (1993) *Racism after 'Race Relations,'* London: Routledge, p. 69.

26 F. J. Glendenning (1973) 'History textbooks and racial attitudes: 1804–1969,' *Journal of Educational Administration and History*, 5, p. 35.

27 Chancellor (1970), p. 240.

28 *Cassell's Class History of England*, cited in Chancellor (1970), p. 122.

29 *Cassell's Class History of England*, cited in Chancellor (1970), p. 122.

30 J. A. Hobson (1902) *Imperialism: A Study*, p. 130, cited in Springhall (1986), p. 49

31 Springhall (1986), p. 49.

32 Springhall (1986), p. 50.

33   M. Dejevsky (2014) 'Britain must accept that Hong Kong is no longer a colony,' *Guardian*, 1 December, www.theguardian.com/commentisfree/2014/dec/01/britain-hong-kong-no-longer-colony-empire-china

34   T. He (n.d.) 'British imperialism in China: a legacy of commerce, addiction, and gunboat diplomacy,' Guided History, http://blogs.bu.edu/guidedhistory/moderneurope/tao-he/

35   K. Tho'mas (1997) 'Opium war: Britain stole Hong Kong from China,' *Workers World*, 10 July, www.serendipity.li/wod/hongkong.html

36   Tho'mas (1997).

37   Rowntree (1905), cited in Tho'mas (1997).

38   Tho'mas (1997).

39   K. Marx (1887) [1965] *Capital*, Vol. 1, Moscow: Progress, p. 752.

40   Tho'mas (1997).

41   He (n.d.).

42   Tho'mas (1997).

43   Cited in Tho'mas (1997).

44   Tho'mas (1997).

45   Cited in B. Porter (2011) 'Where is this England?' *London Review of Books*, 33(21), 3 November, www.lrb.co.uk/v33/n21/bernard-porter/where-is-this-england

46   Porter (2011). The reference is to J. Lovell (2011) *The Opium War: Drugs, Dreams and the Making of China*, London: Picador.

47   Tho'mas (1997).

48   J. Rowntree (1905) *The Imperial Drug Trade*, London: Methuen, cited in Tho'mas (1997).

49   Porter (2011).

50   Tho'mas (1997).

51   R. Klein (1995) 'Law and racism in an Asian setting: an analysis of the British rule in Hong Kong,' *18 Hastings International and Comparative Law Review*, 223.

52   Klein (1995), p. 1.

53   C. H. Nightingale (2012) *Segregation: A Global History of Divided Cities*, Chicago, Ill.: University of Chicago Press.

54   C. H. Nightingale (2013) 'The segregation paradoxes,' www.mascontext.com/issues/17-boundary-spring-13/the-segregation-paradoxes/. Anti-Chinese racism in the United States and Australia is discussed in Chapters 2 and 3 of this book respectively, while racism directed at British Chinese people in the United Kingdom today is discussed later in this chapter.

55   M. Cole (1992) *Racism, History and Educational Policy: From the Origins of the Welfare State to the Rise of the Radical Right*, PhD thesis, University of Essex.

56   G. Lewis (1996) 'Welfare settlements and racialising practices,' *Soundings*, 4 (Autumn), p. 110.

57   W. Beveridge (1942) *Social Insurance and Allied Services*, Cmd 6404, London: HMSO, para. 413.

58   Beveridge (1942), para. 117.

59   Cited in S. Cohen (1985) 'Anti-semitism, immigration controls and the welfare state,' *Critical Social Policy*, 13 (Summer), pp. 88–9.

60   R. Miles and M. Brown (2006) *Racism*, 2nd edn, London: Routledge, p. 131.

61   Miles and Brown (2006), p. 130.

62 P. Fryer (1984) *Staying Power: The History of Black People in Britain*, London: Pluto Press; R. Ramdin (1987) *The Making of the Black Working Class in Britain*, London: Gower.

63 See A. Heath and J. Ridge (1983) 'Social mobility of ethnic minorities,' *Journal of Biosocial Science*, Supplement, 8.

64 W. W. Daniel (1968) *Racial Discrimination in England*, Harmondsworth: Penguin; D. J. Smith (1977) *Racial Disadvantage in Britain*, Harmondsworth: Penguin.

65 Smith (1977).

66 P. Wright (1968) *The Coloured Worker in British Industry*, Oxford: Oxford University Press, pp. 89–144, cited in Miles and Brown (2006), pp. 131–3.

67 Miles and Brown (2006), pp. 132–3.

68 M. Cole and S. Virdee (2006) 'Racism and resistance: from Empire to New Labour,' in M. Cole (ed.), *Education, Equality and Human Rights: Issues of Gender, 'Race,' Sexuality, Disability and Social Class*, 2nd edn, London: Routledge, p. 50.

69 Cole and Virdee (2006), p. 50.

70 Miles (1982), p. 165.

71 *Observer* (1989).

72 Grosvenor (1987), pp. 34–5.

73 L. Althusser (1971) 'Ideology and ideological state apparatuses,' in *Lenin and Philosophy and Other Essays*, London: New Left Books, www.marx2mao.com/Other/LPOE70NB.html, p. 172. Althusser's (1971) theory of interpellation is discussed in the Introduction to this book.

74 Cited in D. Trilling (2013) 'Thatcher: the PM who brought racism in from the cold,' Verso blog, 10 April, www.versobooks.com/blogs/1282-thatcher-the-pm-who-brought-racism-in-from-the-cold

75 Trilling (2013).

76 Trilling (2013).

77 Trilling (2013). A decade earlier, Thatcher's colleague Enoch Powell had used the same logic in a series of speeches prophesying 'rivers of blood' and how white people would soon become a minority in the United Kingdom, with 'the whip hand' held by the immigrant. In 1968, Powell was condemned by the Conservative leader Edward Heath and dismissed from the Shadow Cabinet. Recruits to the NF soared, including right-wing members of Conservative organizations (Trilling, 2013).

78 Cited in Trilling (2013). The Conservatives' hard line on immigration policy extended to refugees, giving rise to the modern stereotype of the 'bogus asylum-seeker' (Trilling, 2013) (see later in this chapter).

79 Trilling (2013).

80 H. Barnard (2011) 'What are the links between poverty and ethnicity,' Joseph Rowntree Foundation, 18 May, www.jrf.org.uk/blog/2011/05/what-are-links-between-poverty-and-ethnicity

81 Barnard (2011).

82 *The Stephen Lawrence Inquiry: Report of an Inquiry by Sir William Macpherson of Cluny* (1999), www.archive.official-documents.co.uk/document/cm42/4262/4262.htm

83 V. Dodd (2012) 'Police up to 28 times more likely to stop and search black people – study,' *Guardian*,12 June, www.guardian.co.uk/uk/2012/jun/12/police-stop-and-search-black-people

84   Cited in R. Stevens (2014) 'UK police make one million stop and searches of young people,' WSWS, 5 July 2014, www.wsws.org/en/articles/2014/07/05/stop-j05.html

85   Centre for Social Justice (2011) *Mental Health: Poverty, Ethnicity and Family Breakdown: Interim Policy Briefing*, February, www.centreforsocialjustice.org.uk/client/downloads/CSJMentalHealth_Final_20110205.pdf.

86   A. Fletcher (2012) 'Racism in football: 'Problems still exist at grassroots level,' BBC Sport, www.bbc.co.uk/sport/0/football/20365922. 'Paki' is an abbreviation for Pakistani, the 'N' word is 'nigger,' and 'park football' refers to informal and semi-formal games played in public parks.

87   P. Kelso (2015) 'Racism allegations in football treble: review,' Sky News, 27 January, http://news.sky.com/story/1415505/racism-allegations-in-football-treble-review

88   S. Adamson, B. Cole and G. Craig, with B. Hussain, L. Smith, I. Law, C. Lau, C. Chan and T. Cheung, (2009) *Hidden from Public View? Racism Against the UK's Chinese Population*, https://lemosandcrane.co.uk/resources/TMG-HiddenFromPublicView.pdf, p. 111.

89   Z. Tong with G. Craig and M. O'Neil (2014) *The Chinese Population in North East England*, Durham: Durham University, School of Applied Social Sciences.

90   E. Thomas (2015) 'British Chinese people say racism against them is "ignored",' *BBC Newsbeat*, 6 January, www.bbc.co.uk/newsbeat/article/30538929/british-chinese-people-say-racism-against-them-is-ignored

91   Cited in Thomas (2015).

92   I use the term 'mainly' because there were settlements of colonial citizens in various parts of the United Kingdom in the colonial era (Fryer, 1984).

93   Antisemitism is discussed in the next section of this chapter.

94   D. O'Hearn (2001) *The Atlantic Economy: Britain, the US and Ireland*, Manchester: Manchester University Press.

95   Not all Irish migrants fell into this limited variety of job categories. For example, the census for Norfolk in 1881 reveals a kaleidoscope of occupations, with Irish people involved in most occupations, right across the social spectrum. London presents a picture of even greater diversity, and has long been a magnet for Irish people working in the professions and the arts: 'Moving here: migration histories – jobs for Irish workers' (n.d.), www.movinghere.org.uk/galleries/histories/irish/working_lives/working_lives.htm

96   The term 'navvy,' originally used to refer to workers on Britain's inland navigation system, has since become a generic description of Irish manual workers.

97   M. J. Hickman (1995) *Religion, Class and Identity*, Aldershot: Avebury.

98   J. Donnelly (2011) 'The Irish famine,' www.bbc.co.uk/history/british/victorians/famine_01.shtml

99   For a discussion, see Donnelly (2011).

100   'Moving here' (n.d.).

101   'Moving here' (n.d.).

102   Data published in June 2011 showed that Irish emigration to Britain had risen by 25 per cent in 2010 (J. Smyth (2011) 'Emigration to Britain up to 25% to almost 14,000 data reveals,' *Irish Times*, 14 June).

103   P. R. Ghosh, (2012) 'Anti-Irish hatred: yes, pockets still exist in Britain,' *International Business Times*, 24 July, www.ibtimes.com/anti-irish-hatred-yes-pockets-still-exist-britain-729873

104   Greenslade Blog (2014) '"Anti-Irish racism" headline in Scots paper over interview with abused journalist,' www.theguardian.com/media/greenslade/2014/jan/12/raceandreligion-rangers

105   All cited in Greenslade (2014).

106   K. McKenna (2014) 'Neil Lennon's persecution shames Scotland,' Guardian, 25 May, www.theguardian.com/commentisfree/2014/may/25/neil-lennon-persecution-shames-scotland-celtic-manager; L. Roberts (2011) 'Neil Lennon: a long-term victim of sectarian abuse,' Telegraph, 20 April, www.telegraph.co.uk/news/uknews/scotland/8462657/Neil-Lennon-a-long-term-victim-of-sectarian-abuse.html

107   McKenna (2014).

108   C. Holmes (1979) Anti-Semitism in British Society 1876 –1939, London: Edward Arnold; P. Thane (1982) Foundations of the Welfare State, London: Longman.

109   Holmes (1979) p. 17.

110   Cohen (1985), p. 75.

111   United States Holocaust Memorial Museum (2012) 'Antisemitism in History: World War 1,' 11 May, www.ushmm.org/wlc/en/article.php?ModuleId=10007166

112   A. Clavane (2012) 'The Nazi chanting of West Ham fans is no resurgence of anti-semitism in football. Truth is, it never went away,' Independent, 28 November, www.independent.co.uk/voices/comment/the-nazi-chanting-of-west-ham-fans-is-no-resurgence-of-antisemitism-in-football-truth-is-it-never-went-away-8364775.html

113   Community Security Trust (2010) 'Antisemitic incidents Jan–June 2010,' www.thecst.org.uk/docs/Incidents%20Report%2010%20-%20First%20six%20months.pdf

114   Clavane (2012).

115   Clavane (2012).

116   M. Taylor (2014) 'Sharp rise in UK antisemitic attacks since start of Gaza conflict,' Guardian, 1 August, www.theguardian.com/society/2014/aug/01/sharp-rise-uk-antisemitic-attacks-gaza-conflict

117   Cited in J. Henly (2014) 'Antisemitism on rise across Europe "in worst times since the Nazis",' Guardian, 7 August, www.theguardian.com/society/2014/aug/07/antisemitism-rise-europe-worst-since-nazis

118   David Latchman has expressed concerns about antisemitism among some parts of the Muslim population in the United Kingdom, and what he describes as 'far Left' antisemitism: 'It is my view that those who claim to be anti-imperialist and anti-Zionist and on the left, but also express antisemitism in any form, are not truly on the left and certainly not modern day Marxists' (2010, cited in M. Reisz (2010) 'Library that helped bring Nazis to justice to relocate,' Times Higher Education, 14 January, www.timeshighereducation.co.uk/story.asp?storyCode=409956&sectioncode=26).

119   Cited in M. Holden (2014) 'Anti-Semitic incidents rise in Britain as Gaza conflict rages' Reuters, 30 July, www.reuters.com/article/2014/07/30/us-mideast-gaza-jewish-idUSKBN0FZ2MF20140730

120   N. Lowles (2014) 'Time to stand in solidarity with Britain's Jewish community,' Hope Not Hate, 24 July, www.hopenothate.org.uk/blog/nick/time-to-stand-in-solidarity-with-britain-s-jewish-community-3910

121   Examples taken from D. Gadher (2014) 'Anti-semitic attacks scar British cities,' Sunday Times, 27 July, p. 1.

122   Cited in Gadher (2014).

123 N. Poulantzas (1978) *State, Power, Socialism*, London: Verso, p. 123. The mode of production in Nazi Germany involved the state exercising ultimate control of the economy, with the seizure of the property of Jewish people. Selected corporations that supported the state in its programme operated with monopoly power. This mode of production also involved the slave labour of Jewish people and others deemed by the fascist state to be subhuman: M. Cole (2011) *Racism and Education in the U.K. and the U.S.: Towards a Socialist Alternative*, New York and London: Palgrave Macmillan, pp. 194–5; see also M. Cole (2012b) 'Capitalist crisis and fascism: issues for educational practice,' in D. R. Cole (ed.), *Surviving Economic Crises through Education*, New York: Peter Lang.

124 I consider anti-Gypsy Roma and Traveller racism under the main heading of 'Non-colour-coded racism' because my focus is the United Kingdom. Many European Roma people have dark skins, and this is a component in the racism directed at them in European countries.

125 Greenfields (2006), pp. 60–1.

126 Greenfields (2006), p. 62.

127 R. Duffy and A. Tomlinson (2009) 'Education on the hoof,' paper presented to the first Centre for Education for Social Justice Seminar at Bishop Grosseteste University College, Lincoln, 19 January, p. 2.

128 Greenfields (2006), p. 63.

129 Duffy and Tomlinson (2009), p. 2.

130 Duffy and Tomlinson (2009), p. 2; Greenfields (2006), p. 65.

131 Greenfields (2006), p. 66.

132 S. Robinson (2011) 'Last stand at Dale Farm as police evict residents,' *Socialist Worker*, www.socialistworker.co.uk/art.php?id=26469

133 Department for Communities and Local Government (2012) 'Count of Gypsy and Traveller Caravans – July 2012,' www.gov.uk/government/uploads/system/uploads/attachment_data/file/11710/caravan.pdf

134 Duffy and Tomlinson (2009), p. 3.

135 Commission for Racial Equality (CRE) (2004) *Gypsies and Travellers: A strategy for the CRE, 2004–2007*, London: CRE.

136 CRE (2006), cited in P. Brown (2012) 'Why we must provide for Gypsy and Traveller communities,' *Guardian*, 13 September, www.guardian.co.uk/housing-network/2012/sep/13/gypsy-traveller-accommodation-cost?newsfeed=true

137 Department for Education (2012) *Gypsy, Roma and Traveller achievement*, 14 November.

138 Duffy and Tomlinson (2009), p. 1.

139 Irish Traveller Movement in Britain (2012) *The Health and Wellbeing of Gypsies and Travellers*, March, http://irishtraveller.org.uk/wp-content/uploads/2012/03/ITMB-Gypsy-and-Traveller-Health-Briefing-March-20122.pdf

140 Clark (2006), pp. 1–2.

141 *Sun*, 27 August 2010, p. 34.

142 See the Introduction to this book for a discussion of Gramscian 'common sense' and 'good sense'.

143 B. Taylor (2011) 'Britain's Gypsy travellers: a people on the outside,' *History Today*, 61 (6), www.historytoday.com/becky-taylor/britains-gypsy-travellers-people-outside

144 Cited in J. Plunkett (2012) '*Big Fat Gypsy Weddings* "has increased bullying of Gypsies and Travellers"', *Guardian*, 16 October, www.guardian.co.uk/media/2012/oct/16/big-fat-gypsy-weddings-bullying-travellers

145 Duffy and Tomlinson (2009), p. 7.

146 Cited in Plunkett (2012).

147 Cited in Plunkett (2012).

148 Brown (2012).

149 Brown (2012).

150 Cited in P. Apps (2014) 'Restricted Gypsy and Traveller definition would face human rights challenges, lawyer says,' Inside housing.co.uk, 23 January, www.insidehousing.co.uk/restricted-gypsy-and-traveller-definition-would-face-human-rights-challenges-lawyer-says/7001767.article

151 For example, Fekete (2009).

152 Fekete (2009), p. 6.

153 Sivanandan (2001), p. 2. Fekete's interpretation of xeno-racism is a wide one that incorporates not just racism directed at European migrant workers, but also Islamophobia (e.g. Fekete (2009), pp. 43–4, p. 69) and anti-asylum-seeker racism (e.g. Fekete (2009), p. 15, p. 19, pp. 41–2). While Sivanandan (2001) does refer to asylum seekers under this definition of xeno-racism, and indeed to those with darker skins from the former colonies, as in the quote to which this note relates, it is my view that conceptually it is better to restrict the term to that form of racism directed at Eastern European migrant workers. Indeed, in the Foreword to Fekete's book, Sivanandan writes of non-colour-coded racism directed at East European workers as follows: 'the treatment meted out to (white) East European immigrants [stems] from a compelling economics of discrimination, effectively racism under a different colour, xeno-racism' (2009, p. viii). There are two reasons for my preference for restricting xeno-racism to (white) Eastern European migrant workers (and their families). First, those Eastern European migrant workers who are inhabitants of an EU country have the right, unlike other migrant workers, to enter and live in the United Kingdom, and the right to work there. Second, xeno-racism thus defined is region-specific, or even country-specific (unlike anti-asylum-seeker racism and Islamophobia, which are not region-specific). Moreover, 'xeno-racism' is of course derived from 'xenophobia,' and if the Online Etymology Dictionary (2001) is correct, the latter was first used just before the First World War, in 1912, and itself had early Eastern European connections. Between 1914 and 1917, in response to xenophobia aimed at citizens of the Austro-Hungarian Empire arising out of the First World War, 8,579 Eastern Europeans were interned.

154 Miles (1993), pp. 130–43.

155 Miles (1993), p. 149.

156 Miles (1982), p. 165.

157 J. Burnett (2012a) *The New Geographies of Racism: Peterborough*, London: Institute of Race Relations, www.irr.org.uk/wp-content/uploads/2012/07/Peterborough.pdf, p. 3.

158 J. Hardy (2009) 'Migration, migrant workers and capitalism,' *International Socialism*, 122, p. 137.

159 I. Fitzgerald (2007) *Working in the UK: Polish Migrant Worker Routes into Employment in the North East and North West Construction and Food Processing Sectors,*

London: TUC; J. Hardy and N. Clark (2007) 'EU enlargement, workers and migration: implications for trade unions in the UK,' Geneva: International Labour Organization; B. Anderson, M. Ruhs, B. Rogaly and S. Spencer (2006) *Fair Enough? Central and East European Migrants in Low-Wage Employment in the UK*, York: Joseph Rowntree Foundation.

160 Hardy (2009), pp. 137–8.

161 Hardy (2009), p. 138.

162 Burnett (2012a), p. 4.

163 John McMurty (1999) *The Cancer Stage of Capitalism*, London: Pluto.

164 Burnett (2012a), p. 6.

165 Burnett (2012a), p. 6.

166 Mail Online (2010) 'Homeless migrants will be ordered to leave,' 7 April, www.dailymail.co.uk/news/article-1263891/Homeless-migrants-living-rough-shanty-towns-told-work-sent-home.html, cited in Burnett (2012a), p. 6.

167 A. Hough (2010) 'Peterborough "under siege" by migrants camps, locals claim,' *Daily Telegraph*, 11 August.

168 Burnett (2012a), p. 5.

169 *Peterborough Evening Telegraph* (2005) 'Homes: ten men had a lock-up for a home,' 20 May, www.peterboroughtoday.co.uk/news/environment/homes-10-men-had-a-lock-up-for-a-home-1-37125, cited in Burnett (2012a), p. 5.

170 D. Pilditch (2010) 'Britain's migrant squatter shambles,' *Daily Express*, 11 August, www.express.co.uk/posts/view/192506/Britain-smigrant-squatter-shambles; S. Reid (2006) 'The town the Poles took over,' *Daily Mail*, 24 August, www.dailymail.co.uk/news/article-402024/Thetown-Poles-took-over.html; V. Allen (2007) 'Peterborough: a city crumbling under pressure from immigrants,' *Daily Mail*, 20 September 20, www.dailymail.co.uk/news/article-482816/Peterborough-A-city-crumbling-pressure-immigrants.html, cited in Burnett (2012a), p. 3.

171 Burnett (2012a), pp. 3–4.

172 S. Reid (2010) 'City that can't cope anymore: while this Czech family are thrilled with their new council house, such largesse is ruining communities,' *Daily Mail*, 10 April, www.dailymail.co.uk/news/article-1264930/Peterborough-struggling-immigration toll.html#ixzz1pvnyPsIF, cited in Burnett (2012a), p. 4.

173 Burnett (2012a), p. 4.

174 'Communism' is discussed in the second paragraph of note 37 to the Introduction.

175 Refugee Council Information (2014) 'Asylum statistics,' May, www.refugeecouncil.org.uk/assets/0002/7887/Asylum_Statistics_May_2013.pdf

176 R. Richardson (2009) 'Islamophobia and anti-Muslim racism – concepts and terms, and implications for education,' *Race Equality Teaching*, 27(1), p. 11.

177 Poynting and Mason (2001).

178 Sivanandan (2009), p. ix.

179 Fekete (2009), p. 109.

180 Fekete (2009), p. 109.

181 Fekete (2009), p. 119.

182 A. Kundnani (2007) *The End of Tolerance: Racism in 21st Century Britain*, London: Pluto, p. 178.

183 Fekete (2009), p. 55.

184 Fekete (2009), p. 50.

185 Fekete (2009), p. 48.
186 Fekete (2009), p. 85.
187 Fekete (2009), p. 125.
188 *New Statesman* (2011) 'Full transcript | David Cameron | Speech on radicalisation and Islamic extremism | Munich,' 5 February, www.newstatesman.com/blogs/the-staggers/2011/02/terrorism-islam-ideology
189 M. Cole (2014) 'Racism and antiracist education,' in D. C. Phillips (ed.), *Encyclopedia of Educational Theory and Philosophy*, London: Sage.
190 N. Copsey, J. Dack, M. Littler and M. Feldman (2013) *Anti-Muslim Hate Crime and the Far Right*, Middlesbrough: Centre for Fascist, Anti-Fascist and Post-Fascist Studies, Teesside University, http://tellmamauk.org/wp-content/uploads/2013/07/antimuslim2.pdf: p. 7 for 2011 stats, p. 14 for 2012–13 stats. Help for Heroes is a charity that provides support to wounded, injured and sick service personnel, veterans, and their families. As I pointed out elsewhere (M. Cole (2014) 'Austerity/immiseration capitalism and islamophobia – or twenty-first century multicultural socialism?' *Policy Futures in Education*, 12(1), p. 83), one of the killers, Michael Adebolajo, a British convert to Islam proclaimed in a video recorded on the mobile phone of an onlooker:

> The only reason we have killed this man today is because Muslims are dying daily by British soldiers. And this British soldier is one. It is an eye for an eye and a tooth for a tooth. By Allah, we swear by the almighty Allah we will never stop fighting you until you leave us alone. So what if we want to live by the Shari'a in Muslim lands? Why does that mean you must follow us and chase us and call us extremists and kill us? Rather you lot are extreme. You are the ones that when you drop a bomb you think it hits one person? Or rather your bomb wipes out a whole family? This is the reality. By Allah if I saw your mother today with a buggy I would help her up the stairs. This is my nature. But we are forced by the Qur'an, in Sura At-Tawba, through many ayah in the Qu'ran, we must fight them as they fight us. An eye for an eye, a tooth for a tooth. I apologise that women had to witness this today but in our lands women have to see the same. You people will never be safe. Remove your governments, they don't care about you. You think David Cameron is going to get caught in the street when we start busting our guns? You think politicians are going to die? No, it's going to be the average guy, like you and your children. So get rid of them. Tell them to bring our troops back so can all live in peace. So leave our lands and we can all live in peace. That's all I have to say. [in Arabic:] Allah's peace and blessings be upon you. (Live Leak (2013) 'Full uncensored version of London Woolwich murderer,' www.liveleak.com/view?i=37e_1369335448)

Adebolajo, I argued, is of course right that Muslims are being killed daily by British soldiers. He is also right that neo-imperialism is 'extreme'. He is further right that the ConDem government doesn't care about ordinary people, that it is the working class who would die in any Islamist insurrection rather than the ruling class. He is finally right that the troops should be brought home, so that all can live in peace. Where he is drastically, hopelessly wrong is in his belief that the solution is to kill individual soldiers on the streets of London – 'an eye for an eye, a tooth for a tooth'.

Just as the ongoing permanent 'war on terror' exacerbates Islamophobia, so does the killing of soldiers on the streets of London.

191 Copsey et al. (2013), p. 27.
192 J. Burnett (2012b) 'Spotlight on racial violence: October–December 2012,' www.irr. org.uk/news/spotlight-on-racial-violence-october-december-2012/
193 J. Burnett (2013) 'Upsurge in anti-Muslim attacks,' Institute of Race Relations, 30 May, www.irr.org.uk/news/upsurge-in-anti-muslim-attacks/.
194 Burnett (2013).
195 K. Rawlinson and K. Gander (2013) 'Half of Britain's mosques have been attacked since 9/11,' *Independent*, 28 June, www.independent.co.uk/news/uk/crime/half-of-britains-mosques-have-been-attacked-since-911-8679304.html
196 I. Awan (2014) 'Islamophobia and Twitter: a typology of online hate against Muslims on social media,' *Policy and Internet*, 6(2), 27 June.
197 C. Marsden (2013) 'The Woolwich killing and the responsibility of Britain's ruling elite,' WSWS, 1 June, www.wsws.org/en/articles/2013/06/01/pers-j01.html
198 My focus here on current anti-asylum seeker racism, under the heading 'Newer Hybridist Racism,' is not of course to underestimate the fact that this form of racism has a long history in the United Kingdom and elsewhere (for an analysis, see e.g. J. Schuster (2002) 'Asylum and the lessons of history,' *Race and Class*, 44(2)). I recognize the problematic nature of the term 'asylum seeker'. It forms part of a 'discourse of derision' (S. Ball (1990) *Politics and Policymaking in Education*, London: Routledge, p. 18) in the media, and in the pronouncements of certain politicians. 'Forced migrants' (J. Rutter (2006) *Refugee Children in the UK*, Buckingham: Open University Press) might be a more appropriate term, but since 'asylum seeker' is the most commonly used and understood term, I use it in this chapter.
199 Ball (1990), p. 18
200 Cited in UNHCR (United Nations High Commission for Refugees (2014) 'The facts: asylum in the UK,' www.unhcr.org.uk/about-us/the-uk-and-asylum.html
201 UNHCR (2014).
202 UNHCR (2014).
203 Cited in UNHCR (2014).
204 UNHCR (2014).
205 Fekete (2009), p. 8.
206 Fekete (2009),p. 23.
207 Fekete (2009), p. 2.
208 Fekete (2009), p. 39.
209 M. Bosworth (2014) *Inside Immigration Detention*, Oxford: Oxford University Press. The following summary of Bosworth's book is by Lucy Williams (2014) 'To unmake, make, remake,' a review of Mary Bosworth's *Inside Immigration Detention*, Oxford University Press, as outlined in *Times Higher Education*, 11 September 2014.
210 Fekete (2009), p. 40.
211 Fekete (2009), p. 15.
212 Fekete (2009), p. 137.
213 Fekete (2009), p. 138.
214 C. Philby (2012) 'Homes, G4S style: rubbish, rising damp… and "roaches",' *Independent*, 14 December, www.independent.co.uk/news/uk/home-news/homes-g4s-style-rubbish-rising-damp-and-roaches-8418089.html

215 G4S (2012) 'Who we are', www.g4s.com/en/Who%20we%20are/

216 According to a picture accompanying an article by B. Guiton (2012) 'G4S contractor evicted heavily pregnant asylum seeker even though they knew she was being
induced the same day', *Independent*, 10 December, www.independent.co.uk/news/
uk/home-news/g4s-contractor-evicted-heavily-pregnant-asylum-seeker-even-
though-they-knew-she-was-being-induced-the-same-day

217 Philby (2012).

218 Guiton (2012).

219 Fekete (2009), p. 37.

220 Kundnani (2007), p. 76.

221 Kundnani (2007), p. 76.

222 Kundnani (2007), p. 76.

223 Kundnani (2007), p. 76.

224 Kundnani (2007), p. 77.

225 Kundnani (2007), p. 88.

226 Home Office (2006) *Asylum Statistics: 2nd Quarter*, London: Home Office, pp. 2,
32; M. Watson and P. Danzelman (1998) *Asylum Statistics United Kingdom 1997*,
London: Home Office, pp. 1, 11, cited in Kundnani (2007), p. 159.

227 IRR (2010) *Driven to Desperate Measures*, London: IRR.

228 Cohen (1973).

229 W. B. Wood (1989) 'The political geography of asylum: two models and a case
study', *Political Geography Quarterly*, 8(2).

230 M. Taylor and P. Lewis (2010) 'Deportation death: "Jimmy Mubenga was a
good man"', *Guardian*, 15 October, www.theguardian.com/uk/2010/oct/15/
jimmy-mubenga-wife-devoted-father

231 Taylor and Lewis (2010).

232 Taylor and Lewis (2010).

233 Taylor and Lewis (2010).

234 J. Hyland (2014) 'Britain: perverse verdict clears security guards of Jimmy Mubenga
killing', WSWS, 20 December, www.wsws.org/en/articles/2014/12/20/mube-d20.
html

235 Hyland, 2014.

236 Cited in Hyland (2014).

237 Hyland (2014)

238 Cited in Hyland (2014).

239 Hyland, 2014.

240 Hyland, 2014.

241 Hyland, 2014.

242 M. Carr (2014) 'The battles of Calais', IRR, 14 August, www.irr.org.uk/news/
the-battles-of-calais/

243 Carr (2014).

244 Carr (2014).

245 *Right to Remain News* (2015) 'Further submissions procedure change, new on the
legal blog & events to put in your diary', 26 January, home@righttoremain.org.uk.

246 K. Fong (2014) 'UK immigration: farce, then tragedy?' *Times Higher Education*, 8
May, www.timeshighereducation.co.uk/comment/columnists/uk-immigration-farce-
then-tragedy/2013138.article

247 Cited in BBC News England (2014) 'Nigel Farage speaks to the UKIP party conference,' 28 September, www.bbc.co.uk/news/uk-england-29382604

248 R. Stevens (2013) 'UK Prime Minister Cameron plays the anti-immigrant card,' WSWS, 29 November, www.wsws.org/en/articles/2013/11/29/came-n29.html

249 EIN (2014a) 'Immigration Bill receives Royal Assent: the Immigration Act 2014 has arrived,' 15 May, www.ein.org.uk/news/immigration-bill-receives-royal-assent-immigration-act-2014-has-arrived

250 Cited in EIN (2014b) 'Movement Against Xenophobia meeting: Immigration Act codifies racism into British law and will become untenable,' 20 May, www.ein.org.uk/news/movement-against-xenophobia-meeting-immigration-act-codifies-racism-british-law-and-will-become. The 'sus laws' refer to Section 4 of the Vagrancy Act of 1824 which allowed police officers to stop, search and arrest people on suspicion that they were going to commit a crime. It was repealed in 1981.

251 S. Hall, C. Critcher, T, Jefferson, J. Clarke and B. Roberts (1978) *Policing the Crisis: Mugging, the State, and Law and Order*, London: Macmillan.

252 UKIP (2014) 'Winston Mckenzie: "After the EU – what next? The Commonwealth",' www.ukip.org/winston_mckenzie_after_the_eu_what_next_the_commonwealth

253 EIN (2014c) 'Yvette Cooper says Labour would scrap net migration target, Miliband forgets section of speech on immigration,' 24 September, www.ein.org.uk/news/yvette-cooper-says-labour-would-scrap-net-migration-target-miliband-forgets-section-speech-immi

254 Cited in EIN (2014c).

255 Quoted in PoliticsHome (2014) 'David Cameron speech to 2014 Conservative Party Conference,' 1 October, www.politicshome.com/uk/article/105662/david_cameron_speech_to_2014_conservative_party_conference.html

256 J. Freedland (2014) 'Scrapping human rights law is an act of displaced fury,' *Guardian*, 3 October, www.theguardian.com/commentisfree/2014/oct/03/scrapping-human-rights-law-european-court-ukip

257 Freedland (2014).

258 ChildLine (2013) *Can I Tell You Something? What's Affecting Children in 2013*, London: National Society for the Prevention of Cruelty to Children (NSPCC), www.nspcc.org.uk/globalassets/documents/research-reports/childline-review-2012-2013.pdf, p. 41.

259 E. Dugan (2014) 'Racist bullying: Far-right agenda on immigration "being taken into classrooms",' *Independent*, 8 January, www.independent.co.uk/news/education/education-news/racist-bullying-farright-agenda-on-immigration-being-taken-into-classrooms-9045148.html

260 Cited in Dugan (2014).

261 BBC News Politics (2014a) 'UK benefits a magnet to migrants, says Calais mayor,' 2 October, www.bbc.co.uk/news/uk-politics-29799733.

262 S. Boseley (2014) 'Keep HIV-positive migrants out of Britain, says Ukip's Nigel Farage,' *Guardian*, 10 October, www.theguardian.com/politics/2014/oct/10/nigel-farage-keep-hiv-positive-migrants-out-britain

263 T. Helm (2014) 'Ed Miliband: we will introduce tougher rules on benefits for new migrants,' *Guardian*, 11 October, www.theguardian.com/politics/2014/oct/11/ed-miliband-toughen-benefit-rules-for-migrants

264 A. Asthana (2014) 'Tory hopeful backs UKIP immigration plan,' Sky News,

16 October, http://news.sky.com/story/1354442/tory-hopeful-backs-ukip-immigration-plan

265 E. Birchley (2014) 'Illegal migrants "too scared" to get treatment,' Sky News, 19 October, http://news.sky.com/story/1355948/illegal-migrants-too-scared-to-get-treatment.

266 M. Battersby (2014) 'Mike Read 'apologises unreservedly' for Ukip Calypso and withdraws it from sale,' Independent, 22 October, www.independent.co.uk/arts-entertainment/music/news/mike-read-apologises-unreservedly-for-ukip-calypso-and-withdraws-it-from-sale-9810106.html; R. Mason (2014a) 'Get Mike Read's Ukip calypso song to number one, urges Nigel Farage,' Guardian, 20 October, www.theguardian.com/politics/2014/oct/20/ukip-calypso-song-number-one-nigel-farage-mike-read

267 T. McTague (2014) '"Some of my best chums are Caribbean": why DJ Mike Read says his "UKIP Calypso" cannot be racist,' Mail Online, 22 October, www.dailymail.co.uk/news/article-2801961/dj-mike-read-says-ukip-calypso-racist-got-chums-caribbean.html#ixzz3PkUCcxdL

268 Guardian (2014) 'Ukip calypso song should be withdrawn, says repentant Mike Read,' 22 October, www.theguardian.com/politics/2014/oct/23/ed-miliband-promises-concrete-immigration-reform

269 R. Mason (2014b) 'Ed Miliband promises concrete immigration reform,' Guardian, 23 October, www.theguardian.com/politics/2014/oct/23/ed-miliband-promises-concrete-immigration-reform

270 T. Helm and D. Boffey (2014) 'Nearly a third of voters prepared to support UKIP,' Guardian, 25 October, www.theguardian.com/politics/2014/oct/25/nearly-third-of-voters-prepared-to-support-ukip

271 A. Travis (2014) 'UK axes support for Mediterranean migrant rescue operation,' Guardian, 27 October, www.theguardian.com/politics/2014/oct/27/uk-mediterranean-migrant-rescue-plan

272 BBC News Politics (2014b) 'UKIP gains first elected MP with Clacton win,' 9 October , www.bbc.co.uk/news/uk-politics-29549414.

273 G. Dale (1999) 'Capitalism and migrant labour,' in G. Dale and M. Cole (eds), The European Union and Migrant Labour, Oxford: Berg, p. 308.

274 BBC News Politics (2014c) 'Nigel Farage: UKIP could do deal with Labour,' 12 November, www.bbc.co.uk/news/uk-politics-30029004

275 J. Chapman (2014) 'Britain can't cope with current immigration: former PM John Major tells Brussels there's 50 per cent chance Britain will quit EU unless borders are tightened,' Daily Mail, 14 November, www.dailymail.co.uk/news/article-2833198/Britain-EU-heading-divorce-Brussels-refuses-act-immigration-Sir-John-Major-warns.html#ixzz3ekmTG5qJ

276 B. Flynn (2014) 'A skint scrap worker from Romania is summoning his wife and kids to join him in the UK – to collect benefits of £25,000-a-year,' Sun, 14 November.

277 L. Mensch (2014) Sun on Sunday, 16 November, p. 27.

278 R. Mason (2014c) 'Reckless claim that EU migrants could be asked to leave over-ruled by Ukip,' Guardian, 19 November, www.theguardian.com/uk-news/2014/nov/19/ukip-mark-reckless-immigrants-rochester-and-strood

279 Press Association (2014) '£10 charge to be introduced for up to 5.5m visitors to the UK, Labour says,' Guardian, 18 November, www.theguardian.com/uk-news/2014/

nov/18/ten-pound-charge-uk-visitors-labour-immigration-travel-border-guards

280 S. Swinford (2014) 'Ed Miliband ridiculed for his "respect" remark over England flags,' *Telegraph*, 21 November, www.telegraph.co.uk/news/politics/ed-miliband/11245673/Ed-Miliband-I-feel-respect-whenever-I-see-a-white-van.html

281 *Star* (2014) 'Ed Miliband urged to apply the "Doncaster North" test on decisions,' 21 November, www.thestar.co.uk/news/local/ed-miliband-urged-to-apply-the-doncaster-north-test-on-decisions-1-6964702

282 Sky News (2014a) 'Net migration to UK Soars by more than 40%,' http://news.sky.com/story/1381360/net-migration-to-uk-soars-by-more-than-40-percent

283 BBC News Politics (2014d) 'David Cameron urges EU support for migration plans,' 28 November, www.bbc.co.uk/news/uk-politics-30224493

284 K. Rawlinson (2014) 'Farage blames immigration for traffic on M4 after no-show at Ukip reception,' *Guardian*, 7 December, www.theguardian.com/politics/2014/dec/07/nigel-farage-blames-immigration-m4-traffic-ukip-reception.

285 C. McDonald-Gibson (2014) 'UN expert slams UK's 'b***' attitude to immigration,' *Independent*, 2 December, www.independent.co.uk/news/world/europe/un-expert-slams-uks-b-attitude-to-immigration-9899049.html.

286 J. Halliday (2014) 'Richard Desmond makes £300,000 donation to Ukip,' *Guardian*, 12 December, www.theguardian.com/media/2014/dec/12/richard-desmond-donation-ukip-nigel-farage#.

287 Sky News (2014b) 'Juncker tells Britain not to 'beat up' migrants,' 13 December, http://news.sky.com/story/1391223/juncker-tells-britain-not-to-beat-up-migrants

288 R. De Peyer (2014) 'Nigel Farage says Ukip candidate in "Chinky" race row is just a rough diamond,' *Standard*, www.standard.co.uk/news/politics/nigel-farage-claims-ukip-candidate-used-offensive-language-because-he-grew-up-in-a-council-house-9935234.html.

289 Sky News (2014c) 'May wants to "send home" foreign graduates,' 21 December, http://news.sky.com/story/1395490/may-wants-to-send-home-foreign-graduates

290 R. Pitel (2015) 'Ukip woman had "a problem with negroes because of their faces",' *The Times*, 8 January, www.thetimes.co.uk/tto/news/politics/article4316972.ece?CMP=Spklr-128282306-Editorial-TWITTER-TimesNewsdesk-20150107&linkId=11612725

291 P. Wintour (2015) 'Muslim Council of Britain objects to Pickles letter to Islamic leaders,' *Guardian*, 19 January, www.theguardian.com/politics/2015/jan/19/uk-muslim-council-objections-eric-pickles-letter

292 Wintour (2015).

293 T. Bale (2015) 'Would Britain accept a Jewish prime minister?' *Telegraph*, 23 January, www.telegraph.co.uk/news/religion/11363294/Would-Britain-accept-a-Jewish-Prime-Minister.html. Benjamin Disraeli, twice prime minister in the nineteenth century, was born into a British Jewish family, but baptized as a Christian by his father to improve his chances in life. He was buried in a churchyard. However, referring to his heritage he once told an opponent in Parliament, according to James Kirkup, 'I am a Jew' (J. Kirkup (2014) 'Britain's "first Jewish PM": does Disraeli have the title?' *Telegraph*, 12 April, www.telegraph.co.uk/news/politics/ed-miliband/10761635/Britains-first-Jewish-PM-does-Disraeli-have-the-title.html).

294 ITV News (2015a) 'Farage outlines "ethical" Ukip immigration plans,' 4 March,

www.itv.com/news/update/2015-03-04/farage-promises-common-sense-immigration-approach/

295 D. Casciani (2015) 'Migrant population "rose 565,000 since 2011"', BBC News, 6 March, www.bbc.co.uk/news/uk-31748422.

296 Sky News (2015a) 'Jeremy Clarkson is "huge talent" says Cameron,' 11 March, http://news.sky.com/story/1442567/jeremy-clarkson-is-huge-talent-says-cameron

297 *Daily Mirror* (2015) 'Motormouth a diplomatic disaster zone,' 14 March, p. 5.

298 F. Strang (2015) 'Nick Clegg calls Top Gear "great television" but it's up to BBC whether they sack Clarkson after "fracas"', *Daily Mirror*, 12 March, www.mirror.co.uk/tv/tv-news/nick-clegg-calls-top-gear-5317818

299 *Guardian* (2015) 'Nigel Farage: British Muslim "fifth column" fuels fear of immigration,' 12 March, www.theguardian.com/politics/2015/mar/12/nigel-farage-british-muslim-fifth-column-fuels-immigration-fear-ukip

300 N. Methven (2015) '*Top Gear* bust-up inquiry: what BBC chiefs will be told,' *Daily Mirror*, 14 March, p. 4.

301 C. Green (2015) 'Jeremy Clarkson ruling: Travellers group objects as BBC Trust says Top Gear presenter's use of "pikey" was not racist,' *Independent*, 16 March, www.independent.co.uk/news/media/tv-radio/jeremy-clarkson-ruling-travellers-group-objects-as-bbc-trust-says-top-gear-presenters-use-of-pikey-was-not-racist-10112115.html.

302 A. Willis (2015) 'Jeremy Clarkson embroiled in fresh row over "lavender oil and sick" remark,' *Metro*, 17 March, http://metro.co.uk/2015/03/17/jeremy-clarkson-embroiled-in-fresh-row-over-lavender-oil-and-sick-remark-5107581/#ixzz3dsesaBhz

303 R. Syal (2015) 'Ukip faces crisis after suspensions and racism claims,' *Guardian*, 20 March, www.theguardian.com/politics/2015/mar/20/ukip-faces-crisis-two-parliamentary-candidates-suspended-one-resigns

304 ITV News (2015b) 'Migrant "health surcharge could cost NHS more"', 17 June, www.itv.com/news/2015-06-17/migrant-health-surcharge-could-cost-nhs-more/

305 K. Rawlinson (2015) 'Farage calls anti-Ukip protesters who forced him out of pub "scum"', *Guardian*, 23 March, www.theguardian.com/politics/2015/mar/22/farage-calls-anti-ukip-protesters-who-forced-him-out-of-pub-scum

306 D. McCaffrey (2015) 'Nigel Farage defends "sensible" HIV remarks' Sky News, 4 April, http://news.sky.com/story/1458835/nigel-farage-defends-sensible-hiv-remarks.

307 Sky News (2015b) 'Nigel Farage: "We want our country back"', 15 April, http://news.sky.com/story/1465316/nigel-farage-we-want-our-country-back

308 Sky News (2015c) 'Farage "insults" audience at leaders' debate,' 17 April, http://news.sky.com/story/1466432/farage-insults-audience-at-leaders-debate

309 P. Kingsley, A. Bonomolo and S. Kirchgaessner (2015) '700 migrants feared dead in Mediterranean shipwreck,' *Guardian*, 19 April, www.theguardian.com/world/2015/apr/19/700-migrants-feared-dead-mediterranean-shipwreck-worst-yet

310 S. Usborne (2015) 'Katie Hopkins has just written a piece so hateful that it might give Hitler pause – why was it published?' *Independent*, 18 April, www.independent.co.uk/voices/katie-hopkins-when-is-enough-enough-10186490.html.

311 D. Gayle (2015) 'New immigrants must speak English, says Ed Miliband,'

Guardian, 18 April, www.theguardian.com/uk-news/2015/apr/18/new-immigrants-must-speak-english-says-miliband

312   A. Bienkov (2015) 'Refugee crisis: only take in Christians insists Nigel Farage,' Politics.co.uk, 22 April, www.politics.co.uk/news/2015/04/22/refugee-crisis-only-take-in-christians-insists-nigel-farage

313   R. Myers (2015) 'Robert Blay: UKIP suspends parliamentary candidate after he threatens to SHOOT Tory rival in shocking video,' *Daily Mirror*, 5 May, www.mirror.co.uk/news/uk-news/robert-blay-ukip-suspends-parliamentary-5641537

314   D. Hill (2012) 'Immiseration capitalism, activism and education: resistance, revolt and revenge,' *Journal for Critical Education Policy Studies*, 10(2), www.jceps.com/PDFs/10-2-01.pdf

315   Cited in Hill (2012).

316   Hill (2012).

317   R. Stevens (2012) 'British Labour backs welfare benefit cuts,' WSWS, 17 December, www.wsws.org/en/articles/2012/12/17/labo-d17.html

318   J, Shaoul (2012) 'Cuts push UK workers' living standards back 30 years,' WSWS, 12 March, www.wsws.org/articles/2012/mar2012/wage-m12.shtml

319   S. Feldman (2012) 'Opportunity blocks,' *Times Higher Education*, 29 November, www.timeshighereducation.co.uk/story.asp?sectioncode=26&storycode=421957&c=1

320   H. Muir (2012a) 'Stephen Lawrence's mother criticises ministers over race discrimination,' *Guardian*, 18 December, www.guardian.co.uk/uk/2012/dec/18/stephen-lawrence-mother-race-discrimination. After these comments were published in the *Guardian*, the prime minister and deputy prime minister replied to Lawrence, but the letter contained little more than platitudes (see H. Muir (2012b) 'Coalition responds to Doreen Lawrence over race equality,' *Guardian*, 23 December, www.guardian.co.uk/uk/2012/dec/23/coalition-respond-doreen-lawrence-equality).

321   T. Ahmed (2012) 'Racism: a very British institution,' *Socialist Review*, 366, February, www.socialistreview.org.uk/article.php?articlenumber=11902

322   T. Scripps (2014) 'UK schools required to actively promote "British values",' WSWS, 19 July, www.wsws.org/en/articles/2014/07/19/valu-j19.html

323   B. Binley (2012) It's a simple message, David: Listen!' 12 December, www.brian binley.com/

324   BBC News (2012) 'Live interview,' 11 December.

325   Ahmed (2012).

2 The United States

1   US Census (2011).

2   The historical analyses in this chapter draw on M. Cole (2011) *Racism and Education in the U.K. and the U.S.: Towards a Socialist Alternative*, New York: Palgrave Macmillan, ch. 3, where the history of racism in the United States is considered in more detail.

3   R. Delgado and J. Stefancic (2001) *Critical Race Theory: An Introduction*, New York: New York University Press, p. 142.

4   Such as Delgado and Stefancic (2001), p. 142.

5   These various forms of resistance to racism, of which space here precludes a

consideration, are discussed in Cole (2011), ch. 3; see also M. Cole (2016c) *Antiracism: A Critical Analysis.*

6   C. Malott and P. Orelus (2015) 'Marxist historiography in the history of education: from colonial to neocolonial schooling in the United States', *Postcolonial Directions in Education,* 4 (1).

7   K. Marx and F, Engels (1848) [2010] *The Manifesto of the Communist Party* (commonly known as *The Communist Manifesto*), www.marxists.org/archive/marx/works/download/pdf/Manifesto.pdf , p. 15.

8   Marx and Engels (1848) [2010], p. 15.

9   Cited in G. Y. Okihiro (1994) *Margins and Mainstreams: Asians in American History and Culture,* Washington: University of Washington Press, p. 17.

10 Okihiro (1994), p. 17.

11 W. M. Denevan (1992) 'Native American populations in 1492: recent research and a revised hemispheric estimate', in W. M. Denevan (ed.), *The Native Population of the Americas in 1492,* 2nd edn, Madison, Wisc.: University of Wisconsin Press, pp. xxviii–xxix, 2010.

12 W. M. Denevan, personal email correspondence, June 2010.

13 Permanent Revolution (2008) 'Columbus and the Discovery of Latin America', 23 August, www.permanentrevolution.net/entry/2267

14 Permanent Revolution (2008).

15 W. E. Coffer (a.k.a. Koi Hosh) (1979) *Phoenix: The Decline and Rebirth of the Indian People,* New York and London: Van Nostrand Reinhold, p. 47; J. Nederveen Pieterse (1986) 'Amerindian resistance: the gathering of the fires', *Race and Class,* 27 (Spring), p. 36.

16 Nederveen Pieterse (1986), p. 38.

17 Nederveen Pieterse (1986), pp. 39–40.

18 Nederveen Pieterse (1986), pp. 41–2.

19 Nederveen Pieterse (1986), pp. 42–3.

20 J. F. Perea, R. Delgado, A. P. Harris, J. Stefancic and S. M. Wildman (2007) *Race and Races: Cases and Resources for a Diverse America,* St. Paul, Minn.: Thomson/West, p. 221.

21 D. Getches, C. F. Wilkinson and R. A. Williams, Jr. (2005) *Cases and Materials on Federal Indian Law,* 5th edn, Eagan, Minn.: West, p. 141.

22 Quoted in Getches et al. (2005), p. 186.

23 Nederveen Pieterse (1986), p. 49.

24 Perea et al. (2007), pp. 222–3.

25 Perea et al. (2007), p. 223.

26 Vine Deloria Jr. and Clifford Lytle, cited in Perea et al. (2007), p. 224.

27 Quoted by Vine Deloria Jr. and Lytle, cited in Perea et al. (2007), p. 224.

28 Ward Churchill (2004) *Kill the Indian, Save the Man: The Genocidal Impact of American Indian Residential Schools,* San Francisco, Calif.: City Lights, p. 1, cited in C. Malott (2011) *Critical Pedagogy and Cognition: An Introduction to a Postformal Educational Psychology,* New York: Springer, p. 96.

29 Malott (2011), pp. 100–1.

30 Ward Churchill (2004), cited in Malott (2011), p. 101.

31 Malott (2011), p. 101.

32 A. Smith (2005) *Conquest: Sexual Violence and American Indian Genocide*, New York: South End Press, cited in Malott (2011), p. 101.

33 Malott (2011), p. 102.

34 Indian Country Diaries (2006) 'Assimilation, relocation, genocide: the Urban Relocation Program,' www.pbs.org/indiancountry/history/relocate.html

35 Indian Country Diaries (2006).

36 T. Williams (2013). 'Quietly, Indians reshape cities and reservations,' *New York Times*. 13 April.

37 Alaska Advisory Committee to the US Commission on Civil Rights (2002).

38 Denise Morris, president, Alaska Native Justice Center, statement before the Alaska Advisory Committee to the US Commission on Civil Rights, community forum, 23 August 2001, transcript, pp. 190–1, cited in Alaska Advisory Committee (2002), www.usccr.gov/pubs/sac/ak0402/ch1.htm

39 Alaska Advisory Committee (2002).

40 Commonwealth North, *Urban Rural Unity Study*, p. 5, cited in Alaska Advisory Committee (2002).

41 Bryan Cooper (1973) *Alaska: The Last Frontier*, New York: William Morrow, p. 23, cited in Alaska Advisory Committee (2002); Steve Douglas (2000) 'The Alaska pipeline,' March, www.miavx1.muohio.edu/~kaufmadg/alaska.html

42 Quoted in Alaska Public Lands Information Centers (n.d.) 'World War II in Alaska,' www.alaskacenters.gov/wwii.cfm

43 Alaska Public Lands Information Centers (n.d.).

44 Alaska Advisory Committee (2002).

45 Gary Charles Patten, Copper River Tlingit, statement, 23 August 2001 transcript, pp. 236–7.

46 Indian Country Today Media Network (ICTMN) Staff (2013).

47 Indian Country Diaries (2006).

48 Williams (2013).

49 D. Stokes (2014a) 'Anti-Indian racism is everywhere in America,' 5 October, http://indiancountrytodaymedianetwork.com/2014/10/05/anti-indian-racism-every-where-america. The sentimentalized images Stokes refers to also deflects attention from real living conditions of Native Americans.

50 Stokes (2014a).

51 Stokes (2014a).

52 D. Stokes (2014b) '5 studies that prove Dan Snyder is wrong about "Redskins",' 21 April, http://indiancountrytodaymedianetwork.com/2014/04/21/5-studies-prove-dan-snyder-wrong-about-redskins. Studies mentioned include J. A. Steinfeldt, B. D. Foltz, M. C. Steinfeldt, J. K. Kaladow, T. N. Carlson, L. A. Pagano, Jr. and E. Benton (2010) 'Racism in the electronic age: role of online forums in expressing racial attitudes about American Indians' cultural diversity and ethnic minority psychology'; J. Chaney, A. Burke and E. Burkley (2011) 'Do American Indian mascots = American Indian people? Examining implicit bias towards American Indian people and American Indian mascots'; S. Freng and C. Willis-Esqueda (2011) 'A question of honor: Chief Wahoo and American Indian stereotype activation among a university based sample,' *Journal of Social Psychology*, 151(5); A. R. LaRocque, J. D. McDonald, J. N. Weatherly and F. R. Ferraro (2011) 'Indian sports nicknames/logos: affective

difference between American Indian and non-Indian college students,' *American Indian Alaskan Native Mental Health Research*, 18(2).

53   Steinfeldt et al. (2010), quoting E. J. Staurowsky (2007) '"You know, we are all Indian": exploring White power and privilege in reactions to the NCAA Native American mascot policy,' *Journal of Sport and Social Issues*, 31.

54   J. E. Black (2002) 'The "mascotting" of Native America,' *American Indian Quarterly*, 26, cited in Steinfeldt et al. (2010).

55   Stokes (2014b).

56   Quoted in S. Horwitz (2014) 'Native Americans struggle with high rate of youth suicides,' *Washington Post*, 16 March, www.bostonglobe.com/news/nation/2014/03/15/native-americans-struggle-with-high-rate-youth-suicides/Lh38oMic3BQoG2K2WDnwyN/story.html

57   Horwitz (2014).

58   Horwitz (2014).

59   Quoted in Horwitz (2014).

60   Horwitz (2014).

61   Cited in Horwitz (2014).

62   Eric Huntington (2014) 'Racism alive and well on the last frontier,' *Alaska Dispatch News*, 9 May, www.adn.com/article/20140509/racism-alive-and-well-last-frontier

63   D. Bron Davis (2006) *Inhuman Bondage: The Rise and Fall of Slavery in the New World*, Oxford: Oxford University Press, p. 124.

64   P. Kolchin (1995) *American Slavery 1619–1877*, London: Penguin, pp. 3–4.

65   D. Eltis (2007) 'A brief overview of the Trans-Atlantic slave trade,' www.slavevoyages.org/tast/assessment/essays-intro-08.faces

66   D. Eltis (2008) 'The U.S. transatlantic slave trade, 1644–1867: an assessment,' *Civil War History*, 54(4), p. 353.

67   Kolchin (1995), p. 20.

68   Kolchin (1995), p. 21.

69   Quoted in D. P. Mannix with M. Cowley, 1788 [1962] *Black Cargoes: A History of the Atlantic Slave Trade, 1518–1865*, New York: Viking, p. 117.

70   Kolchin (1995), p. 21.

71   Finley (1967), p. 10, cited in Genovese (1969), p. 246.

72   Zinn (1995), cited in Perea et al. (2007), p. 101.

73   Zinn (1995), cited in Perea et al. (2007), p. 101.

74   I. Berlin (2010) T*he Making of African America: The Four Great Migrations*, London: Penguin.

75   Kolchin (1995), p. 96.

76   Marx and Engels (1846) [1977], p. 665.

77   Quoted in Perea et al. (2007), p. 136.

78   Kolchin (1995), pp. 200–1.

79   Kolchin (1995), pp. 205–7.

80   Kolchin (1995), pp. 210–11.

81   Kolchin (1995), p. 224.

82   Kolchin (1995), pp. 224, 219.

83   Malott (2011), p. 80.

84   W. H. Watkins (2001) *The White Architects of Black Education: Ideology and Power*

in America, 1865-1954, New York: Teachers College Press, p. 46, quoted in Malott (2011), p. 80.

85   The origin of the term 'Jim Crow' is often attributed to 'Jump Jim Crow,' a 'song- and- dance' caricature of African Americans first performed by a white actor in 1832. 'Jim Crow' subsequently became a derogatory expression for black Americans. Hence the racial segregation laws became known as 'Jim Crow laws' (C. Woodward and W. McFeely (2001) *The Strange Career of Jim Crow,* Oxford: Oxford University Press, p. 7).

86   C. Vann Woodward (1966) 'Seeds of failure in radical race policy,' *Proceedings of the American Philosophical Society,* 110 (1), p. 1. 'White supremacy' is used here in its traditional, and in my view correct sense, as opposed to the CRT usage that uses the term to describe, in certain contexts, everyday racism experienced by people of colour (see the Introduction to this book).

87   Perea et al. (2007), p. 148.

88   L. Litwack (1961) *North of Slavery: The Negro in the Free States,* Chicago, Ill.: University of Chicago Press, p. 97.

89   Perea et al. (2007), p. 155.

90   Kolchin (1995), p. 235.

91   Perea et al. (2007), p. 155.

92   F. Chapman (2010) 'Some sobering notes on African American equality' *People's World,* 21 April, http://peoplesworld.org/some-sobering-notes-on-african-american-equality/

93   PrisonIndustrialComplex.org, www.prisonindustrialcomplex.org/ (n.d.). So who is making the money out of the prison-industrial complex today? One of the largest companies is Corrections Corporation of America (CCA). CCA is the largest owner and operator of for-profit correctional and detention facilities and one of the largest prison operators in the United States, behind only the federal government and three states. CCA currently owns and operates more than 65 facilities including 47 company-owned facilities, with a design capacity of more than 90,000 beds in 19 states and the District of Columbia. Its 2012 revenue was $1.77 billion, 100 per cent of which comes from taxpayers via government contracts. Its highest paid executives earned $2,772,435 and $1,415,655 (In the Public Interest (2013) *Criminal: How Lockup Quotas and 'Low-Crime Taxes' Guarantee Profits for Private Prison Corporations,* www.inthepublicinterest.org/wp-content/uploads/ Criminal-Lockup-Quota-Report.pdf).

94   M. Marable (2006) 'Globalization and racialization,' *Synthesis/Regeneration,* 39, www.greens.org/s-r/39/39-06.html

95   Marable (2006).

96   Philip Bump (2014) 'The source of Black poverty isn't black culture, it's American culture,' *The Wire,* 1 April, www.thewire.com/politics/2014/04/the-source-of-black-poverty-isnt-black-culture-its-american-culture/359937/

97   K. Randall (2014a) 'US prison population increases for first time since 2009,' WSWS, 23 September, www.wsws.org/en/articles/2014/09/23/pris-s23.html

98   Randall (2014a).

99   Randall (2014a).

100   Randall (2014a).

101 ACLU (2013) 'The war on marijuana in black and white,' New York: ACLU, www.aclu.org/files/assets/061413-mj-report-rfs-rel4.pdf

102 Randall (2014a).

103 M. Mitchell and M. Leachman (2014) *Changing Priorities: State Criminal Justice Reforms and Investments in Education*, Center on Budget and Policy Priorities, 28 October, www.cbpp.org/research/changing-priorities-state-criminal-justice-reforms-and-investments-in-education

104 K. Randall (2014b) 'US state prison population soars as education spending plummets,' WSWS, 4 November, www.wsws.org/en/articles/2014/11/04/cbpp-n04.html

105 *Independent* (2014) 'Eric Garner death: Father of six dies in police custody after "chokehold" arrest,' 20 July, www.independent.co.uk/news/world/americas/eric-garner-death-father-of-six-dies-in-police-custody-after-chokehold-arrest-9617390.html

106 P. Martin (2014) 'Police, media smear victim of Missouri police shooting,' WSWS, www.wsws.org/en/articles/2014/10/20/ferg-o20.html

107 A. Damon (2014a) 'Obama administration signals reluctance to bring civil rights charges against killer cop in Missouri,' WSWS, 20 October, www.wsws.org/en/articles/2014/10/20/ferg-o20.html

108 T. Gaist (2014) 'Autopsy shows St. Louis teenager Vonderrit Myers was gunned down by police while fleeing,' WSWS, 25 October, www.wsws.org/en/articles/2014/10/25/myer-o25.html

109 Amnesty International, 'On the streets of America: human rights abuses in Ferguson,' www.amnestyusa.org/research/reports/on-the-streets-of-america-human-rights-abuses-in-ferguson. Cited in A. Damon (2014b) 'Amnesty International: Ferguson police crackdown violated US and international law,' WSWS, 25 October, www.wsws.org/en/articles/2014/10/25/ferg-o25.html

110 R. Hackman (2014) 'New wave of protests reveal anger at high unemployment for black Americans,' *Guardian*, 15 October, www.theguardian.com/us-news/2014/oct/15/-sp-ferguson-protests-undercurrent-economic-inequality

111 US Department of Labor; Bureau of Labor Statistics, 2014.

112 Cited in Hackman (2014).

113 M. Karenga (2014) 'Defending Marlene Pinnock and ourselves: issues of justice, agenda and struggle,' *Los Angeles Sentinel,* 17 July, http://lasentinel.net/defending-marlene-pinnock-and-ourselves-issues-of-justice-agenda-and-struggle.html

114 Karenga (2014).

115 Karenga (2014).

116 BBC News (2015) 'The damning report that made Ferguson's police chief quit,' 12 March, www.bbc.co.uk/news/world-us-canada-31849421

117 Anna Brown and Eileen Patten (2014) 'Statistics portrait of Hispanics in the United States, 2012,' Pew Research Center, 29 April, www.pewhispanic.org/2014/04/29/statistical-portrait-of-hispanics-in-the-united-states-2012/#population-by-race-and-ethnicity-2000-and-2012

118 Perea et al. (2007), p. 288. People of Latina/o heritage have lived in what is now the United States since early colonization in St Augustine in 1565.

119 Horseman (1981), cited in Perea et al. (2007), pp. 290–1.

120 Quoted in Perea et al. (2007), p. 292.

121   Quoted in Perea et al. (2007), p. 292.
122   Cited in Horseman (1981), in turn cited in Perea et al. (2007), p. 292.
123   Cited in Horseman (1981), in turn cited in Perea et al. (2007), p. 292.
124   Cited in Horseman (1981), in turn cited in Perea et al. (2007), p. 293.
125   Encylopaedia Britannica (2010).
126   Perea et al. (2007), p. 301.
127   Carrasco (1997), cited in Perea et al. (2007), p. 341.
128   Carrasco (1997), cited in Perea et al. (2007), p. 341.
129   Carrasco (1997), cited in Perea et al. (2007), p. 342.
130   Carrasco (1997), cited in Perea et al. (2007), pp. 343–4.
131   Carrasco (1997), cited in Perea et al. (2007), p. 344.
132   Carrasco (1997), cited in Perea et al. (2007), p. 345.
133   Carrasco (1997), cited in Perea et al. (2007), p. 347.
134   Carrasco (1997), cited in Perea et al. (2007), p. 348.
135   Carrasco (1997), cited in Perea et al. (2007), p. 349.
136   Perea (2004), cited in Perea et al. (2007), pp. 329–33.
137   Perea (2004), cited in Perea et al. (2007), p. 330.
138   Perea (2004), cited in Perea et al. (2007), p. 340.
139   See my discussion of racism in the Introduction to the book.
140   Quotes are from Weston (1972), cited in Perea et al. (2007), pp. 370–1.
141   Fox News Latino (2013) 'U.S.-based Puerto Ricans want equality, right to vote, statehood back home,' 1 December, http://latino.foxnews.com/latino/politics/2013/12/01/in-florida-puerto-ricans-want-equality-right-to-vote-statehood-back-home/
142   Quoted in Fox News Latino (2013).
143   Huff Post Latino Voices (2014) The sign is shown on www.huffingtonpost.com/2013/01/07/racist-playground-sign-delaware-anti-latino-sign_n_2427133.html
144   S. G. Bauman (2014) 'Key economic issues for Latinos in 2014,' Huffington Post, 18 January, www.huffingtonpost.com/2014/01/18/economic-issues-latinos_n_4623333.html
145   K. Semple (2014) 'Latino drivers report thefts by officers,' *New York Times*, 2 March, www.nytimes.com/2014/03/03/nyregion/latino-drivers-report-thefts-by-officers.html?_r=0
146   Baumann (2014).
147   Baumann (2014).
148   A. Gonzalez-Barrera and J. M. Kroqstad (2014) 'U.S. deportations of immigrants reach record high in 2013,' Pew Research Center, www.pewresearch.org/fact-tank/2014/10/02/u-s-deportations-of-immigrants-reach-record-high-in-2013/
149   Gonzalez-Barrera and Kroqstad (2014).
150   J. M. Krogstad, A. Gonzalez-Barrera and M. H. Lopez (2014) 'Children 12 and under are fastest growing group of unaccompanied minors at U.S. border,' Pew Research Center 22 July www.pewresearch.org/fact-tank/2014/07/22/children-12-and-under-are-fastest-growing-group-of-unaccompanied-minors-at-u-s-border/
151   Van Auken (2014) 'Defend the rights of immigrant workers, youth!,' *Herald*, www.herald.co.zw/defend-the-rights-of-immigrant-workers-youth/

152 N. Diaz (2014) 'Obama announces increased border security and stepped-up deportations', WSWS, 7 July, www.wsws.org/en/articles/2014/07/07/immi-j07.html

153 Van Auken (2014).

154 Diaz (2014).

155 Van Auken (2014).

156 Van Auken (2014).

157 Martin (2014).

158 Quoted in Martin (2014).

159 Martin (2014).

160 United States Census 2010 (www.census.gov/). Other Asian Americans with a total population of over a quarter of a million include Pakistani Americans (409,163), who began arriving in the early 1900s after Pakistani independence in 1947 (J. Singh (2003) 'Bangladeshi & Pakistani Americans', *Asian-Nation: The Landscape of Asian America*, www.asian-nation.org/bangladeshi-pakistani.shtml) and people migrating to the United States as a result of the protracted war between the United States and South Vietnam that ended in 1975. These include Cambodian Americans (276,667) who, as refugees, settled in the United States in the 1980s, following the overthrow of the Khmer Rouge regime by Vietnam in 1979 (C. L. Bankston III (2010) 'Cambodian Americans', www.everyculture. com/multi/Bu-Dr/Cambodian-Americans.html); Hmong Americans (260,073), whose origins are in China, but who migrated to South-East Asia, and who entered the United States from refugee camps after the war (H. Zia (2000) *Asian American Dreams*, New York: Farrar, Straus & Giroux, p. 256); Thai Americans (237,583), allies of the United States and South Vietnam who also migrated to the United States both during and after the war; and Laotian Americans (232,130) who fled the region as a result of the war (R. Takaki (1989) *Strangers from a Different Shore: A History of Asian Americans*, Boston, Mass.: Little, Brown, pp. 460–1).

161 Takaki (1989), p. 80.

162 See my discussion of racism in the Introduction to this book.

163 Quoted in G. Kraus (1969) 'Chinese laborers and the construction of the Central Pacific', *Utah Historical Quarterly*, 37(1), http://cprr.org/Museum/Chinese_Laborers.html

164 Quoted in Kraus (1969).

165 M. Zhou (2003) 'Chinese Americans', *Asian-Nation*, www.asian-nation.org/chinese.shtml

166 McClain (1994), pp. 12–20, cited in Perea et al. (2007), p. 400.

167 Sandmeyer (1991), p. 57, cited in Perea et al. (2007), p. 405.

168 Zhou (2003).

169 Quoted in Sandmeyer (1991), p. 65, cited in Perea et al. (2007), p. 406.

170 Zhou (2003).

171 Zhou (2003). Ellen Wu has argued that, unsurprisingly given the preceding analysis, Chinese culture was perceived as disgusting and vile, with Chinatowns seen 'as depraved colonies of prostitutes, gamblers and opium addicts bereft of decency' (E. D. Wu (2014) 'Asian Americans and the "model minority myth"', *Los Angeles Times*, 23 January, www.latimes.com/opinion/op-ed/la-oe-0123-wu-chua-model-minority-chinese-20140123-story.html).

172 Zhou (2003).

173 Zhou (2003).

174 Zhou (2003).

175 US Immigration Legislation Online, 2007; Zhou (2003).

176 Ling-chi Wang (2010) 'Chinese Americans,' encylopedia.com, www.encyclopedia.com/topic/Chinese_Americans.aspx

177 Ling-chi Wang (2010).

178 Takaki (1989), p. 315.

179 M. Dela Cruz and P. Agbayani-Siewert (2003) 'Filipino Americans,' *Asian-Nation,* www.asian-nation.org/f ilipino.shtml

180 Takaki (1989), p. 315.

181 Takaki (1989), p. 327.

182 Quoted in Takaki (1989), p. 327.

183 Philippine History Site (n.d) 'The Philippine History Site' (n.d.) http://opmanong.ssc.hawaii.edu/filipino/riots.html) From 1913 to 1948, 30 out of the then 48 states of the United States prohibited 'interracial couples'. This included whites and blacks, and in many states, also relationships and the intermarriage of whites with Native Americans or Asians (Loving Day, 2009 'Legal Map,' http://lovingday.org/legal-map). Anti-miscegenation legislation continued in some states until the outlawing of 'interracial' relationships and marriage was made illegal in 1967.

184 Dela Cruz et al. (2003).

185 K. V. Rao, E. Lai and D. Arguelles (2003) 'Indian Americans,' *Asian-Nation,* www.asian-nation.org/indian.shtml; S. Chan (1991) *Asian Americans: An Interpretive History,* Boston, Mass.: Twayne, p. 18.

186 Rao et al (2003).

187 Rao et al (2003).

188 Zia (2000), pp. 90–1, 221.

189 Zia (2000), pp. 219–20.

190 Takaki (1989)p.449

191 Takaki (1989), p. 452.

192 Takaki (1989), pp. 453–4.

193 *East Asian Times* (2010) 'Vietnamese fishermen fear rougher waters ahead after spill,' www.eastasiantimes.com/vietnamese-fishermen-fear-rougherwaters-ahead-after-spill.htm

194 Zia (2000), p. 52.

195 Zia (2000), p. 52.

196 E. T. Chang (2003) 'Korean Americans,' *Asian-Nation,* www.asian-nation.org/korean.shtml

197 S. Shinn Sunoo (2002) *Korean Picture Brides: 1903–1920: A Collection of Oral Histories,* Bloomington, Ind.: Xlibris.

198 Chang (2003).

199 Chan (1991), p. 52.

200 Perea (1995), cited in Perea et al. (2007), p. 1,101.

201 F. H. Wu (2002) *Yellow: Race in America Beyond Black and White,* New York: Basic Books, p. 72.

202 Zia (2000), p. 182.

203 Perea (1995), cited in Perea et al. (2007), pp. 1,101–2. The 'model minority' myth is discussed in the next subsection of this chapter and also under the heading

'Asian Americans today'. Perea goes on to identify a fourth media image: groups of Latina/o people rushing from stores clutching stolen goods. He points out how this image works to mask the fact that Latina/o people were also part of the riots. He points out that this is hardly surprising since half the population of South Central Los Angeles was Latina/o and faced similar life conditions to African Americans. The needs of Latina/o communities there, however, were not part of the picture.

204 Perea et al. (2007), p. 428.
205 United States History (n.d.) 'Immigration Act of 1924,' www.u-shistory.com/pages/ h1398.html
206 Takaki (1989), p. 218.
207 Perea et al. (2007), p. 436.
208 *Report of the Commission on Wartime Relocation and Internment of Civilians*, 1982, cited in Perea et al. (2007), p. 436.
209 Congressional Information Service (2000) 'Wartime relocation of civilians,' http:// bss.sfsu.edu/internment/congressional%20records/19880415.html
210 W. Petersen (1966) 'Success story, Japanese-American style,' *New York Times*, 9 January, http://inside.sfuhs.org/dept/history/US_History_reader/Chapter14/ modelminority.pdf. His *New York Times* article on the 'achievement orientation' of Japanese Americans was followed later in the same year with an article in *US News & World Report* which stated that at a time:

> when Americans are awash in worry over the plight of racial minorities … Chinese-Americans … [are] winning wealth and respect by dint of …[their] own hard work …. Still being taught in Chinatown is the old idea that people should depend on their own efforts – not a welfare check – in order to reach America's 'promised land'. Visit 'Chinatown U.S.A.' and you find an important racial minority pulling itself up from hardship and discrimination to become a model of self-respect and achievement in today's America (cited in R. S. Chang (1993) 'Toward an Asian American legal scholarship: critical race theory, post-structuralism, and narrative space,' *California Law Review*, October), http://modelminority. com/joomla/index.php?option=com_content&view=article&id=394:legal-implications-of-the-model-minority-myth-&catid=42:law&Itemid=56).

211 Delgado and Stefancic (2001), p. 151.
212 Delgado and Stefancic (2001), pp. 81–2.
213 Professor Frank Wu, cited in BAMN (Coalition to Defend Aff irmative Action, Integration, and Immigrant Rights and Fight for Equality by Any Means Necessary) (2001) 'Asian Pacif ic Americans and aff irmative action: from the trial transcript of Professor Frank Wu,' www.bamn.com/doc/2001/010212-apas-and-aa-wu-excerpts pdf
214 Wu, cited in BAMN (2011). The idea that all Asian Americans all live in nuclear families is itself a stereotype and untrue.
215 R. S. Chang (2000) 'Toward an Asian American legal scholarship: critical race theory, post-structuralism, and narrative space,' in R. Delgado and J. Stefancic (eds), *Critical Race Theory: The Cutting Edge*, 2nd edn, Philadelphia, Pa.: Temple University Press, p. 359.

216 B. Chang and W. Au (2007/8) 'Unmasking the myth of the model minority,' *Rethinking Schools,* 22(2), pp. 15–16.

217 BAMN (2001).

218 Lam (2011).

219 National Coalition for Asian Pacific American Community Development (NCAPACD) (2013) 'Asian American and Pacific Islander poverty grows in wake of recession,' 21 June, www.nationalcapacd.org/press-room/asian-american-and-pacific-islander-poverty-grows-wake-recession. Native Hawaiian or Other Pacific Islanders (people having origins in any of the original peoples of Hawaii, Guam, Samoa or other Pacific islands) are listed as a separate category in the US Census from 2000 onwards. In 1898, Hawaii became an 'official territory' of the United States, having had its monarchy overthrown some five years earlier by US naval forces. In 1959 Hawaii became the 50th state of the United States. The Samoan Islands comprise American Samoa and Samoa. The former sends a delegate to the US Congress; the latter is an independent country. After Samoans, the next largest NHPI group are natives of the island of Guam (also known as Chamorro). Although Guamanian people have US citizenship, they cannot vote in US presidential elections (Cole (2011), pp.110–11).

220 NCAPACD (2013).

221 NCAPACD (2013).

222 ChangeLab, www.changelabinfo.com/about/#.VeGGIPlVhBc

223 S. Nakagawa (2014a) 'MSNBC is doing Asian Americans no favors' Race Files, ChangeLab, Oakland, Calif., 14 March, www.racefiles.com/2014/03/14/msnbc-is-doing-asian-americans-no-favors/

224 Cited in S. Nakagawa (2014b) 'Asian Americans on the Sunday shows: what they talk about when they talk about us,' Oakland, Calif.: ChangeLab, www.change-labinfo.com/reports/ChangeLab_Asian-Americans-on-the-sunday-shows.pdf

225 S. Nakagawa (2014c) 'Model minority suicide: five reasons, five ways,' Race Files, ChangeLab, Oakland, Calif, 16 Apri, www.racefiles.com/2014/04/16/model-minority-suicide-five-reasons-five-ways/

226 Z. Ali (2010) 'Islamophobia did not start at ground zero' *The Root,* 7 September, www.theroot.com/articles/culture/2010/09/islamophobia_did_not_start_at_ground_zero.html

227 Ali (2010).

228 H. Elver (2012) 'Racializing Islam before and after 9/11: from melting pot to Islamophobia,' *Transnational Law and Contemporary Politcs,* 21(119), http://lesliecaton.com/tlcp/wp-content/uploads/2013/03/racializing.pdf, p. 137.

229 J. Zogby (1984) *Taking Root, Bearing Fruit: The Arab American Experience,* Washington DC: ADC Research Institute, cited in L. A. Cainkar (2011) *Homeland Insecurity: The Arab American and Muslim American Experience After 9/11,* New York: Russell Sage Foundation, p. 90.

230 K. Moore (1995) *Al-Mughtaribun: American Law and the rransformation of Muslim life in the United States,* Albany, N.Y.: State University of New York Press, p. xi, cited in Elver (2012), p. 137.

231 Elver (2012), p. 138

232 M. Posner (2006) 'Human Rights in the Post-September 11 Environment,' *Seattle Journal for Social Justice,* (1), note 95, p. 186, cited in Elver (2012), p. 142.

233 Posner (2006) note 95, p. 186 (citing Rachel L. Swarns, 'Program's value in dispute as a tool to fight terrorism,' *New York Times*, 21 January 2004, cited in Elver (2012), p. 143).

234 D. Kumar (2011) 'Political Islam: a Marxist analysis,' *International Socialist Review* 76, http://isreview.org/issue/76/political-islam-marxist-analysis

235 Muslim Public Affairs Council (n.d.) 'Statistics: what you need to know,' www. mpac.org/programs/hate-crime-prevention/statistics.php. The Council argues that statistics are likely to under-represent the total number of hate crimes actually committed because many victims of hate crimes are reluctant to contact law enforcement owing to, for example, distrust of the government as a result of post-9/11 policies and programmes, lack of knowledge about the criminal justice system, fear of retaliation, linguistic and cultural barriers, immigration status, apathy towards recourse, and prior negative experience with government agencies.

236 Southern Poverty Law Center (2011) 'A list of anti-Muslim hate crimes and bias incidents collected by the SPLC from news reports since 9/11,' 29 March, www splcenter.org/news/2011/03/29/anti-muslim-incidents-sept-11-2001

237 O. Memarian (2009) 'Q & A Islamophobia alive and well in the U.S.', Interpress Service News Agency, http://ipsnews.net/news.asp?idnews=46620

238 CAIR (2014a) 'About us,' www.islamophobia.org/about.html

239 CAIR (2014b) 'Islamophobia reports,' www.islamophobia.org/islamophobia-reports.html

240 CAIR (2014b).

241 Quoted in CAIR (2014b).

242 Quoted in CAIR (2014b).

243 CAIR (2014c) 'Islamophobic organizations,' www.islamophobia.org/islamophobic-organizations.html

244 CAIR (2014c).

245 J. Chasmar (2014) 'Who is Jessica Chasmar?' https://foolmenever.wordpress.com/about/

246 Chasmar (2014).

247 T. Green (2015a) *The Fear of Islam: An Introduction to Islamophobia in the West* Minneapolis, Minn.: Fortress Press.

248 http://www.ricksantorum.com/home

249 Cited in T. Green (2015b) 'Is America becoming more Islamophobic?' Huffington Post, 26 June, www.huffingtonpost.com/todd-green-phd/is-america-becoming-more-_b_7658942.html

250 www.paul.senate.gov/about-rand/meet

251 The mosque, which opened in 2011 two blocks from the site of the 9/11 attack (11 September 2001), was opposed by some on the grounds that 'it could become a shrine to the Islamic extremists'. Supporters of the project, which will feature interfaith workshops, said 'it would serve to promote a better understanding of the Muslim-American community and its history in New York City'(Reuters, (2014) 'Park51, so-called "Ground Zero Mosque" site, has been requested for demolition Huffington Post, 9 June, www.huffingtonpost.com/2014/04/09/park51-ground zero-mosque_n_5113092.html); Green (2015b).

252 www.lindseygraham.com/

253 Green (2015b).

254 www.mikehuckabee.com/index.cfm?p=mikehuckabeepledge

255 Green (2015b).

256 A. D. Dixson (2006) 'The fire this time: jazz research and critical race theory,' in A. D. Dixson and C. K. Rousseau (eds), *Critical Race Theory in Education: All God's Children Got a Song*, New York: Routledge.

257 P. Martin (2014) 'ISIS atrocities and US imperialism,' WSWS, 4 September, www.wsws.org/en/articles/2014/09/04/pers-s04.html

258 Martin (2014).

259 Martin (2014).

260 Martin (2014).

261 P. R. Carr (2016) 'Afterword: Pygmalion President, Military Commander-in-Chief, Cheer Leader for Wall Street, and Head of the Empire: Obama, hegemony and the promise for hope and change,' in P. Orelus *Race, Power and the Obama Legacy*, New York: Routledge.

262 Carr (2015).

263 Carr (2015).

264 Quoted in www.washingtonpost.com/wp-dyn/articles/A19751-2004Jul27.html

265 P. Orelus (2016) *Race, Power and the Obama Legacy*, New York: Routledge.

266 D. Grubin (n.d.) 'Anti-Semitism in America,' Washington DC: *The Jewish Americans*, www.pbs.org/jewishamericans/jewish_life/anti-semitism.html

267 Virtual Jewish Library (2014) 'Anti-Semitism in the United States: statistics on religious hate crimes,' December, www.jewishvirtuallibrary.org/jsource/anti-semitism/hatecrimes.html. The URL link tracks antisemitic and anti-Islamic hate crimes back to 1996.

268 Southern Poverty Law Center (SPLC) (2014).

269 Southern Poverty Law Center (SPLC) (2014).

270 B. Paddock, E. Sandoval, R. Schapiro and C. Siemaszko (2015) 'Dylann Roof shot all nine Charleston massacre victims "multiple times," court papers charge,' *New York Daily News*, 19 June, www.nydailynews.com/news/national/dylann-roof-confesses-charleston-church-shooting-report-article-1.2263668

271 SPLC (2015) 'Hate map,' www.splcenter.org/hate-map#s=SC

272 F. Boyle (2015) 'The west has normalised racist wars – but you can't solve complex problems with 1,000lb bombs,' *Guardian*, 30 June, www.theguardian.com/commentisfree/2015/jun/30/west-racist-wars-bombs-radicalisation-frankie-boyle

3   Australia

1 Australian Council of Social Service (2014) *Poverty in Australia*, www.acoss.org.au/images/uploads/ACOSS_Poverty_in_Australia_2014.pdf

2 Australian Council of Social Service (2014).

3 Unpublished estimates provided by Azpitarte from the Brotherhood of St Laurence, in R. McLachlan, G. Gilfillan and J. Gordon (2013) *Deep and Persistent Disadvantage in Australia*, rev. edn, Productivity Commission Working Paper, Canberra: Commonwealth of Australia, www.pc.gov.au/research/completed/deep-persistent-disadvantage/deep-persistent-disadvantage.pdf, p. 84.

4 S. Ballyn (2011) 'The British invasion of Australia: convicts: exile and dislocation,' in M. Rennes (ed.), *Lives in Migration: Rupture and Continuity*, www.ub.edu/

dpfilsa/2ballyn.pdf. Prior to Cook's invasion, there is evidence of Chinese and indigenous Indonesian presence in the fifteenth century, and further Indonesian trading in the sixteenth century which continued up to the beginning of the twentieth century when it was stopped by the Australian government in 1906. In addition there were clashes between the Dutch (the first Europeans to set foot in Australia) and Australian Aboriginal people in the seventeenth century. The Spanish also sailed through the Torres Strait in the seventeenth century (Creative Spirits/Jens Korff (2015a) 'Aboriginal history timeline (1400–1769),' www.creativespirits.info/aboriginal culture/history/aboriginal-history-timeline-1400-1769#axzz3g46LReda).

5   Aboriginal Heritage (2015) 'A brief Aboriginal history,' www.aboriginalheritage. org/history/history/

6   Aboriginal Heritage (2015).

7   Treaty Republic (2012a) 'Terra nullius,' http://treatyrepublic.net/content/terra-nullius-0

8   E. Elklund (2001) 'Terra nullius and Australian colonialism,' in Treaty Republic (2012a).

9   Elklund (2001).

10 Elklund (2001).

11 For a list of languages, see Creative Spirits/Jens Korff (2015b) 'Loss of Aboriginal languages,' www.creativespirits.info/aboriginalculture/language/loss-of-aboriginal-languages#toc2

12 Aboriginal Heritage (2015)

13 Aboriginal Heritage (2015).

14 Ballyn (2011).

15 Aboriginal Heritage (2015).

16 Aboriginal Heritage (2015).

17 Bishop Polding, 1845, cited in Aboriginal Heritage (2015).

18 Treaty Republic (2012b) 'History of Australian Aboriginal massacres,' http:// treatyrepublic.net/content/history-australian-aboriginal-massacres

19 A. K. Cantrill (1963) 'Sheep' in A. H. Chisholm (ed.), *Australian Encyclopedia, Vol. 8*, Sydney, NSW: Grolier Society of Australia, p. 96; F. O'Loghlen (1963) 'Cattle industry,' in Chisholm, *Australian Encyclopedia, Vol. 2*, p. 295; R. L. Heathcote (1987) 'Images of a desert? Perceptions of arid Australia,' *Australian Geographical Studies* 25, cited in A. G. Paterson (2005) 'Historical interactions between Aborigines and European pastoralists in Australia's drylands,' in M. A. Smith and P. Hesse (eds), *23 Degrees South: Archaeology and Environmental History of the Southern Deserts*, Canberra: National Museum of Australia, www.academia.edu/795494/ Historical_Interactions_between_Aborigines_and_European_Pastoralists_ in_Australias_Drylands, p. 256.

20 Paterson (2005), p. 255.

21 B. Reyburn (1988) 'The forgotten struggle of Australia's Aboriginal people,' *Cultural Survival Quarterly*, 12(3), www.culturalsurvival.org/publications/cultural-survival-quarterly/australia/forgotten-struggle-australias-aboriginal-people

22 Reyburn (1988).

23 T. Anthony (2004) 'Labour relations on northern cattle stations: feudal exploitation and accommodation,' *The Drawing Board*, 4(3), www.australianreview.net/journal/ v4/n3/anthony.pdf, p. 120.

4 P. Anderson (1978) *Passages from Antiquity to Feudalism*, London: Verso, p. 153, cited in Anthony (2004), p. 124.

5 B. Rosser (1985) *Dreamtime Nightmares: Biographies of Aborigines Under the Queensland Aborigines Act*, Canberra: Australian Institute of Aboriginal Studies, p. 1, cited in Anthony (2004), p. 128.

6 F. Merlan (1978), '"Making people quiet" in the pastoral north: reminiscences of Elsey Station,' *Aboriginal History*, 2(1), p. 74, cited in Anthony (2004), p. 126.

7 Anthony (2004), p. 126.

8 G. Buchanan (1933) *Packhorse and Waterhole: With the First Overlanders to the Kimberleys*, Sydney, NSW: Angus & Robertson, p. 117, cited in Anthony (2004), p. 124.

9 Anthony (2004), p. 124. The source of the quote from Bird is J. Bird (1988) 'They can't break us down,' in P. Marshall (ed.), *Raparapa Kularr Martuwarra ... all right, now we go 'side the river, along the sundown way: Stories from Fitzroy River Drovers*, Broom, WA: Magabala, p. 98.

0 D. May (1983) *From Bush to Station: Aboriginal Labour in the North Queensland Pastoral Industry*, Townsville, QLD: James Cook University, p. 20, cited in Anthony (2004), p. 122.

1 The Torres Strait Islander peoples are indigenous peoples of the Torres Strait Islands, a group of nearly 400 small islands in the Torres Strait, separating Australia's Cape York Peninsula and the island of New Guinea. The islands are mostly part of the state of Queensland.

2 E. Brennan (2011) 'On this day: indigenous people get citizenship,' *Australian Geographic*, 27 May, www.australiangeographic.com.au/blogs/on-this-day/2011/05/on-this-day-indigenous-people-get-citizenship/

3 Brennan (2011).

4 Reyburn (1988).

5 Reyburn (1988).

6 Reyburn (1988).

7 Reyburn (1988).

8 Reyburn (1988).

9 T. Lee Ack (2012) 'Who is to blame for racism in Australia,' *Marxist Left Review*, 4 (Winter), www.marxistleftreview.org/index.php/no4-winter-2012/78-who-is-to-blame-for-racism-in-australia6

0 Reyburn (1988).

1 Creative Spirits/ Jens Korff (2015c) 'A guide to Australia's stolen generations,' www.creativespirits.info/aboriginalculture/politics/a-guide-to-australias-stolen-generations#axzz3g46LReda

2 Creative Spirits/Jens Korff (2015c).

3 J. Pilger (2014) 'Another stolen generation: how Australia still wrecks Aboriginal families,' *Guardian*, 21 March, www.theguardian.com/commentisfree/2014/mar/21/john-pilger-indigenous-australian-families

4 Pilger (2014).

5 Reyburn (1988).

6 Aboriginal Peak Organisations Northern Territory, cited in Pilger (2014).

7 Quoted in Pilger (2014).

8 M. Cole (1986) 'The Aboriginal struggle: an interview with Helen Boyle,' *Race and Class*, 28(4), p. 23.

49   Creative Spirits/Jens Korff (2015d) 'Aboriginal prison rates,' www.creativespirits. info/aboriginalculture/law/aboriginal-prison-rates#axzz3g46LReda

50   Creative Spirits/Jens Korff (2015d).

51   Indigenous Observatory (2014) 'Mortality and life expectancy of Indigenous Australians 2008 to 2012,' www.aihw.gov.au/indigenous-observatory/reports/ mortality/

52   P. Anderson (2014) 'We need to get past the myth that everything significant on this continent began in 1788,' Sovereign Union, http://nationalunitygovernment. org/content/we-need-get-past-myth-everything-significant-continent-began-1788

53   Anderson (2014).

54   Anderson (2014).

55   Cole (1986), p. 23; Better Health Channel (2015) 'Eyes – trachoma,' Melbourne: Better Health Channel, www.betterhealth.vic.gov.au/bhcv2/bhcarticles.nsf/pages/ trachoma

56   Better Health Channel (2015).

57   Australian Indigenous HealthInfoNet (2015) 'Summary of Australian Indigenous health,' www.healthinfonet.ecu.edu.au/health-facts/summary

58   S. Allan (2014) 'Australia: Eleven-year-old Aboriginal boy commits suicide,' WSWS, 8 December, www.wsws.org/en/articles/2014/12/08/suic-d08.html

59   Australian Bureau of Statistics, cited in Allan (2014).

60   Cited in Allan (2014).

61   Allan (2014).

62   Allan (2014).

63   Anderson (2014).

64   O. W. Parnaby (1964) *Britain and the Labour Trade in the Southwest Pacific*, Durham, N.C.: Duke University Press, p. 203, cited in R. Mortensen (2000) 'Slaving in Australian courts: blackbirding cases, 1869–1871,' *Journal of South Pacific Law*, 4, www.paclii.org/journals/fJSPL/vol04/7.shtml

65   Mortensen (2000).

66   J. H. Galloway (1989) *The Sugar Cane Industry*, Cambridge: Cambridge University Press, p. 234; Queensland Cane Growers' Council (QCGC) (1965) *Sugar Country*, Brisbane: QCGC, pp. 13–14, cited in Mortensen (2000).

67   Mortensen (2000).

68   Harold Finch-Hatton in 1886, quoted in R. Evans, K. Saunders and K. Cronin (1988) 'A Queensland plantation owner,' in *Race Relations in Colonial Queensland. A History of Exclusion, Exploitation and Extermination*, St Lucia, QLD: University of Queensland Press, p. 158, cited in Australian Human Rights Commission (AHRC) (2003) 'A history of South Sea Islanders in Australia,' www.humanrights gov.au/erace-archives-history-south-sea-islanders-australia

69   E. Roberts (2013) 'It seemed too good to be true and it was: the exploitation of Pacific Island labourers in "White Queensland",' http://eview.anu.edu.au/ burgmann/issue2/pdf/ch07.pdf , p. 48.

70   K. Saunders (1976) 'The Pacific islander hospitals in colonial Queensland: the failure of liberal principles,' *Journal of Pacific History*, 1(1), p. 40, cited in Roberts (2013), p. 48.

71   Roberts (2013), p. 47.

72   L. Megarrity (2006) '"White Queensland": the Queensland government's ideologica

position on the use of Pacific island labourers in the sugar sector 1880–1901,' *Australian Journal of Politics and History*, 52(1), p. 2, cited in Roberts (2013), p. 47.

73 Saunders (1976), pp. 32–3, cited in Roberts (2013), p. 48.

74 P. Corris (1970) 'Pacific Island labour migrants in Queensland,' *Journal of Pacific History*, 5(1), p. 43; Saunders (1976), pp. 32–3, cited in Roberts (2013), p. 49.

75 Saunders (1976), pp. 32–3, cited in Roberts (2013), p. 49.

76 Parnaby (1964), p. 146, cited in D. Scarr. (1967) 'Recruits and recruiters: a portrait of the Pacific Islands labour trade,' *Journal of Pacific History*, 2(1), p. 8.

77 Saunders (1976), p. 37, cited in Roberts (2013), p. 49.

78 P. M. Mercer (1981) *'The survival of a Pacific Islander population in North Queensland, 1900–1940'*. PhD thesis, Australian National University, p. 37, cited in Roberts (2013), p. 49.

79 Documenting a Democracy (n.d.). 'Pacific Island Labourers Act Amendment Act 1884 (Qld),' www.foundingdocs.gov.au/item-sdid-53.html

80 ABC Online, cited in AHRC (2003).

81 Documenting a Democracy (n.d.).

82 Richmond River Historical Society (1978) *The Sugar Industry on the Richmond River*, p. 5, cited in *The Call for Recognition*, p. 19, cited in AHRC (2003).

83 Maclellan (2012), cited in Roberts (2013), p. 50.

84 Mercer (1981), p. 37, cited in Roberts (2013).

85 AHRC (2003).

86 AHRC (2003).

87 ABC Online, cited in AHRC (2003).

88 P. Mercer (1992) *White Australia Defied: A Centennial History of Pacific Islander Settlement in North Queensland*, Townsville, QLD: James Cook University, p. 140, cited in *The Call for Recognition*, p. 18, cited in Documenting a Democracy (n.d.).

89 AHRC (2003).

90 AHRC (2003).

91 AHRC (2003).

92 AHRC (2003).

93 Roberts (2013).

94 K. Worthington (2014) 'Australia's South Sea Islander community launches campaign for united government lobby group,' ABC Radio Australia, 31 March, www.radioaustralia.net.au/international/2014-03-30/australias-south-sea-islander-community-launches-campaign-for-united-government-lobby-group/1287466

95 Queensland Government (2014) Queensland Australia South Sea Islander Community Survey, Rockhampton: Queensland Government, www.communities.qld.gov.au/resources/multicultural/communities/assi-community-survey-report.pdf, p. 7.

96 Queensland Government (2014), p. 8.

97 Sutherland, cited in M. Maddison (2015) 'South Sea islanders see little improvement in housing, health, education,' ABC News, 14 April, www.abc.net.au/worldtoday/content/2015/s4216132.htm

98 Maddison (2015).

99 Australian Government (2015) 'The Australian gold rush,' www.australia.gov.au/about-australia/australian-story/austn-gold-rush

100 Australian Government (2015).

101 P. Griffiths (2002) 'The road to White Australia: economics, politics and social

control in the anti-Chinese laws of 1877–88,' unpublished, p. 1. http://philgriffiths.id.au/writings/articles/Road%20to%20white%20australia.rtf

102 Welch (200?), p. 191.

103 Griffiths (2002), p. 3. Ann Curthoys has discussed how Chinese settlers became a vital and largely accepted part of the rural economy in NSW (cited in Griffiths, 2002, p. 3).

104 Griffiths (2002), p. 34.

105 J. Supple (2010) 'Racism in Australia: the working class is not to blame,' Solidarity net.au, 6 October, www.solidarity.net.au/marxist-theory/racism-in-australia-the-working-class-is-not-to-blame/

106 Gold! (n.d.). 'Anti-Chinese riots and rorts,' www.sbs.com.au/gold/story.php?storyid=56 (Gold! is a Victorian Cultural Collaboration (VCC) project website).

107 Griffiths (2002), pp. 31–2.

108 Chi-tse Tseng (1887), cited in Griffiths (2002), p. 32.

109 *Sydney Morning Herald*, 15 October 1887, quoted in Richard Fletcher (1964) 'The role of the immigration question in gaining for the labour movement recognition by society in the period 1877 to 1890 in New South Wales,' MA thesis, Sydney University, p. 123.

110 Griffiths (2002), p. 32.

111 Duncan Gillies, premier of Victoria, writing to the secretary of state for the colonies, 11 April 1888, cited in P. Griffiths (2015) 'The "necessity" of a socially homogeneous population: the ruling class embraces racial exclusion,' *Labour History*, 108 (May), p. 123.

112 Griffiths (2015), pp. 123, 125.

113 While Australians elected their own parliament which made Australian laws, foreign policy and defence remained under British control. Australia did not have its own navy and it could not make treaties with other nations (S. Thompson, 2011, '1901 Immigration Restriction Act,' www.migrationheritage.nsw.gov.au/exhibition/objectsthroughtime/immigration-restriction-act/).

114 Thompson (2011).

115 P. Griffiths (2007) 'The making of White Australia: ruling class agendas, 1876–1888,' PhD thesis, Australian National University, http://hdl.handle.net/1885/47107, p. 401; Griffiths (2002), p. 18.

116 Supple (2010). Both Griffiths and Supple argue against the conventional arguments by both Left and Right that anti-Chinese racism emanated from the working class. Supple summarizes this position, which I would attribute to successful ruling class interpellation of white Australian workers and 'divide and rule' tactics:

> There certainly were a series of racist campaigns against Chinese immigration in the years leading up to 1901 involving workers. But the first scare about boat people, directed against Chinese migrants who arrived aboard the *SS Afghan* in 1888, was whipped up by establishment newspapers and politicians. The working class certainly bought into these racist campaigns. The Labor Party was a strong supporter of White Australia, and included it in its first Federal Objective in 1905. But this served a purpose for the rulers. While white workers believed that their interests lay with the Australian nation, not with their class, they were much easier to divide and weaken. Many employers knew this. (Supple, 2010)

117 C. Cooper (2012) 'The immigration debate in Australia: from Federation to World War One', Canberra: Government of Australia, www.aph.gov.au/About_Parliament/Parliamentary_Departments/Parliamentary_Library/pubs/BN/2012-2013/ImmigrationDebate

118 J. Jupp (2002) *From White Australia to Woomera: the story of Australian immigration*, Cambridge: Cambridge University Press, p. 8, cited in Cooper (2012).

119 Cooper (2012).

120 Quoted in Cooper (2012).

121 P. Griffiths (2004) 'Racism: whitewashing the class divide', in R. Kuhn (ed.), *Class and Struggle in Australia*, French's Forest, NSW: Pearson Education, https:/digitalcollections.anu.edu.au/bitstream/1885/42702/2/Anti-immigrant_racism.pdf, p. 165.

122 J. Collins (1991) *Migrant Hands in a Distant Land: Australia's Post-war Immigration*, 2nd edn, Sydney and London: Pluto Press.

123 G. Bottomley and M. de Lepervanche (1989) *Ethnicity, Class and Gender in Australia*, Sydney, NSW: Allen & Unwin.

124 Griffiths (2004), p. 7

125 In the ensuing argument, the other sponsor, married to a Fijian woman, tried to placate the racist by pleading, 'But you like Shanti, don't you?'

126 Gizen-no-Teki (Edward William Foxall) (1903) *Colorphobia: an exposure of the 'White Australia' fallacy*, Sydney, NSW: R. T. Kelly, pp. 104–5, cited in Griffiths, p. 7.

127 Griffiths (2004), p. 7.

128 J. Mordike (2002) '*We should do this thing quietly': Japan and the great deception in Australian defence policy 1911-1914*, Aerospace Centre, Fairbairn, cited in Griffiths (2004), p. 7.

129 Cited in T. W. Burkman (2008) *Japan and the League of Nations: Empire and World Order, 1914–1938*, Honolulu: University of Hawai`i Press, p. 83.

130 M. Kajima (1980) *The Diplomacy of Japan 1894–1922*, Vol. 3, Tokyo : Kajima Institute of International Peace, p. 405, cited in P. G. Lauren (1988), *Power and Prejudice: The Politics and Diplomacy of Racial Discrimination*, Boulder, Colo.: Westview Press, p. 90.

131 Griffiths (2004), p. 7.

132 Quotes and information from C. Piper (2014) 'Japanese internment a dark chapter of Australian history', *Sydney Morning Herald*, 15 August, www.smh.com.au/comment/japanese-internment-a-dark-chapter-of-australian-history-20140813-103ldy.html

133 Griffiths (2004), pp. 7–8.

134 Both quoted in J. Blakkarly (2014) 'Does Australia have a racism problem?' Al-Jazeera, 7 October, www.aljazeera.com/indepth/features/2014/10/does-australia-racism-problem-2014105111751199936.html

135 H. McQueen (1970) *A New Britannia: An Argument Concerning the Social Origins of Australian Radicalism and Nationalism*, Ringwood, VIC: Penguin, p. 53, cited in Griffiths (2004), p. 7.

136 T. Bramston (2014) 'Shorten's speech plumbs the depths', *The Australian*, 11 September, www.theaustralian.com.au/opinion/columnists/bill-shortens-submarine-speech-plumbs-the-depths/story-fnbcok0h-1227054614440.

137 Reappropriate (2014) 'Video catches Australian woman's angry, racist & very public anti-Asian meltdown,' 3 July, http://reappropriate.co/2014/07/video-catches-australian-womans-angry-racist-anti-asian-meltdown/

138 C. Takeuchi (2014) 'Racist attacks against Asian transit passengers in Australia,' *The Georgia Straight* 25 August, www.straight.com/blogra/310456/racist-attacks-against-asian-transit-passengers-australia

139 C. Dunn (1998) 'The attempted assassination of Prince Alfred at Clontarf 1868,' Internet Family History Association of Australia (IFHAA) Perspectives on Australian History, www.historyaustralia.org.au/ifhaa/history/princealfred.htm

140 Hall (1868), cited in Dunn (1998).

141 Dunn (1998).

142 J. Shaw (1999) 'Sir Henry Parkes,' *Australian Society for the Study of Labour History (ASSLH),* http://asslh.org.au/hummer/vol-3-no-2/sir-henry-parkes/

143 Dunn (1998).

144 Quoted in Shaw (1999).

145 Shaw (1999).

146 Griffiths (2015), p. 143.

147 S. Langan (2014) 'Updated: Irishman who caused $500K in damage to Australian hotel found dead,' *Irish Central,* 8 May, www.irishcentral.com/news/Drunk-Irishman-guilty-of-flooding-Australian-hotel-causing-500000-in-damage.html

148 E. Hahessy (2014) 'Why is it OK to be racist to the Irish Down Under?' *Independent. IE,* 9 May, www.independent.ie/opinion/why-is-it-ok-to-be-racist-to-the-irish-down-under-30260579.html

149 S. Pollack and C. Kenny (2014) 'Leprechaun cartoon was "irreverent and a bit of fun",' *Irish Times,* 13 August, www.irishtimes.com/news/world/asia-pacific/leprechaun-cartoon-was-irreverent-and-a-bit-of-fun-1.1895929

150 A. Markus (2004) '"Mapping social cohesion", The Scanlon Foundation Surveys, Summary Report 2011,' http://arts.monash.edu.au/mapping-population/--documents/mapping-social-cohesion-summary-report-2011.pdf, p. 112, cited in Lee Ack (2012).

151 Lee Ack (2012).

152 T. Orsag (2013) 'The New Guard: when Australia's rulers flirted with fascism,' *Solidarity.Net.Au,* 10 October, www.solidarity.net.au/mag/back/2013/61/the-new-guard-when-australias-rulers-flirted-with-fascism/

153 Quoted in Orsag (2013).

154 Quoted in Orsag (2013).

155 Orsag (2013).

156 A. Moore, *The Right Road? A History of Right-wing Politics in Australia,* Oxford University Press, South Melbourne, 1995, p. 8, quoted in Lee Ack (2012).

157 Lee Ack (2012).

158 Moore (1995), p. 46 cited in Lee Ack (2012).

159 Lee Ack (2012).

160 Markus (2004), p. 112, cited in Lee Ack (2012).

161 M. Aarons (1989) *Sanctuary,* Melbourne: William Heinemann ch. 1, cited in Lee Ack (2012).

162 J. Levi (2014) 'Anti-Semitsm on the rise,' *Australian Jewish News,* 14 November, www.jewishnews.net.au/anti-semitsm-on-the-rise/38421

163 *Jerusalem Post* (2013) 'Anti-Semitism in Australia,' 27 October, www.jpost.com/ Opinion/Editorials/Anti-Semitism-in-Australia-329882

164 Levi (2014).

165 Executive Council of Australian Jewry (ECAJ) (2014) 'Report on Antisemitism in Australia, 1 October 2013–30 September 2014,' www.ecaj.org.au/wp-content/ uploads/2012/08/2014_antisemitism_report.pdf , p. 6.

166 ECAJ (2014), p. 8.

167 ECAJ (2014), p. 8; Levi (2014).

168 ECAJ (2014), p. 8.

169 ECAJ (2014), pp. 7–9; Levi (2014).

170 D. Randall (2014) 'Challenging anti-Semitism on Gaza demonstrations,' *Workers' Liberty*, 28 July, www.workersliberty.org/node/23455

171 Randall (2014).

172 Randall (2014).

173 S. Poynting (2015), comments on this chapter.

174 C. Cunneen, D. Fraser and S. Tomsen (1997) *Faces of Hate: Hate Crime in Australia*, Sydney, NSW: Hawkins Press, p. 35.

175 Cunneen et al. (1997), p. 35.

176 Poynting (2015).

177 A. Jakubowicz (1985) 'Racism, multiculturalism and the immigration debate in Australia: a bibliographic essay,' *SAGE Race Relations Abstracts*, 10(3), London: Institute of Race Relations, www.multiculturalaustralia.edu.au/doc/jakubowicz_7. pdf, p. 3.

178 Lee Ack (2012).

179 M. Grewcock (2009) *Border Crimes. Australia's war on illicit migrants*, Sydney, NSW: Institute of Criminology Press (Sydney Institute of Criminology Series 29), p. 107, cited in Lee Ack (2012).

180 Lee Ack (2012).

181 G. Blainey (1984) *All For Australia*, Sydney, NSW: Methuen Haynes, p. 55, cited in Jakubowicz (1985), pp. 2, 3.

182 Grewcock (2009), p. 109, cited in Lee Ack (2012).

183 S. Ozdowski (2012) 'Australian multiculturalism: the roots of its success,' Third International Conference on Human Rights Education: Promoting Change in Times of Transition and Crisis, Jagiellonian University, Krakow, Poland, 6–10 December 2012, www.uws.edu.au/equity_diversity/equity_and_diversity/tools_ and_resources/reportsandpubs/australian_multiculturalism_the_roots_of_its_ success

184 Tavan (2006), p. 5.

185 Ozdowski (2012).

186 Jakubowicz (n.d.).

187 Ozdowski (2012).

188 S. Poynting and V. Mason (2008) 'The new integrationism, the state and Islamophobia: retreat from multiculturalism in Australia,' *International Journal of Law, Crime and Justice*, 36(4), p. 244.

189 AustralianPolitics.Com (1996) 'Pauline Hanson's maiden speech in the House of Representatives,' 10 September, http://australianpolitics.com/1996/09/10/pauline-hanson-maiden-speech.html

190 AustralianPolitics.Com (1996).

191 AustralianPolitics.Com (1996). Thatcher stated in 1978 in the run-up to the 1979 General Election that she won:

> there was a committee which looked at [immigration] and said that if we went on as we are then by the end of the century there would be four million people of the new Commonwealth or Pakistan here. Now, that is an awful lot and I think it means that people are really rather afraid that this country might be rather swamped by people with a different culture and, you know, the British character has done so much for democracy, for law and done so much throughout the world that if there is any fear that it might be swamped people are going to react and be rather hostile to those coming in. (Margaret Thatcher Foundation, 27 January 1978)

192 A. Calwell (1949) 'Can be no half-measures about White Australia,' *The Argus* (Melbourne), 24 October, www.australianculture.org/can-be-no-half-measures-about-white-australia-1949/. As Calwell puts it:

> We will avoid the evils that plague America, that distress South Africa, that embitter Malaya, and that worry Fiji. Ingredients of an explosive character are inherent in the conditions existing in all those countries, and when the explosion occurs ... there is civil war. The evils of miscegenation always result in rioting and bloodshed. We have avoided them in this country, thanks to the foresight of our forebears and our own innate common sense.

193 AustralianPolitics.Com (1996).

194 Lee Ack (2012).

195 Quoted in Supple (2014).

196 Lee Ack (2012).

197 Robert Manne (ed.) (1998) *Two Nations: The Causes and Effects of the Rise of the One Nation Party in Australia*, Melbourne, VIC: Bookman Press, p. 4, cited in Lee Ack (2012).

198 Supple (2014).

199 Brennan (1997).

200 B. Stevenson (1996) *The Wik Decision and After: Research Bulletin 4/97*, Brisbane, QLD: Queensland Parliamentary Library, www.parliament.qld.gov.au/documents/explore/ResearchPublications/researchBulletins/rb0497bs.pdf, p. 19.

201 Lee Ack (2012).

202 Lee Ack (2012).

203 ABC News, 'WA pastoralists back Government abuse plan for NT,' 27 June 2007, quoted in Lee Ack (2012).

204 Quoted in A. Davies (2008) 'Apology was a mistake, says feisty Howard,' *The Age*, 12 March, www.theage.com.au/articles/2008/03/11/1205125911264.html

205 Supple (2014); R. Omond (2009) 'The evils of temporary protection,' *Amnesty International Australia*, 17 September, www.amnesty.org.au/refugees/comments/21704/ The term 'boat people' originated in the 1970s, when it was used to describe migrants fleeing from Vietnam. It is currently used to describe refugees who, secretly and illegally, leave their home countries on overcrowded, unseaworthy

vessels (Jacqueline Marie Hall, *Sink or Swim: The Deadly Consequences of People Smuggling*, cited in P. Fox (2010) 'International asylum and boat people: the Tampa affair and Australia's "Pacific solution"', *Maryland Journal of International Law*, 25(356), http://digitalcommons.law.umaryland.edu/mjil/vol25/iss1/17).

206 Fox (2010).

207 Supple (2014).

208 Lee Ack (2012).

209 L. Tenenbaum (2012) 'The rise and decline of Pauline Hanson's One Nation', WSWS, 9 March, www.wsws.org/en/articles/1999/03/hans-m09.html

210 Lee Ack (2012).

211 Lee Ack (2012).

212 S. Verghis (2009) 'Australia: attacks on Indian students raise racism cries', *Time*, 10 September, http://content.time.com/time/world/article/0,8599,1921482,00.html

213 Verghis (2009).

214 Lee Ack (2012).

215 Quoted in Lee Ack (2012).

216 *Herald-Sun*, 9 October 2010, cited in Lee Ack (2012).

217 K. Hagan (2009) 'Man "looking to kill blacks" murdered Sudanese', *Sydney Morning Herald*, 1 October, www.smh.com.au/national/man-looking-to-kill-blacks-mur-dered-sudanese-20090930-gcr5.html. Given that Liep Gony was both a refugee and came from a country where nearly 100 per cent of the population is Muslim, there could be grounds that the discussion of racism in this section should fall under a different heading. However, as indicated by the actions of the murderer before the killing, the reason for the murder of Gony was clearly that he was a black African. The boundaries of racism are of course fluid, as I argued in the Introduction to this book.

218 *The Age*, 'Minister cuts African refugee intake', 2 October 2007, cited in Lee Ack (2012).

219 Bec Smith and Shane Reside, "'Boys, you wanna give me some action?" Interventions into policing of racialised communities in Melbourne', report of the 2009/10 Racism Project, www.fitzroy-legal.org.au/cb_pages/files/ LegalAid_RacialAdol_FA2.pdf, cited in Lee Ack (2012).

220 *The Age*, 4 May 2012, cited in Lee Ack (2012).

221 The reason I use the term 'hybridist' is explained in the Introduction (that this racism that can be either colour-coded or non-colour-coded).

222 D. Marr and M. Wilkinson (2003) *Dark Victory*, Crows Nest, NSW: Allen & Unwin, cited in Lee Ack (2012).

223 Lee Ack (2012).

224 J. Holland (2010) 'Howard's war on terror: a conceivable, communicable and coercive foreign policy discourse', *Australian Journal of Political Science*, 45 (4), p. 643.

225 Poynting and Mason (2008), p. 238.

226 PM (2005) 'Teach Australian values or "clear off", says Nelson. PM program', ABC Radio, 24 August. Reporter: Samantha Hawley, www.abc.net.au/pm/content/2005/s1445262.htm, cited in Poynting and Mason (2008), p. 238

227 Poynting and Mason (2008), pp. 238–9.

228 P. Daley (2013) 'Cronulla riots: there's still the capacity for Anzac name to be taken in vain', *Guardian*, 10 December, www.theguardian.com/world/postcolonial/2013/dec/11/still-capacity-for-cronulla-riot

229 New South Wales Police (n.d.) *Strike Force Neil Cronulla Riots: Review of the Police Response – Report and Recommendations*, Parramatta, NSW: New South Wales Police.

230 Daley (2013).

231 Daley (2013).

232 Quoted in Lee Ack (2012.

233 J.,Wells, P. Lloyd and wires (2012) 'Jones forced to apologise over racist comments,' ABC News, 13 December, www.abc.net.au/news/2012-12-13/jones-to-apologise-after-calling-lebanese-muslims-vermin/4426692

234 ABC News Online (2005) 'Police on alert after Sydney race riot,' 2 December.

235 Racismnoway (2015) 'Australian communities: Lebanese Australians' www.racism-noway.com.au/teaching-resources/factsheets/55.html

236 N. Kabir, 'The Cronulla riot: how one newspaper represented the event,' in B. Curtis, S. Mathewman and T. McIntosh (eds), *Public Sociologies: Lessons and Trans-Tasman Comparisons*, papers from TASA/SAANZ Conference, Department of Sociology, University of Auckland, 4–7 December 2007, cited in Lee Ack (2012).

237 Lee Ack (2012).

238 Poynting and Mason (2008), p. 238.

239 Quoted in Poynting and Mason (2008), p. 238.

240 J. Gordon and J. Topsfield (2006) 'Our values or go home: Costello'. *The Age*, 24 February, www.theage.com.au/news/national/our-values-or-go-home-costello/2006/02/23/1140670207642.html, cited in Poynting and Mason (2008), p. 238.

241 Howard (2006), cited in Poynting and Mason (2008), p. 238.

242 *AM* (2006) 'Aust imams recommend Muslim clerics preach in English.' ABC Radio, 18 September. Reporter: Michael Edwards, www.abc.net.au/am/content/2006/s1743077.htm, cited in Poynting and Mason (2008), p. 239.

243 Poynting et al. (2004); S. Poynting, G. Noble, P. Tabar and J. Collins, (2004) *Bin Laden in the Suburbs: Criminalising the Arab Other*, Sydney, NSW: Institute of Criminology. 333+xii pp. Currently available for download through the Sydney eScholarship Repository at http://hdl.handle.net/2123/8593; S. Poynting and V. Mason (2006), '"Tolerance, freedom, justice and peace"? Britain, Australia and anti-Muslim racism since 11th September 2001', *Journal of Intercultural Studies* 27(4), November,

244 P. Tabar, G. Noble and S. Poynting (2003) 'The rise and falter of the field of ethnic politics in Australia: the case of Lebanese community leadership,' *Journal of Intercultural Studies* 24 (3), cited in Poynting and Mason (2008), p. 239.

245 See Poynting et al. (2004).

246 Poynting and Mason (2008), p. 240.

247 Quoted in Poynting and Mason (2008), p. 243.

248 Poynting and Mason (2008), p. 244. See also Poynting and Perry (2007).

249 P. Hoffman (2004) 'Human rights and terrorism,' *Human Rights Quarterly*, 26, p. 935, cited in Poynting and Mason (2008), p. 244

250 Quoted in Ozdowski (2012).

251 Quoted in Ozdowski (2012).

252 R. Phillips (2014) 'Burqas banned in Australian parliament,' WSWS, 10 October, www.wsws.org/en/articles/2014/10/10/veil-o10.html

253 Phillips (2014).

254 Quoted in L. Bourke and J. Massola (2014) 'Controversial Parliament House burqa ban dumped,' *The Age*, 20 October, www.theage.com.au/federal-politics/political-news/controversial-parliament-house-burqa-ban-dumped-20141019-118j5h

255 Quoted in Bourke and Massola (2014).

256 B. Pitt (2014) 'Australian broadcaster ordered to pay $10,000 for racial vilification,' *Islamophobia Watch*, 29 December, www.islamophobiawatch.co.uk/category/australia/

257 E. Karlsen (2015) 'Refugee resettlement to Australia: what are the facts?' Canberra: Parliament of Australia, www.aph.gov.au/about_parliament/parliamentary_departments/parliamentary_library/pubs/rp/rp1415/refugeeresettlement

258 DIAC, *Seeking asylum within Australia*, fact sheet no. 61, www.immi.gov.au/media/fact-sheets/61asylum.htm, cited in J. Phillips and H. Spinks (2012) 'Boat arrivals in Australia since 1976,' www.aph.gov.au/About_Parliament/Parliamentary_Departments/Parliamentary_Library/pubs/BN/2011-2012/BoatArrivals

259 N. Viviani (1984) 'The long journey: Vietnamese migration and settlement in Australia,' Melbourne, VIC: Melbourne University Press, 1984, p. 79, cited in Phillips and Spinks (2013).

260 M. Steketee (2008) 'Howard in war refugee snub: Fraser,' *The Australian*, 1 January, www.theaustralian.com.au/in-depth/cabinet-papers/howard-in-war-refugee-snub-fraser/story-e6frgd9x- 1111115225044

261 Phillips and Spinks (2013).

262 Fraser, cited in Steketee (2008).

263 Steketee (2008).

264 Fraser, cited in Steketee (2008).

265 K. Betts (2001) 'Boatpeople and public opinion in Australia,' *People and place*, 9(4), p. 37, cited in Philipps and Spinks (2013).

266 Human Rights and Equal Opportunity Commission (HREOC) (1998) *Those who've come across the seas: Detention of unauthorised arrivals*, Commonwealth of Australia, May, www.hreoc.gov.au/pdf/human_rights/asylum_seekers/h5_2_2.pdf cited in Philipps and Spinks (2013).

267 Phillips and Spinks (2013).

268 A. Delitt (2002) 'How the "children overboard" lie developed' *Green Left Weekly*, 6 March, www.greenleft.org.au/node/25781

269 Human Rights and Equal Opportunity Commission (HREOC), (2004) *A Last Resort? National Inquiry into Children in Immigration Detention*, Commonwealth of Australia, April, www.hreoc.gov.au/human_rights/children_detention_report/index.html, cited in Phillips and Spinks (2013).

270 Phillips and Spinks (2013).

271 Phillips and Spinks (2013).

272 K. Bem, N. Field, N. Maclellan, S. Meyer and T. Morris (2007) *A Price Too High: The Cost of Australia's Approach to Asylum Seekers*, Glebe,NSW: Oxfam Australia, p. 3.

273 Bem et al. (2007), p. 5.

274 Phillips and Spinks (2013).

275 Phillips and Spinks (2013).

276 Lee Ack (2012). 'Stop the boats' was used as a slogan by Abbott in his 2013 election campaign.

277 A. Pha (2012) 'Australia's asylum seeker shame indefinite mandatory detention,'

CPA Guardian, 1561, 22 August, www.cpa.org.au/guardian/2012/1561/01-australias-asylum-seeker-shame.html

278 Pha (2012).

279 Wright, quoted in Pha (2012).

280 Pha (2012).

281 B. Doherty and N. Evershed (2014) 'Manus Island detainees being put in medical isolation at rate of one a day,' *Guardian,* 30 December, www.theguardian.com/australia-news/2014/dec/30/manus-island-detainees-being-put-in-medical-isolation-at-rate-of-one-a-day

282 Quoted in Doherty and Evershed (2014).

283 Doherty and Evershed (2014).

284 Cited in P. Kelly (2014) 'Australia: Senate inquiry whitewashes killing at Papua New Guinea refugee camp,' WSWS, 17 December, www.wsws.org/en/articles/2014/12/17/manu-d17.html

285 M. Head (2014) 'Australian sailors say Labor government ordered them not to rescue refugees,' WSWS, 5 December, www.wsws.org/en/articles/2014/12/05/refu-d05.html

286 H. Regan (2014) 'Australia approves temporary protection visas for refugees' *Time*, 5 December, http://time.com/3619649/australia-temporary-protection-visas-refugees-boat-people/

287 Quoted in Regan (2014).

288 Quoted in Regan (2014).

289 T. Cook (2014) 'UN torture report criticises Australia's refugee policies,' WSWS, 19 December, www.wsws.org/en/articles/2014/12/19/refu-d19.html

290 G. McGregor (2013) 'Broken toilets, no shoes, limited water: the daily humiliations of life on Manus,' *Guardian,* 16 December, www.theguardian.com/commentisfree/2013/dec/16/broken-toilets-no-shoes-limited-water-the-daily-humiliations-of-life-on-manus

291 W. Morrow (2015) 'Hunger strike in Australian refugee detention camp on Manus Island,' WSWS, 17 January, www.wsws.org/en/articles/2015/01/17/manu-j17.html

292 M. Head (2015) 'Australian High Court rubberstamps detention of refugees at sea,' WSWS, 5 February, www.wsws.org/en/articles/2015/02/05/refu-f05.html

293 A. White (2014) 'The pro-white gangs spreading race hate across Australia' *Herald Sun,* 7 October, www.heraldsun.com.au/news/law-order/the-prowhite-gangs-spreading-race-hate-across-australia/story-fni0fee2-1227082897992

Conclusion

1 US Government (2012) 'The American Indian and Alaska Native Population: 2010,' 2010 Census Briefs, www.census.gov/prod/cen2010/briefs/c2010br-10.pdf, p. 3; Australian Bureau of Statistics (2012) '2011 Census Counts – Aboriginal and Torres Strait Islander Peoples,' www.abs.gov.au/ausstats/abs@.nsf/lookup/2075.0main+features32011

2 In a pamphlet put out by the Australian Council on Population and Ethnic Affairs in 1982 entitled *Multiculturalism for All Australians*, it states:

Multiculturalism is ... much more than the provision of special services to minority ethnic groups. It is a way of looking at Australian society, and involves living together with an awareness of cultural diversity. We accept our differences and appreciate a variety of lifestyles rather than expect everyone to fit into a standardised pattern. Most of all, multiculturalism requires us to recognise that we each can be 'a real Australian,' without necessarily being 'a typical Australian.' (*Multiculturalism for all Australians: Our Developing Nationhood*, Canberra: Australian Government Publishing Service, May, p. 17, cited in J. Stratton and I. Ang (1994) 'Multicultural imagined communities: cultural difference and national identity in Australia and the USA,' *Continuum*, 8(2), www.mcc. murdoch.edu.au/ReadingRoom/8.2/Stratton.html)

The Australian government's latest statement of provision is Department of Human Services (2015) *Delivering Services to Multicultural Australia 2013–2015*, www.humanservices.gov.au/corporate/publications-and-resources/delivering-services-to-multicultural-australia-2013-2015. To a large extent, all of the important aspects of Australian multiculturalism in the above quote have been effectively undermined since the Howard government, not just 'the provision of special services to minority ethnic groups'. As Australian sociologist of racism, nationalism and ethnic relations Scott Poynting puts it, the ideological trick was to define multiculturalism as it were just the provision of 'special services,' then to cast these as 'special privileges,' thereby ditching equity principles at the same time as, and along with, cultural diversity ones (his comments on this Conclusion).

3   Stratton and Ang (1994).
4   B. Anderson (1991) *Imagined Communities: Reflections on the Origin and Spread of Nationalism*, rev. edn, London: Verso.
5   Stratton and Ang (1994).
6   Stratton and Ang (1994).
7   Stratton and Ang (1994).
8   C. Marsden (2015) 'Imperialist war, the "war on terror" and the end of democracy,' WSWS, 14 January, www.wsws.org/en/articles/2015/01/14/pers-j14.html
9   Quoted in Marsden (2014).
10   International Committee of the Fourth International (ICFI) (2014) 'Socialism and the fight against imperialist war: statement of the International Committee of the Fourth International,' WSWS, 3 July, www.wsws.org/en/articles/2014/07/03/icfi-j03.html
11   Marsden (2015).
12   K. Sheridan (2013) 'Iraq death toll reaches 500,000 since start of U.S.-led invasion, new study says,' *World Post*, www.huffingtonpost.com/2013/10/15/iraq-death-toll_n_4102855.html
13   Marsden (2015).
14   ICFI (2014).
15   Marsden (2015).
16   Thatcher (1986), cited in A. Memom (2015) 'Thatcherism lives on,' Centre for Policy Studies, 8 April, www.cps.org.uk/blog/q/date/2014/04/08/thatcherism-lives-on/
17   Martin (2014).
18   Cited in L. Elliott and E. Pilkington (2015) 'New Oxfam report says half of global wealth held by the 1%,' *Guardian*, 19 January, www.theguardian.com/

business/2015/jan/19/global-wealth-oxfam-inequality-davos-economic-summit-switzerland

19   Elliott and Pilkington (2015); T. Piketty (2014) *Capital in the Twenty-First Century*, Cambridge, Mass.: Harvard University Press

20   A. Damon (2015) 'Oxfam: Richest one percent set to control more wealth than the bottom 99 percent', WSWS, 20 January, www.wsws.org/en/articles/2015/01/20/oxfa-j20.html

21   Quoted in Martin (2014).

22   G. Gold (2014) 'Osborne's declaration of war on the people', *A World To Win*, http://aworldtowin.net/blog/Osbornes-declaration-of-war-on-the-people.html

23   Martin (2014).

24   Martin (2014).

25   ICFI (2014).

26   ICFI (2014).

27   Damon (2015).

28   H. Magdoff (1973) 'Introduction' to Pierre Jalée, *Imperialism in the Seventies*, New York: Third Press, pp. xvii–xviii.

29   R. Dunbar-Ortiz (2003) 'The grid of history: cowboys and Indians', *Monthly Review*, 55(3), http://monthlyreview.org/2003/07/01/the-grid-of-history-cowboys-and-indians/

30   S. C. Motta and M. Cole (eds) (2013) *Education and Social Change in Latin America*, New York: Palgrave Macmillan; and S. C. Motta and M. Cole (2014) Constructing *Twenty-First Century Socialism in Latin America: The Role of Radical Education*, New York: Palgrave Macmillan.

31   See the second paragraph of note 37 to the Introduction.

Index